Interrogating Social Justice

Politics, Culture and Identity

edited by
Marilyn Corsianos
Kelly Amanda Train

Canadian Scholars' Press Inc.   Toronto   1999

Interrogating Social Justice: Politics, Culture and Identity
edited by Marilyn Corsianos and Kelly Amanda Train

First published in 1999 by
Canadian Scholars' Press Inc.
180 Bloor Street West, Ste. 1202
Toronto, Ontario
M5S 2V6

We acknowledge the financial support of the Government of Canada through the Book Publishing Industry Development Programme for our publishing activities.

Canadian Cataloguing in Publication Data

Corsianos, Marilyn
    Interrogating social justice: politics, culture and identity

Includes bibliographical references.
ISBN 1-55130-162-8

1. Social Justice—Canada. 2. Political ethics—Canada. 3. Social ethics—Canada. 4. Equality—Canada. I. Train, Kelly Amanda, date. II. Title.

HM216.C67 1999   303.3'0971   C99-932079-3

Page layout and cover design by Brad Horning

In memory

of

Timothy P. Rouse

(1950-1998)

Contents

Acknowledgments

We would like to thank all of the contributing authors for their terrific work and for sharing in our desire to think critically and inspire change. To Tim Rouse, your memory will live on in your work; we will not forget you.

We would also like to express our gratitude to the publishers for their support in undertaking this project, their editorial comments, and for realizing the significance in voicing social justice concerns.

Lastly, we would like to thank our families for their support and encouragement. I would especially like to thank my mentors in life, Demetre and Rena Corsianos.

Biographies of Contributors

Marilyn Corsianos is an Assistant Professor in the department of Sociology and Anthropology at Central Michigan University in Mount Pleasant, Michigan.

Colleen Anne Dell is a Ph.D. candidate in the department of Sociology and Anthropology at Carleton University in Ottawa, Ontario, Canada.

Susan T. Marcus-Mendoza is an Associate Professor and Interim Chair in the Master of Human Relations Department at the University of Oklahoma in Norman, Oklahoma.

Robynne Neugebauer is an Assistant Professor in the department of Sociology at York University in Toronto, Ontario, Canada.

Deborah Plechner is a Ph.D. candidate at the Center for Crime and Justice Studies at the University of California, Riverside.

Mike Presdee is a reader at the School of Social and International Studies at the University of Sunderland in Sunderland, United Kingdom.

Timothy P. Rouse was an Associate Professor in the department of Sociology, Anthropology and Social Work at Middle Tennessee State University in Murfreesboro, Tennessee.

Jeffrey Arnold Shantz is a Ph.D. candidate in the department of Sociology and Anthropology at Carleton University in Ottawa, Ontario, Canada.

Susan F. Sharp is an Assistant Professor in the department of Sociology at the University of Oklahoma in Norman, Oklahoma.

Kelly Amanda Train is a Ph.D. candidate in the department of Sociology at York University in Toronto, Ontario, Canada.

Peter J. Venturelli is an Associate Professor in the department of Sociology at Valparaiso University in Valparaiso, Indiana.

Reece Walters is a senior lecturer at the Institute of Criminology at Victoria University of Wellington in Wellington, New Zealand.

Britta B. Wheeler is a Faculty Fellow and Assistant Professor in the Draper Interdisciplinary Master's Program for Humanities and Social Thought at New York University in New York, New York.

Preface

The concept of social justice encompasses a huge body of literature that surmounts various disciplines and interests. Social justice has traditionally involved studies in criminology, specifically with respect to policing, social order, crime and incarceration. Yet, within this literature, criminality has been defined along the lines of mainstream notions of crime and deviance. For example, we think of the use of illicit or street drugs as deviant, needing to be curbed and eradicated without questioning the nature of their illegality. In this sense, we do not give a forum for the recognition of possible benefits of the use of, for example, marijuana as a source of relief and therapy for cancer patients. More fundamentally, we accept the illegal label of drug use as a given, and therefore do not give ourselves the arena to critically interrogate common sense notions of deviance.

Historical social forces and dominant ideologies are responsible for shaping certain "truths" relating to the construction of "social justice" concerns; that is, the hegemonic constructs of legitimate versus illegitimate issues. The themes presented in the various chapters of the collection are at the margins. In other words, the topics are not unique as they have been discussed before, but are unique in their presentation and orientation. They offer different realities, different truths, by exposing the power dynamics that ultimately construct and define our social order. "Politics" is at the centre of all of the essays where attention is given to social structures that are erected to silence, control and/or blind the populace from alternative ways of thinking and acting.

In this volume, social justice has been interpreted in a number of ways; from notions of freedom and democracy to issues of economic, social, gender and racial equality. More specifically, we see an analysis of power imbalances and the expression of diverse realities and experiences that disrupt and challenge dominant ideologies and hegemonic practices as essential to moving towards forms of social justice.

Rather than simply adding to the vast body of already existing literature on social justice, this collection intends to broaden the boundaries of the ways we think about what constitutes criminality and interrogate issues of social justice and power in new, innovative and critical ways. To do so, we have combined a wide range of essays which seek to examine a variety of themes.

Marilyn Corsianos looks at how the notion of "justice" must be explored in relationship to an analysis of freedom and equality. She asks two questions. Firstly, how does the discourse on freedom limit the possibilities for equality? Secondly, to what extent does the discourse on equality minimize the attainment of freedom? She argues that these concepts are antithetical and, therefore, what constitutes justice can be determined only after one is able to place certain values on various degrees of freedom and equality. Through her analysis of both schools of thought, Corsianos argues that the goal of social justice can only be realized through a society where there is equal access to social and material resources.

Jeffrey Arnold Shantz suggests that social justice can be achieved through various forms of anarchist resistance. Shantz focuses on the peaceful resistance activities of egalitarian, self-governed anarchist communities that have come under the increasingly "watchful eye" of the state and, in consequence, have been subject to police brutality. Shantz suggests that the principles and activities of anarchist resistance, such as equality, self-government and peaceful expressions of dissent, offer tenets by which we can move closer towards forms of social justice.

Mike Presdee and Reece Walters examine the relationship between the contract research that academics undertake and the range of regulations placed upon the research findings. They interrogate social justice in their examination of the "politics" involved in the processes and production of criminological knowledge. They argue that criminological research is becoming less and less critical as we experience the continual emergence of politically safe research. In their struggle to publish critical findings based on government funded research, Walters and Presdee contest that criminological research must not become information gathering for government policy that is not prepared to critique the role of the state.

Deborah Plechner asks the question: Is a feminist criminology theoretically possible? This question forms the basis of Plechner's argument that a viable feminist criminology must take into account the complex and interlocking ways in which race, class and gender structure women's lives and experiences differently with respect to the criminal justice system and society in general. For Plechner, the first step towards goals of social justice necessitates the recognition that a feminist criminology must be inclusive, and therefore must acknowledge difference between among women to be able to begin to address the lives of all women.

Colleen Anne Dell proposes that constructs of femininity have direct implications upon the ways in which women are located within the criminal justice system. Dell interrogates how stereotypes and images of female behaviour are erected and applied to construct women as either "victims" or female "violent" offenders. To move towards forms of social justice, Dell expresses that it is necessary to breakdown these stereotypes and recognize how normative constructs of femininity are used to excessively punish women's behaviour that falls outside of these boundaries.

Kelly Amanda Train is concerned with how the image of criminality is used to regulate the boundaries around Jewish community membership. Community membership is policed through the metaphor of criminality, which serves to legitimate the exclusion and marginalization of Russian Jews who have sufficient criteria to claim membership, yet their identity does not fit the ideal mould or "authentic" identity of that ascribed by the hegemonic forces within the community. For Train, social justice is about rethinking community as an inclusive, rather than exclusive, place.

Britta B. Wheeler examines how funding decisions construct artwork that is seen outside the traditional forms of art as "deviant" or "criminal". This imagery of criminality and deviance is ascribed upon artwork that challenges, and even threatens, the normative dominant culture. This stigmatization legitimates the lack of funding of this art, and through this process, deems this art as "worthless" and "inappropriate". For Wheeler, social justice means re-evaluating how funding decisions are made and emphasizing the need to recognize and value difference and diversity within and among different art.

Timothy P. Rousse's conception of social justice emphasizes that cancer patients must have easy accessibility to marijuana for immediate medicinal relief in order to counteract the harsh side-effects of chemotherapy. He argues that state enforced criminality of marijuana use not only infringes upon the immediate and overall quality of life for cancer patients but deems such patients as criminal in the process. This stigmatization leaves cancer patients in the precarious, complex and even contradictory position of needing to engage in "criminal conduct" in order to attain a sense of physical relief and wellness.

Peter J. Venturelli asks: Why do people initiate the use of illicit drugs, and why do they continue to use drugs? In exploring this issue through numerous in-depth interviews and oral histories, Venturelli argues that single discipline focused theories cannot properly begin to comprehend and explain this phenomenon because they are too narrowly focused. This obstacle leads the author towards a discussion that the issue of drug use must be theorized through a multiplicity of combined interdisciplinary theories. For Venturelli, social justice means critically re-examining how we victimize or blame drug users through widely accepted theories that explain drug use in narrowly construed ways.

Susan Sharp, Susan Marcus-Mendoza, et al. examine the consequences of incarceration of male and female drug offenders on their families. They emphasize the detrimental effects of incarceration upon inmates' families and specifically focus upon gender differences in the imprisonment of women and men and their different effects upon familial life and survival. For the authors, social justice means that there is great need to seek out alternate forms of corrections whereby the family is not directly punished through the effects of the state's imposed imprisonment of familial primary caregivers and/or primary breadwinners.

Robynne Neugebauer analyzes the differential treatment of First Nations communities by police. She focuses on the police labelling

First Nations peoples as "criminals" while dismissing their experiences as victims of crime. It is argued that community participation is essential to the improvement of relations between police and First Nations people as well as other visible minority communities. For Neugebauer, social justice refers to the creation of programs of action including heightened police accountability, increased representation of First Nations officers and anti-racist organizing and coalition-building with other interest groups.

By interrogating social justice issues in a variety of themes, this anthology aims to discover and encourage marginalized discourses and practices with the purposes of opening dialogue, challenging dominant ideologies, and bringing forth change.

Freedom Versus Equality:
Where Does Justice Lie

Marilyn Corsianos
Central Michigan University

The word equality is rather complex and widely debatable in our day-to-day social interactions. It is a concept that conjures up various meanings and interpretations to different people at different times. It is a term that has come to preoccupy much of my time recently as I have struggled to apply it to my individual life, to various institutions, diverse groups of people and the political economy. At the same time, I have realized that equality cannot be discussed without juxtaposing it to an analysis of freedom and justice. To attempt to engage in a critical analysis and, therefore, an understanding of one without the other, would be an unjust exercise. However, the question that arises is to what extent does the discourse on freedom and justice minimize the attainment of equality; or, to what extent does the discourse on equality and justice minimize the attainment of freedom? Justice, which is commonly defined as rightfulness or fairness, can refer to equality of membership in society, or, it can refer to freedom of society's members depending on whom one asks. This paper will explore the above questions by critically assessing the three particular themes (i.e., equality, freedom and justice) and positing equality and freedom as antithetical concepts when put into practice. "Justice" by the definition given above, becomes associated with notions of equality or freedom depending on the values and interpretations applied to them. Specifically, these concepts will be debated and explored at a theoretical and conceptual level and then applied empirically through the use of various examples such as economic systems and the criminal justice system. It will be argued that the notion of justice largely depends on one's economic state. In other words, those with economic power (i.e., possessing money, resources, assets) are able to attain their own freedom and define their own justice. The less powerful (i.e., the less wealthy), on the other hand, are vulnerable and in many instances succumb to the dominant ideologies that reflect the interests of the powerful, and therefore cannot alter certain aspects of their lives. Furthermore, Marx's theory of economic equality as the goal of a just society will be critically analyzed and contested against the argument that equality of opportunity should be the goal of a just society.

To begin with, the term equality is often associated with the same quantity, degree, merit etc. or having the same rights, privileges, etc. However, when the term is applied to society, to what does it pertain specifically? Does it refer to equal access to education or equal amount of education? Alternatively, does it refer to equal access to material possessions and property or equal ownership of material possessions and property? Or does it perhaps refer to equal treatment of people or an equal acceptance of diverse treatment, diverse values and morality? To what extent is equality shaped by the economic state of a particular society?

Equality issues play a major role in political, economic and social debates. However, consensus about the meaning of equality continues to be elusive. Some theorists, as well as practitioners, have argued that in order to experience equality, society must witness the elimination of formal legal barriers of exclusion based on characteristics such as gender, race, sexual orientation, physical disabilities, ethnicity, religion etc. However, in order to achieve equality we must strive to eradicate inequality on a far broader scale. The elimination of formal barriers to full participation in social and economic life is not sufficient to create an equal society; that is, a society where there is equal social and economic opportunity. Various theorists, practitioners and activists have argued that equality of opportunity is not enough. For instance, two people may be given the opportunity to attend university, however, one may be more successful in obtaining a particular job as a result of his/her family contacts, his/her "good looks" or even perhaps because of his/her talent in public speaking. Presently, in Canada and the United States there is formal equality guaranteed under the Charter of Rights and Freedoms and the Bill of Rights, but we do not yet have equal social and economic opportunity. For example, the Charter protects women from sexual discrimination, however in practice women continue to earn 60-70% of what men earn, and gender differences continue to be socially constructed. Therefore, formal mechanisms do not lead to equality in practice. What must change is the very foundation of the social and economic order to attain a semblance of equality.

According to Aristotle, "Justice is equality" (Nichomachean Ethics). A just society is an equal society, but equal doesn't necessarily mean having the same because people have different interests, different desires, different attitudes towards work, life etc. Therefore *equal* should refer to *equal access to*, providing we live in a world where differences are not socially constructed (e.g., gender and racial differences). Unfortunately we do not live in that type of world. Plato's beliefs are still echoed loudly today. He said, "Everywhere there is one principle of justice, which is the interest of the stronger." Larry Temkin, in *The Just Society*, discusses the differential treatment of "identifiable" people from "statistical" people:

> An entire nation, or even an entire world can get caught up in efforts to prevent the imminent death of some sailors lost at sea or a little girl trapped underground while remaining largely, if not wholly, unmoved by the knowledge that a greater number of statistically predictable lives could be saved if the same resources were spent on improving a dangerous intersection, reducing toxic emissions, or making a vaccine more widely available. (Temkin 1995:88)

Similarly, parallels can be drawn to the criminal justice system. For example, there are public demands for an arrest whenever there is a bank robbery, and the police are well equipped to investigate such a case; the robberies are the "identifiable" crimes, however, where corporate crime is concerned, the public is very rarely made aware of the extent of corporate crimes (i.e., the number of occurrences and the level of seriousness) and police are neither trained nor encouraged to police such cases. Police also lack accessibility. Taxpayers' money is spent policing identifiable crimes as opposed to statistical crimes, and people predominantly perceive blue-collar crimes as being more serious than white-collar crimes. Therefore, there are structures in place (e.g., the criminal justice system) that produce inequalities, and unless changes are actually made to the structures and the ideologies themselves, any attempt to change is simply window dressing. Thus the criminal justice system is a derivative of larger concerns relating to the social economic order.

According to Rosenberg:

> It might be argued that just because we cannot attain some end—for instance complete equality—it does not follow that we need not try to attain it. Thus, even if complete equality is an unattainable ideal, it might nevertheless be obligatory to strive for it. For pursuing an unattainable goal may be the best way or the only way to achieve some other attainable goal. Pursuing the unattainable goal of complete equality could be the best way of achieving the attainable goal of minimizing social unrest. (1995:55)

Rosenberg makes the argument that it is impossible to compensate or tax to attain real equality of outcome in welfare benefits, goods, income, wealth and advantages that people seek. Firstly, people have a variety of talents and/or disabilities. Rosenberg asks, for instance, how much money should a blind person be given to compensate for his/her sightlessness. He says,

> ...making up for differences in talents and disabilities in order more nearly to approach equality of outcomes is just a disguised way of equalizing for welfare, since what counts as a marketable talent or an earning-depressing disability is a function of the preferences of members of the society in which a talented or a disabled agent lives. (ibid.:56)

But aside from the debate on equalizing the naturally occurring differences, Rosenberg says that we must "equalize for humanly imposed differences in abilities which generate obstacles to equality" (ibid.: 57). For example, equalizing for differences in resources available to certain ethnic and racial children or equalizing for differences in wealth to African-Americans as a result of years of slavery. But the question is how much is enough. How do we, for instance, place a dollar figure on years of slavery of African-Americans?

And should we necessarily be talking abut compensation in dollar terms? According to Rosenberg, "outcome equality means that the just society will have to equalize for natural and social advantages and disadvantages in order to ensure the attainment of equal outcomes" (ibid.). He further argues that the causes of inequalities must be identified and then removed by society or compensated for them. But, he also says that there is such a thing as earned or deserved abilities and disabilities. He further argues against radical egalitarianism because he says that in order for something to be earned or deserved it must be free from deterministic causes. However, if we started at zero differences and at some point there was difference in outcome of welfare among people, then there must be a cause; that is, a difference in character, personality or make-up. However, these differences do not lie in the individual's control; they too are the result of natural or human (social) causes (ibid.: 58).

> If radical egalitarianism requires that we equalize for difference not under agents' control, it requires that we equalize for these differences in character. But in doing so, radical egalitarianism excludes desert, and has no room for the possibility that outcomes might be earned, that agents are autonomous and responsible for their own choices to a degree that makes any difference in the material quality of their lives. (ibid.)

> In addition to preventing agents from employing their benefits to others, radical outcome-egalitarianism will have to prohibit or offset the differential effects of domestic up-bringing and socialization on the earning-power and welfare-attaining powers of individuals. Since no one deserves the family, friends, or primary schools he has, or the good or bad upbringing they provide, equality of undeserved outcomes in welfare will require interference with domestic arrangements, both to improve upbringing and sometimes to worsen it, so that all end up with upbringings that equalize welfare. (ibid.: 59)

But a concern here is how does one measure good versus bad upbringing, and while some would define a particular person's upbringing as "bad", that person may have become more successful in terms of wealth, for instance, than a person with a "good" upbringing. Therefore, Rosenberg says that equality of welfare—outcome is not a reasonable responsibility of a just society. However, what about equalizing for income or wealth? According to Rosenberg, equalizing for wealth or income involves a continuing and massive interference in individual lives (ibid.: 60), and therefore the creation of a Marxist state. He does not deny the fact that great discrepancies in wealth combined with political organizations can enable people to control and exploit others; however, he believes that there are many other ways, aside from equality in wealth and income, to prevent these kinds of outcomes from materializing (ibid.: 62).

According to philosopher Harry Frankfurt,

> A concern for economic equality, construed as desirable in itself, tends to divert a person's attention away from endeavoring to discover—within his experience of himself and of his life—what he himself really cares about and what will actually satisfy him.... Exaggerating the moral importance of economic equality is harmful, in other words, because it is alienating. (Frankfurt 1988:135-36)

Therefore, society must strive for equality of opportunity, says Rosenberg. And in order to create real equality of opportunity, there must be equalization of socially constructed barriers and naturally generated ones. However, equalizing opportunity does not only require the removal of human(social) or natural obstacles:

> It would mean weighing and balancing sets of different obstacles that face individuals and determining whether they are equal. It requires us to burden some with extra obstacles if we cannot remove the obstacles from others; it requires us to withdraw advantages when they are unequally distributed, or to add burdens if these advantages cannot be withdrawn. (Rosenberg 1995: 63)

Rosenberg says that ultimately equality of opportunity requires statistical equality of outcome as its test and, therefore, in the end requires equality of outcome in wealth and/or income (ibid.: 64-65). But according to Frankfurt, as mentioned earlier, this would distract us from truly discovering ourselves and our limitations.

Equality of opportunity seems to allow for inequality of outcome due to an individual's autonomy. In other words, people may be given an equal chance of attaining a specific goal (i.e., equality of opportunity as a result of equalization of socially constructed barriers and naturally generated ones), but whether they achieve it rests on their individual efforts (Rosenberg 1995: 62). However, empirically, how can society strive towards equalization of socially constructed barriers and naturally generated ones? Variables such race, gender, ethnicity, religion, dress, physical attributes, dis/abilities etc. play a vital role in everyday life in determining, for instance, whether a person is hired for a job even though the individual possesses the required academic qualifications. Today in North America, equality of opportunity may be granted in certain social settings (e.g., admissions committees at universities that equally assess students based on past grades), however, people do not have equal access to these social settings (e.g., an individual's economic position enables him or her to apply to a university in the first place, or life events that influence or inspire a person to attend university). Moreover, since equality of opportunity only exists in certain social settings, then restrictions or limitations are placed on one's level of equality on a far broader scale (e.g., the university degree one achieves does not necessarily lead to specific employment) and hence equality of outcome is not the end result. As stated earlier, Rosenberg argues that in order to achieve real equality of opportunity, there would have to be equality of outcome in wealth and/or income as its test which would mean, for example, women were not only attaining university degrees but were also being hired for decision-making, male-dominated jobs. And in order to measure equality of opportunity, he says that statistical equality of outcome must be used as its test. Therefore, if African-Americans comprise 5% of the population, then 5% of African-Americans should be represented in all sectors in society (ibid.: 64). The question, however, still remains whether these types of equality constitute justice.

The concept of justice has come to be defined as the administration of what is right and fair. According to Cupit, once we adopt the notion of justice as fittingness, then we accept that justice is determined by avoiding treating people as less or more than they are (Cupit 1996:4). He says that there is a distinction between comparative and non-comparative justice. Cupit does not support the argument that in order to treat someone as equal it is necessary to treat him or her in the same way, and therefore to treat as unequal it is necessary to treat in a different way. Cupit argues that cases can be treated differently without treating them as different and therefore still treating them as equals (ibid.: 30). In an example given to us by Feinberg, in *Rights, Justice and the Bounds of Liberty,* God arbitrarily chooses to save some human beings even though none deserved to be saved (Feinberg 1980:281-2). Cupit argues that there has been no non-comparative injustice since no human deserved to be saved; however, he asks whether it is still unjust because it is comparatively unjust seeing that some were saved over others (Cupit 1996:30). According to Cupit, " ... justice is not always comparative: injustice does not arise only through failures to treat equals as equals and unequals as unequals. It remains to be seen whether all non-comparative injustice has the form which justice as fittingness requires" (ibid.: 33). Cupit argues that utilitarianism is sufficient to treat all as equals (ibid.: 32). According to Mill (1962), utilitarianism does not consider one's interests as more important than another's, and therefore one does not have superior status to anyone else (Mill 1962:319-20).

> If adopting utilitarianism is indeed sufficient to treat all as equals, then utilitarianism can be successfully defended against the charge that it may lead to injustice—in so far as injustice is supposed to arise from a failure to treat all as equals. Conversely, if we accept that utilitarianism is sufficient to treat all as equals, but still wish to argue that utilitarianism is consistent with injustice, we must show that in some other way utilitarianism treats people as less than they are. It will not be our equality which utilitarianism fails to respect, but some determinant of our non-comparative status. That is, we will need to show how utilitarianism treats us all as less than we are. (Cupit 1996:32-3)

Notions of "justice" necessarily entail a set of values. For instance, justice can refer to equality between people or freedom of the people to act, depending on whom one asks. However, to what extent is the definition of justice the result of the economic state? It seems that those who have the money, resources or assets are able to attain their own freedom and define their own justice. In the words of Kolm, "economic justice is not only a very large part of justice in society, it can also be seen a all of it, since desires, interests, conditions, and rivalries between them can be expressed in economic terms" (Kolm 1996:3).

Now to what extent does the discourse on equality and justice minimize the attainment of freedom? According to Kolm, the central application of distributive justice is the allocation of services, goods, resources or commodities that are scarce and raise rival desires; this he refers to as economic justice (Kolm 1996:32). On the other hand, Buddhists abandon material wealth in order to free themselves from "attachments." Therefore, freedom for the Buddhists is not valued a means for what it enables one to obtain (ibid.: 42). But in capitalist society, is freedom a means to equality or an end in itself? In North American society freedom is perceived as a means to achieving certain goals in life. Capitalism and technology have given people certain freedoms and rights but at what costs? Some academics, as well as some lay persons, have argued that this "freedom" has enslaved people; that human beings have become slaves to this money-based economy where they must work long hours in order to be able to attain certain "attachments" (e.g., cars, homes, computers, etc.). Aggressive advertising tells people how much they need these "attachments" and that they are entitled to them just as much as anyone else living in a capitalist society and, therefore, they continue to put themselves further into debt in order to buy material possessions that they cannot afford.

Karl Marx, in *The German Ideology*, believed that freedom would only lead to inequalities as some people moved up the economic ladder while others were left behind. Moreover, for those who moved up the hierarchy, their power and their contacts (associating with others at the "top") would empower them and enable them to further make more and more money thus continuing to widen the gap between rich and poor to the point where people at the bottom of the economic ladder could not possibly "catch up." One must not look far to see examples of this in our society; for example, monopolies such as Bell Canada where there is practically no competition. In other words, what are the chances that a "middle-class" person (let alone someone from a lower socio-economic group) would be able to start a phone company! Kolm, on the other hand, believes that freedom is the means required to obtain desired consequences and for exercising one's capacities for movement, action, choice, reason, decision or will power. Basically, freedom/liberty is choice, says Kolm, and (intentional) action. Liberty permits choice and choice requires liberty (ibid.: 44). Liberty, according to Kolm, is not an arbitrary ethical stance, but rather just the opposite; its essence is non-arbitrariness, and it is a logical requirement of rationality and not simply an ethical position. Therefore, Kolm argues that justice refers to practical reason and is intended for choice (ibid.: 35-36). Kolm uses one of Alexis de Tocqueville's (1836) statements to support his argument. Tocqueville said, "He who wants freedom for anything but itself does not deserve it and will soon lose it." Therefore, according to Kolm, freedom from values and possibilities is not possible or rather is not practical. This can be interpreted to mean that there must be a purpose to demand certain freedoms in society. Kolm recognizes that freedom is by nature a means to achieving certain things (ibid.: 42); however, he raises a profound question when he asks,

> Can one sensibly take a means as an end value? This is indeed possible for a means of individuals and an end value of a conception of justice, as a mere sharing of responsibility between the individuals and the policy that implements redistributions or respects or protects the "spontaneous" allocation. However, the above remarks suggest that liberty can also be valued in its own right by the concerned individuals, who attribute to it an intrinsic, final or end value.... (ibid.)

Freedom enables people to think and act; in other words, it is a means for exercising one's capacities for reason, choice and action. Freedom enables people to obtain the desired consequences. However, complete freedom, where we could obtain any consequence we desired, would obviously mean living in a very frightening world and quite an unorganized and chaotic world seeing that there would be those, for example, who would resort to violence to settle arguments, murder for honour, revenge or even for pleasure or drive their automobiles in any direction and at any speed. This complete freedom can be referred to as full-act freedom (ibid.: 87-88).

On the other hand, full-process freedom, which is the central and founding theory of the modern world, allocates the product to its producer, allows for freedom of exchange and allocates natural resources by free collective or individual choice (ibid.: 64). In simpler terms, this theory, according to Kolm, says, "this is mine because I made it, because I bought it with well-earned money, or because I was given it" (ibid.).

Elizabeth Anderson explores the dialectic relationship between equality and freedom by applying them to the production of knowledge in academia. She states that the traditional liberal strategy for maintaining both equality and freedom in society has been through sphere differentiation. She says, "The liberal separation between public and private spheres aims to secure individual freedom and equality by insulating citizens' practices from political intervention and state favouritism" (Anderson 1995:186). By making this argument she fails to recognize that the public and private spheres intersect; there's a dialectic relationship between the two and they cannot be separated. Moreover, the private sphere is largely shaped by the public sphere (i.e., economic), as individuals are products of the environment that surrounds them. However, she argues that this strategy of sphere differentiation does not work if some groups exercise power over others. By applying this liberal tactic to academia, Anderson notes that racist, sexist and other intolerant groups can operate and maintain themselves privately without the interference and threat of the state, and as a result, this practice can jeopardize the freedom of other people in learning (ibid.: 186-187). Moreover, she says the idea that unregulated speech maximizes freedom of speech is an illusion; however, liberal sphere differentiation offers an alternative to enhancing freedom of speech (ibid.: 217-218).

> Instead of trying to 'maximize' freedom of speech, we can create a variety of social spaces in which many different kinds of expressive freedom can find a home. Academic freedom is one such expressive freedom, the flourishing of which requires social spaces of universal access on terms of equality. Thus, the demand for justice, understood as equality of respect in the academy, cannot be seen as an external political demand threatening academic freedom. It is a political demand generated internally by the aims of the academy itself. (ibid.: 219)

Therefore, in order to strive towards a just society, people must strive towards a just world where there are certain freedoms guaranteed and where everyone constantly interrogates one another's actions in order to ensure less inequalities. There must be a social contract that people voluntarily accept for the betterment of society. According to Rousseau's *Social Contract*, there was a "General Will" amongst people and therefore a social contract was formed by free and equal individuals. Rousseau believed that people could be freed if they could be released from a particular form of society. The problem was to find a type of society that would protect all people via the united power of an entire political organization, and where every person remains free and equal. Rousseau felt that the government can be a constant threat to people's freedom, which is in a position to undermine the sovereignty of the people, and as a result, believed that an "aristocracy," which was a balance between a democracy and a monarchy, would be the best form of government. This "aristocracy" type of government would consist of a minority chosen on the basis of age and experience and would govern with patience and divine wisdom (Rousseau, 1968).

Hegel, on the other hand, in the *Phenomenology of Mind* (1807), recognized that there is no intrinsic reason why one group of people should subordinate themselves to the will of another group of people, and therefore each person is free to decide for himself his personal objectives in life (Hegel refers solely to males; he believed females possessed a different social status). A premise to his political philosophy is that freedom is a value for all people. However, the question that he was concerned with is the question I seem to be always obsessing about, that is, what form of political organization is most appropriate for free individuals. What justifies the power/authority of a particular government body and its demands and limitations or even at time restrictions of certain actions and therefore certain freedoms? And to what extent does the discourse on freedom and justice minimize the attainment of equality?

According to Karl Marx, striving towards equality is the goal of a just society and more specifically, economic equality. The emphasis on freedom, according to Marx, will lead to inequalities as the few will be able to exploit the many leading to an ever-increasing gap between rich and poor. Modern day liberalists, however, argue just the opposite; that the goal of a just society is freedom rather than equality. The abolition of capitalism is the abolition of individuality and freedom; freedom to produce commodities and engage in free trade (i.e., free selling and buying), according to the bourgeoisie (Marx and Engels 1996/1848:27). In addition,

> But if selling and buying disappears, free selling and buying disappears also. This talk about free selling and buying, and

all other 'brave words' of the bourgeoisie about freedom in general, have a meaning, if any, only in contrast with restricted selling and buying, with the fettered traders of the Middle Ages, but have no meaning when opposed to the Communistic abolition of buying and selling, of the bourgeois conditions of production, and of the bourgeoisie itself (ibid.: 27).

According to Marx, the industrial revolution in the 1800s had replaced feudalism with capitalism. Societies in England, Germany, France and America were as a result divided into two main groups: the bourgeoisie and the proletariat. The bourgeoisie were the ruling class and the owners of the means of production as well as employers of wage labour, while the proletariat were the working class who were forced to sell their labour power for money as a means of subsistence (ibid.: 3, 20). Members of the lumpenproletariat were not considered a class according to Marx; they were the vagabonds and the criminals, that is, those who did not work and resorted to stealing from others in order to survive. In *The German Ideology*, Marx and Engels state that the division of labour enslaves people as people are forced to do one particular job if they want to have a means of livelihood (Marx and Engels 1970/1846:53). They further state that the working class under capitalism is exploited and is "pushed down" below the conditions of existence of its own class (Marx and Engels 1996/ 1848:21). Moreover, they believed that the ruling class was not only the ruling material force of society but also the ruling intellectual force. In other words, the ruling class possesses the power to shape the ideologies that are in their own best interest (i.e., dominant material relationships), and the working class is subject to these ideologies because they do not possess full consciousness, unlike the ruling class (Marx and Engels 1970/1846:64-54). And in order to maintain their power, the ruling class represents its interests as the common interests of society and represents them "as the only rational, universally valid ones" (ibid.: 66). Marx and Engels argued that behind laws, morality and religion lied the interests of the bourgeoisie (Marx and Engels 1996/1848:20). However, they argued that in a communist state, private property would be eliminated and would be replaced by public ownership of land and property (Marx and Engels 1970/1846:93). Communism would deprive people the power to appropriate the products of society and to exploit the labour of others turning workers themselves into commodities (Marx and Engels 1996/1848:28).

With respect to education, Marx believed that a communist state would ensure an education free from the influence of the bourgeoisie and that family relations would change; no longer would a bourgeois family's foundation be based on capital and private gain and the children of the proletariat would no longer be transformed into mere instruments of labour (ibid.: 30). In a communist state, according to Marx and Engels, equality would be the end result. There would be:

1. Abolition of property in land and application of all rents of land to public purposes.
2. A heavy progressive or graduated income tax.
3. Abolition of all right of inheritance.
4. Confiscation of the property of all emigrants and rebels.
5. Centralization of credit in the hands of the State, by means of a national bank with State capital and an exclusive monopoly.
6. Centralization of the means of communication and transport in the hands of the state.
7. Extension of factories and instruments of production owned by the State; the bringing into cultivation of wastelands, and the improvement of the soil generally in accordance with a common plan.
8. Equal liability of all to labour. Establishment of industrial armies, especially for agriculture.
9. Combination of agriculture with manufacturing industries; gradual abolition of the distinction between town and country, by a more equable distribution of the population over the country.
10. Free education for all children in public schools. Abolition of children's factory labour in its present form. Combination of education with industrial production, &c., &c. (ibid.: 35-36).

Under communism, one class would exist; one "association" in which "the free development of each is the condition for the free development of all," according to Marx and Engels (ibid.: 36).

However, to what extent have Marx's writings been put into practice and to what extent have his goals of equality been achieved? How practical are his theories given the complexity and diversity of humanity as well as the influence of a global economy on all countries?

When looking at the former Soviet Union for instance and present communist countries, we see the virtual elimination of unemployment. Work in these countries becomes defined as a right guaranteed to all people, and a duty for all those who are able-bodied. Moreover, variations in wages and salaries are much smaller than in capitalist societies. No individual owns property valued at hundreds of millions or billions of dollars but rather only own personal possessions such as clothes, household furnishings and, in some cases, automobiles. There is no ownership of the means of production; there is access to health care for all, as well as access to schooling for all. Schooling is seen as an end in itself rather than a means to an end. In other words, one may choose to pursue an education or specialize in a particular field for the love of learning because one enjoys it, or for the interest and/or passion for that particular field, and not because it will simply bring him or her money and material possessions. However, at what costs have these apparent equalities come into being? Have there been restrictions or limitations on individual or collective development, physically and intellectually? Has there been exploitation of people by those in government under Communism? What we have witnessed in present and former communist societies is not the vision that Karl Marx described; not the apparent equality and improved living conditions of all people. Rather, what we have seen is control not only on people's economic and political lives but also on their social lives including religious beliefs, family values and intellectual freedom. For instance, Lenski, Nolan and Lenski provide us with some examples from the former Soviet Union where children were encouraged to "turn in" their parents if they were found speaking against Communism. Also these people were not allowed to attend university for fear of corrupting others, and as a result of their anti-Communist sentiments faced severe repercussions (Lenski et al. 1995:419-420). There was also control on arts and sciences; not the freedom Marx talked about. For instance, the study of sociology was illegal in the Soviet Union and Communist China for decades; when it was later re-introduced, only courses in Marxist ideologies were taught. And there were also strict controls placed on the media, that is, on what was printed, published and reported (ibid.: 419). Furthermore, public ownership of the means of production did not mean that everyone shared equally in the control of these enterprises (i.e., what will be produced, how much will be produced and sold, etc.), but rather control was always in the hands of the Communist Party leaders. Marx had said that under communism the state would become small and less powerful simply overseeing the wishes of the people, and, according to Thompson, "in time, Marx sometimes suggests, human relations and consciousness will develop to the point where individuals will freely endeavour to satisfy each other's needs without the governance of either external authorities or an internal sense of duty" (Thompson 1992:65). However, in communist countries we have witnessed very large, complex and powerful governments and as a result political inequality has increased. According to Lenski, Nolan and Lenski, in the former Soviet Union, the political elite had special stores and other facilities such as hospitals, schools and resorts available to them and not to the general public. Therefore, even though their incomes were not much higher than other workers, they had many benefits, hence creating inequalities. Moreover, we found out after the collapse of the Soviet Union, some politicians had Swiss accounts and some were even involved in illegal deals (e.g., illegal arms sales with third world countries) (Lenski et al. 1995:414). Moreover, millions have been imprisoned or executed for possessing anti-Communist sentiments. According to G. Lenski, "the best available estimates today indicate that as many as 40 million individuals were imprisoned and 20 million were executed or died in prison in the years before Gorbachev" (Lenski 1984:202). Furthermore, in China, Communist authorities "in recent years have acknowledged that approximately 20 million people in their country were unjustly imprisoned or executed during the quarter century of Chairman Mao's rule" (Lenski et al. 1995:421).

In addition, the living conditions of people were not significantly improved. Some have argued that the standard of living for the working class under capitalism has risen and is much higher than in communist societies, and that is why the collective revolution of all workers has not taken place. According to Lenski, Nolan and Lenski, there is a flawed assumption concerning human nature in Marxist theorists:

> They assume that people are inherently good and only become greedy and selfish when the means of production (land, factories, machines and other tools) are privately owned. Thus, they believe that if only the institution of

> private property were abolished, human beings would all
> become hardworking, socially responsible individuals who
> share the costs and benefits of society equally. (Lenski et al.
> 1995:424)

Others argue that people have not rebelled as a collective because it is difficult to unite; there are too many divisions in today's society. And then, of course, is the argument that the populace is blinded by the dominant ideologies to the point where they do not realize they are being exploited.

Dominant ideologies are powerful social forces in society that influence and shape people's lives. These ideologies limit or restrict people's freedom and level of equality. For example, when looking at the criminal justice system people "buy into" the "justice for all" motto not realizing the extent to which the "justice system" favours the wealthy in society.

> Criminal justice plays an ideological role in support of
> capitalism because people do not recognize that the
> principles governing criminal justice are reflections of
> capitalism. The principles of criminal justice appear instead
> to be the result of pure reason, and thus a system that
> supports capitalism is (mistakenly) seen as an expression of
> rationality itself! (Reiman 1998:197)

According to Foucault, people accept the present penal system as a method of punishing or reforming criminals; however, he notes that prison fails to eliminate crime and therefore one should perhaps view the prison as an organization that produces delinquency "extremely well" (Foucault 1979:277). Therefore, he argues that "delinquency, solidified by a penal system centred upon the prison, thus represents a diversion of illegality for the illicit circuits of profit and power of the dominant class" (ibid.: 280). According to Foucault, in an article printed in *La Phalange* on December 1, 1838:

> there is not, therefore, a criminal nature, but a play of forces
> which, according to the class to which individuals belong,
> will lead them to power or to prison: if born poor, today's
> magistrates would no doubt be in the convict-ships; and the
> convicts, if they had been well born, 'would be presiding in
> the courts and dispensing justice'. (ibid.: 289)

According to Antonio Gramsci (1957), people are governed by the dominant ideologies in society, that is, the ideologies of the powerful, and people consent to this because they are made to feel that these values, laws and morality are in their best interest. People consent to the coercive nature of law because they think it is common sense. They come to believe that the law serves all people equally rather than seeing the law as the legitimator of the values of the dominant class. And they come to believe that this ethos of individualism, represented under capitalism, is in their best interest, and they consent to this praxis because they see it as being common sense rather than critically analyzing and questioning it.

The dominant class is successful in producing a number of illusions in order to legitimate their position of control, and one method utilized in creating illusions to camouflage positions of power is through the use of language. As H. Gadamer stated, "language is the fundamental mode of operation of our being-in-the world, and the all embracing form of the constitution of the world" (Gadamer 1976:3). Expressions such as "justice for all", "land of opportunity" and "democratic government" are utilized by those in power to present society as **free** and therefore **just** where every person has **equal** opportunity to attain his or her goals providing he or she is willing to work hard and therefore dedicate personal energy and time to fulfilling his or her objectives. At the manifest level, these common expressions indicate justice and freedom for all people, while at the latent level they affirm conformation to the economic order, competition, exploitation and discrimination. Therefore, language expresses equality amongst people while simultaneously covertly operating to fulfil the hidden agenda in protecting the present economic order.

A society with a capitalist government system has the potential of becoming less unjust by ensuring less inequalities and, therefore, transforming into a more cooperative society with an acceptance of diversity of people and people's values; however, there would have to be specific limitations placed on those in power (e.g., the illegalization of monopolies, the illegalization of false and aggressive advertising, the illegalization of so-called "classified information" by governments). Marx would of course disagree with this seeing that he believed that a capitalist society would undoubtedly bring about war, that is, war could not be avoided under this economic system and it would eventually bring about the destruction of all. However, in *Justice and World Order: A Philosophical Inquiry*, Janna Thompson states that modern day critics of capitalism argue that capitalism doesn't necessarily generate wars and injustice but is a system that encourages greed and exploitation; it rewards those who are greedy and makes it difficult if not impossible for those who are vulnerable (less wealthy) to change their situation. Moreover, it is a system that makes it unlikely for those in power to respond to the demands for justice by the less powerful in society (Thompson 1992:72). Similarly, under its present form, it is a system that predominantly demands a certain set of values, ideologies and morality; and these reflect the interests of the powerful. Liberalist democratic ideology suggests that individual rights are protected and people are made to think of law and morality as being synonymous. According to Gadamer, the authority becomes dogmatic power, in other words, it becomes not negotiable; it is seen as legitimate and legal and hence accepted as reality. In order for a cooperative reformed capitalist society to exist, there needs to be an acceptance of diverse values and morality; that is not to suggest that we must all subscribe to these values/morality, but rather that we need to recognize that there **are** differences and provide people with the freedom to reach a level of individuality (humanity) that best suits them providing there is no direct physical harm caused to others (indirect harm especially indirect psychological harm would be difficult to assess and therefore control). People must be allowed certain freedoms in order to achieve desired consequences; the result will mean differences in people whether it be in levels of education, wealth, family structure etc. However, the economic and social order would have to change in order to ensure that all people had equality of opportunity to pursue personal goals; moreover, there would have to be limits placed on just how much money an individual could earn in order prevent the present situation where the economic gap between rich and poor is continuously widening. It is fair to say that the higher level of difficulty rests on making "some money", however, when one has obtained the "some money" then it becomes less difficult to make "more money". Besides, it is reasonable to assume that people in society could collectively agree on how much money would constitute "more than enough". Most people would agree that Bill Gates's fortune has become an "insanity"; that is, there are only so many homes a person can buy and reasonably expect to live in; there are only so many clothes one can buy and reasonably expect to wear, etc. Furthermore, the social order would have to change to eliminate the ways in which gender, race, culture, sexuality, religion, age, dis/ability and one's profession (i.e., social status) become socially constructed. And there would have to be an acceptance of diverse value systems seeing that morality relies on subjective interpretation and, therefore, morality, so long as it imposes duties on us, is perceived as a restriction of people's freedom rather than an enhancement of it.

Therefore, to attempt an exploration of what constitutes "justice", the complex nature of equality must be pursued in association with the concept of freedom. There is a dialectical relationship between equality and freedom; when applied, they are antithetical concepts and, therefore, what constitutes justice can be determined only after one is able to place certain values on various degrees of freedom and equality. Under various social economic orders (e.g., capitalism, communism, etc.), equality, freedom and "justice" have all, to some level, been determined by economics. It is obvious that a large part (if not all) of people's level of freedom and their status as "equals" in society is determined by the social economic order, and therefore justice comes to be defined in a manner that best suits those in power. Furthermore, it was argued that material equality is not a reasonable expectation of a just society seeing that it would involve a continuous and massive interference in people's lives and secondly, a concern with material equality may divert a person's attention away from experiencing particular phenomena that he or she really cares about. Moreover, equality of outcome is also not a reasonable expectation of a just society because there are differences in people's levels of interest, personal time dedicated to performing particular tasks, talents, etc. However, society must strive towards creating a world where there is equality of opportunity, and in order to accomplish this, changes must be made to the economic and social order. In other words, causes of certain inequalities must be identified and then removed by society and there must be equalization of socially constructed barriers and naturally generated ones.

Bibliography

Anderson, Elizabeth S. 1995. "The Democratic University: The Role of Justice in the Production of Knowledge." In Ellen Frankel Paul, Fred D. Miller, Jr., and Jeffrey Paul, (Eds.), *The Just Society*, 186-219. Cambridge: Cambridge University Press.

Aristotle. 1962 (1934). *The Nichomachean Ethics* (trans., H. Rackman). Cambridge: Harvard University Press.

Cupit, Geoffrey. 1996. *Justice as Fittingness*. New York: Oxford University Press.

Feinberg, J. 1980. *Rights, Justice and the Bounds of Liberty*. Princeton: Princeton University Press.

Foucault, Michel. 1979. *Discipline & Punish: The Birth of the Prison* (trans., Alan Sheridan). New York: Vintage Books.

Frankfurt, Harry. 1988. "Equality as a Moral Ideal." In Frankfurt, *The Importance of What We Care About*, 134-58. Cambridge: Cambridge University Press.

Gadamer, H. 1976. *Philosophical Hermeneutics*. Berkley: University of California.

Gramsci, Antonio. 1957. *The Modern Prince and Other Writings*. New York: International Publishers.

Hegel, G.W.F. 1931 (1807). *Phenomenology of Mind* (trans., J.B. Baillie), 2nd edition. London: Allen & Unwin.

Kolm, Serge-Christophe. 1996. *Modern Theories of Justice*. Massachusetts: Massachusetts Institute of Technology.

Lenski, Gerhard. 1984. "Income Stratification in the United States: Toward a Revised Model of the System," *Research in Social Stratification and Mobility* 3:202.

Lenski, G., Patrick Nolan and Jean Lenski. 1995. *Human Societies: An Introduction to Macrosociology*—Seventh Edition. New York: McGraw-Hill Inc.

Marx, Karl and Friedrich Engels. 1996 (1848). *The Communist Manifesto*. London: Phoenix.

Marx, Karl and Friedrich Engels. 1970 (1846). *The German Ideology*. C.J. Arthur (Ed.). New York: International Publishers.

Mill, J.S. 1962. *Utilitarianism: On Liberty; Essay on Bentham* (introduction by Mary Warnock). London: Wm. Collins Sons & Co. Ltd.

Reiman, Jeffrey. 1998. *The Rich Get Richer and the Poor Get Prison: Ideology, Class and Criminal Justice*—Fifth Edition. Boston: Allyn and Bacon.

Rosenberg, Alexander. 1995. "Equality, Sufficiency, and Opportunity in the Just Society." In Ellen Frankel Paul, Fred D. Miller, Jr., and Jeffrey Paul, (Eds.), *The Just Society*, 54-71. Cambridge: Cambridge University Press.

Rousseau, Jean-Jacques. 1968. *The Social Contract* (trans. and introd. by Maurice Cranston). Harmondsworth: Penguin Books.

Temkin, Larry S. 1995. "Justice and Equality: Some Questions About Scope." In Ellen Frankel Paul, Fred D. Miller, Jr., and Jeffrey Paul, (Eds.), *The Just Society*, 72-104. Cambridge: Cambridge University Press.

Thompson, Janna. 1992. *Justice and World Order: A Philosophical Inquiry.* London: Routledge.

Tocqueville, Alexis de. 1980 (1836). *Selected Writings on Democracy, Revolution and Society* (edited and with an introd. by John Stone and Stephen Mennell). Chicago: University of Chicago Press.

Countering Convention: Active Resistance and the Return of Anarchy

Jeffrey Arnold Shantz
Carleton University

Introduction

.The final weeks of August 1996 saw a dubious cast of miscreants, rascals and social misfits descend upon the city of Chicago. The Democratic Party's National Convention (DNC) did not pass unopposed, however. Outside the comfortable confines of the convention site an unlikely script was being crafted under the working title "Active Resistance: A Counter-Convention" (AR). A ten-day anarchist conference, held alongside the DNC, AR was the largest anarchist gathering in North America since 1989,[1] attracting more than 700 participants from North America and Europe. On the surface, activists were motivated by immediate concerns with Democratic Party policies regarding criminal justice, corporate welfare, health care, education, homelessness and immigrant rights. Specific issues such as prison abolition, policing practices, immigration, the "war on drugs" and the wide-ranging impacts of neo-liberal policies were addressed. Behind AR's non-violent demonstrations against the Democrats lay a much deeper critique of State authority. Response was swift and direct: sixteen participants were arrested. In addition activists reported being gassed, video cameras used to document police actions were confiscated and communal living spaces were raided. The festival accentuated the paradoxical relationships of governance, community-buildng and social change.

That the anarchists of AR should run afoul of the authorities is hardly surprising. Indeed, anarchism has a long history of direct conflict with State institutions and their defenders. Some of the most striking images from this history are the caricatures of black trenchcoat wearing "bomb throwers" who owe their fame to activities at the turn of the century. Novels such as Conrad's *The Secret Agent* and Harris's *The Bomb* have kept the character of the fanatic alive, while more recently the Unabomber has suggested its return. In the popular imagination, the spectre of anarchy still conjures notions of terror, chaos, destruction and the collapse of civilization (Marshall 1993).

Of course, few anarchists have ever engaged in terrorism or even advocated violence. The charcterization stems largely from the startling bombings and assassinations which arose from the despair of the 1890s (Marshall 1993). Certainly, anarchism has counted assasins and bomb-makers among its number, figures like Ravachol and Emile Henry during the nineteenth century and Leon Czolgosz who assassinated President McKinley in 1901. Some contemporary anarchists choose as an element of style to play up this image, dressing entirely in black and printing "zines" with such titles as "The Blast"[2] and "Agent 2771."[3]

While anarchist history has not been free of violence, anarchism has been largely a peaceful tradition (Woodcock 1962; Marshall 1993; Kornegger 1996). The writings of people such as Godwin, Proudhon, Kropotkin and Reclus are moved by sentiments of mutuality, conviviality, affinity and affection. Most anarchist practical initiatives have been directed towards building new communities and institutions. If anything, the history of anarchism shows that it is anarchists themselves who have fallen victim to political violence. As Marshall (1993: ix) notes, anarchism "appears as a feeble youth pushed out of the way by the marching hordes of fascists and authoritarian communists" (not to mention the hordes of nationalists and populists). Anarchists are certainly not lacking when it comes to martyrs (The Haymarket Martyrs, Joe Hill, Frank Little, Gustav Landauer, Sacco and Vanzetti, the Kronstadt sailors and the Maknovists of Ukraine are only a few of the anarchist victims of State violence).

It is no surprise, of course, that rulers should so desire to construct anarchists as nihilistic fanatics because they question the very legitimacy of rulership itself. As Marshall (1993: x) notes, the radical implications of anarchism have not been lost on rulers (of the Left or Right) or ruled, "filling rulers with fear, since they might be made obsolete, and inspiring the dispossessed and the thoughtful with hope since they can imagine a time when they might be free to govern themselves."

This history of conflict and criminalization at least partly explains why criminologists have been far ahead of sociologists in paying attention to anarchist activities—this and the legacy of Marxism which from the beginning[4] established its distaste for the lumpen flavour of anarchist direct action and propaganda of the deed. The result has been that sociology has largely excluded anarchist movements, politics and analyses from its history.

Recently, criminologists have shown some interest in taking anarchism seriously as politics. Ferrell (1997) suggests that becoming attuned to anarchist practice and the anarchist critique of the State is especially relevant in the current context. In his view, close attention to anarchism should encourage criminologists to develop a criminology of resistance. This criminology of resistance would take seriously the criminalized activities undertaken by anarchists (and others), e.g., graffiti, squats, pirate radio, sabotage, "as means of investigating the variety of ways in which criminal or criminalized behaviours may incorporate repressed dimensions of human dignity and self-determination, and lived resistance to the authority of state law" (Ferrell 1997: 151). These behaviours should no longer be dismissed as symptomatic of an "infantile disorder,"[5] or "banditry,"[6] but taken for what they are—political acts. This, of course, requires making a break with assumptions of privileged forms of resistance and received notions about activism.

The present work documents the novel forms of anarchist resistance transforming the political landscape. Such creativity, largely ignored by sociologists, is expressed through autonomous zones (community centres based on anarchist principles), "rags" and "zines" (self-publishing efforts), internet actions and experimentation in music and art. Participants' conservator lifestyles are built around practices of mutual aid aimed toward the difficult tasks of establishing self-governed communities organized on an egalitarian basis.

Anarchy Now (and Again)

The presence of several hundred people participating in an anarchist conference may be cause for much surprise. After all, anarchism was supposed to have died, at least as a relevant "movement" or "politics," by the beginning of World War II. Repression of the industrial workers of the world (Wobblies), the Russian Revolution and the hegemony of Leninism,[7] the brutal defeat of the anarcho-syndicalists during the Spanish Revolution,[8] the rise of mass (and legal) labour movements and social democratic parties supposedly spelled the end for poor old "pre-political,"[9] prefigurative anarchism.

The 1940s and 1950s were grim periods for anarchist politics. Movements had collapsed, revolutionary internationalism had waned and the only ongoing anarchist projects were book clubs and study groups. By the early 1960s three major histories of anarchism (Woodcock 1962; Horowitz 1964; Joll 1964) came to the same conclusion: anarchism as a movement was dead, its vision remaining only as a reminder of how much had been lost.

Reports of anarchism's demise would prove premature, however. The corpse soon began to stir. By the mid-1960s the New Left, with its emphasis upon decentralization, direct action and mutual aid, and the counter-culture, through its experiments in alternative communities and its libertine sensibilities resurrected fundamentally anarchist themes (See Marshall 1993). Soon explicitly anarchist movements began to emerge again. The Situationist International (SI) in France offered a compelling mix of councilism and anarchy.[10] Developing a more nuanced analysis of power beyond the State and capital they demanded a "revolution of everyday life"[11] in order to resist the passifying tendencies which rendered people mere consumers of "spectacular society."[12] Situationist-inspired rebellions in the summer of 1968 almost brought down the ruling government of France.[13] While the SI itself dissolved in the early 1970s, its message and tactics were taken up by others elsewhere. In Britain, the situationists played some influence in the emergence of punk (Marcus 1989) and in the extremist rhetoric of the class war federation.

In the 1970s the anarchist tide began to subside once more. Rather than simply disappearing, however, anarchist themes became more diffuse, turning up in the activities of the peace and feminist movements. Concern with questions of hierarchy, domination, representation and consensus became key components of the new social movements (NSMs) of the 1980s.[14] While much of NSM practice emphasized traditionally anarchist themes and forms, e.g., direct action, affinity groups and participatory democracy, few of the movements or organizations were explicitly anarchist. Rather, they were largely reformist, seeking primarily to effect legislative change through appeals to the State.

Consciously anarchist politics did not re-emerge with any force until the mid-1980s. This re-emergence was largely driven by the explicitly anarchist practices and ideas of radical environmentalism. Ecological crises and a re-thinking of nature/society relations led some ecology activists to develop radical analyses of social relations of hierarchy and domination, and their relationship to the exploitation of nature. Dissatisfaction with the capacity and willingness of states to deal with environmental degradation contributed to a newfound appreciation for anarchist traditions. Anarchist insights were important in the early formulation of ecology and Tolstoyan anarchism found a welcome place in animal rights movements. Perhaps of greatest significance for the re-emergence of anarchism has been Murray Bookchin's "social ecology," which draws inspiration from the anarchist geographers Peter Kropotkin and Elisée Reclus.

Since the early 1990s anarchism as a self-aware political force has enjoyed a rather remarkable resurgence. Global economic transformations, along with the social dislocations and ecological crises accompanying them, have impelled a rediscovery of anarchism by people seeking alternatives to both capitalism and communism. The simultaneous collapse of state capitalism in the Soviet Union and the move of Western social democratic parties to the Right have left socialism discredited as an alternative to neo-liberal capitalism. These remnants of Leninism and Social Democracy respectively, which had supposedly put anarchism to rest, have themselves suffered death blows recently. With the political Left in dissaray, anarchism presents to many an overlooked alternative to both liberal democracy and Marxism.

Recent transformations to bring the State more in line with the needs of global capital have led to the emergence of a minarchist state which claims to be feeble in the face of global forces while flexing its muscles against the poor and disadvantaged. Ruling elites have been hard at work removing reforms won from capital, through great struggles, over the past century. Social programs continue to be dismantled with cuts to health care and public education, the introduction of anti-labour legislation, restrictions upon social assistance (and workers' compensation and unemployment insurance) and "loosened" environmental regulations rank among the more familiar minarchist initiatives.

Notably these policies have been embraced by each of the mainstream political parties. The Democratic Party has routinely adopted positions quite similar to the Republicans on matters such as welfare, affirmative action and NAFTA. In response to this convergence, anarchists refer to the "Republicrats," signifying their belief that there is no difference between these parties of the ruling classes. Anarchists mobilize against Republicrat policies that advocate building more prisons and developing tougher sentencing practices including mandatory terms. For anarchists such policies appeal only to "racist crime hysteria" (Subways 1996: 11) and sentiments that demonize the poor.

These transformations have given shape to an austerity politics with the conversion of the welfare state into a penal state, the primary function of which is understood to serve as a law and order mechanism. Worthy social services now include boot camps, workfare, changes to young offenders legislation and violent repression of peaceful demonstrations and contravention of previously recognized rights to freedom of speech and assembly. Dismantling of the welfare state, without simultaneously developing adequate alternatives, has meant an increase in poverty and more extreme disparities between rich and poor (Heider 1994). These conditions have been ideologically justified through a vigorous redeployment of *laissez-faire* discourses. The broken record of neo-liberal policies, in harmony with manipulated debt "crises" and a chorus of pleas for competitiveness, have provided the soundtrack for the current box office smash, "Return to Nineteenth-Century Capitalism."

"Don't Go in the Pit! Our Power's in the Street"[15]

AR was born in the minds of activists at a midwest anarchist gathering at the time that the location for the Democrats' convention was announced in 1994 (Solnit 1996). Organizers envisioned a proactive gathering which would not limit itself to a simple protest of the Democrats but provide a more generalized critique of the politics of neo-liberalism. AR was viewed by its organizers as an opportunity to make a major contribution to the advancement of anarchist organizing and community-building in North America by building networks, sharing skills and bringing together otherwise isolated projects (Solnit 1996; Subways 1996).

Chicago Mayor Richard Daley Jr. had other ideas. For Mayor Daley, the convention provided an opportunity to make up for the infamous fiasco of 1968 when his father, then mayor of Chicago, had ordered the clubbing and tear-gassing of anti-war activists by police and National Guard troops. Daley denied that the convention would be violent, even speaking to his officers personally about the events of 1968. Police counsellors conducted "sensitivity training" sessions which included videos from 1968 and assurances were given that a no-arrest policy would be in effect throughout the convention (Sand 1996). As a gesture of reconciliation the mayor welcomed "former Students for a Democratic Society organizers to a rally called 'Return to Chicago '68/'96,' complete with a 38-member cast revival of the musical 'Hair'" (Subways 1996: 11). The City of Chicago spent millions preparing the city for the arrival of the Democrats. Flowers and trees were planted, bridges were painted and vacant lots were cleared.

Less widely reported, police moved homeless people from high traffic streets such as Michigan Avenue (Solnit 1996; Sand 1996). "Despite his public non-confrontational attitude, Daley demonstrated his control of the city with and overwhelming police presence" (Sand 1996: 23). An area of several blocks around the United Center was fenced in by the Chicago Police Department and rows of police guarded entranceways (Sand 1996). Citing possible "terrorist" action, police restricted access to delegates and members of the mainstream media alone. "Police officers stood on every corner for several blocks around the United Center; police cruisers raced toward every type of suspicious activity" (Sand 1996: 23-24).

The convention itself was held on the city's west side at the United Center, a new facility bordered by the deeply impoverished Henry Horner housing project. In the time leading up to the convention three of the Horner apartment towers were demolished and their residents provided only temporary housing vouchers as alternatives (Solnit 1996). Chicago Housing Authority Police warned residents not to do anything which might disrupt the convention. "Housing police and marked FBI agents spread word of a curfew during the DNC; most residents heeded the intimidation and Horner Homes was relatively quiet during the convention" (Sand 1996: 24). The convention was choreographed to the smallest detail. In the eyes of AR participants it was nothing but a phony "publicity event designed to create a mask of electoral democracy concealing the corporate elites that control both parties and most of the wealth, government and media in [the U.S.]" (Solnit 1996: 1). A major part of this choreography involved carefully managing images of dissent. In an effort to contain demonstrations beyond the media eye, the City of Chicago and the National Democratic Commitee established a "protest pit," a giant chain-link enclosed parking lot within sight of the United Center but well away from the delegates, as the "official" free speech area (Sand 1996; Solnit 1996; Subways 1996). "These cages were large enough to make all the protests look small, and far enough away from the action to allow all of the delegates to forget about the presence of demonstrators and [their] issues" (Subways 1996: 11). City officials tried to do their part by initially refusing to grant permits for any march except ones which stayed to the sidewalks. After a legal challenge, the "Not On the Guest List"[16] coalition won a court decision permitting street demonstrations.

Actions began Sunday, August 25th. One hundred and fifty anarchists joined more than 500 Latino activists from *Pueblo Sin Fronteras* (People Without Borders), a Chicano/a group along with groups from the Puerto Rican Cultural Center in the "*Una Voz/* One Voice March for Immigrant Rights" march against anti-immigration laws (Sand 1996; Subways 1996; Solnit 1996). Signs expressed the common plea of *Ni Estados, Ni Fronteras* (No State, No Borders). Several anarchists carried a representation of the U.S./Mexico border, with flames along the bottom and heads and hands poking through concertina wire on top (Solnit 1996). Others from Active Resistance displayed a large red banner which read, "Anarchist Solidarity, Viva Zapata, No One is Illegal; No Borders" and a large puppet carried a "No One is Illegal" sign (Solnit 1996). As the demonstration neared the "protest pit" the anarchists, refusing to go in, took up positions at the entrance and chanted, "Don't go in the pit! Our power's in the streets!" as members of the other groups passed through the gates.

Tuesday, August 27th, over 300 anarchists took part in the "No Justice, No Peace" march organized by "Not On the Guest List." The march was intended as a protest against "Clinton and the Democrats' politics of repression and brutality" in order to "stand up against the racism and classism of the criminal justice system, free all political prisoners, stop police brutality and abolish the death penalty" (Solnit 1996: 3; Subways 1996). The more immediate goal of activists was to block buses transporting delegates to the convention site. Anarchists formed a puppet procession featuring a thirty-foot tall "Corporate Power Tower," a hybrid high-rise office building and corporate executive covered in company logos. The tower, pulling the strings on ten-foot high puppets of Bill Clinton and Bob Dole, was dragged by costumed figures identified as "voters," "taxpayers," "workers" and "consumers"—all those who consent to capitalism. Following behind in chains were the overlooked casualties of capitalism, including single moms, endangered species and tree stumps along with body bags containing health care and education. Activists dressed as police with giant pig heads and cardboard "barricades" mingled with real police and shouted orders at marchers. As the march moved along people residing in nearby housing projects "enthusiastically joined, identifying with the group's issues" (Subways 1996: 14).

As the procession came within sight of the United Center, marchers chanting "rise up" staged an uprising against the Corporate Power Tower tearing off its four walls to reveal a giant red fist and murals illustrating anarchist visions of a free society. Two liberation puppets were released and circled the crowd. While police prevented the march from reaching the convention centre, people stayed in the streets and managed to slow delegate buses for an hour without any arrests being made (Subways 1996).

The main anarchist-organized demonstration was a festive street theatre parade, the "Festival of the Oppressed," timed to coincide with the convention's close. The anarchists, unlike other protesters "decided not to march to the United Center public relations farce, but creatively appeal to the community [they] were in" (Solnit 1996: 3). Accordingly, marchers chose a visible route throught the Wicker Park neighbourhood to display all of their creations from the previous week.

These demonstrations, which refused the confines of "the pit" and the regulation of protest by the State, were the most inspiring and successful (Subways 1996: 11). Significantly they moved outside of the limited circle of organizers and brought together people from a variety of social and economic groups.

In addition to lively demonstrations and protests participants took part in daily workshops and discussions concerning some of the crucial issues facing contemporary anarchism: community organizing, alternative economics and conceptions of "revolutionary" politics. "The organizers' goals were for activists to network and share skills learned from [their] often-isolated projects, and to facilitate the effort to build a better-organized anarchist movement" (Subways 1996: 11). According to the AR pamphlet, the intention was to "approach the future" through self-education and sharing ideas about "developing counter-institutions and oppositional politics which offer the most profound impact on our daily existence" (A-Zone 1996: n.p.). Anarchists discussed such crucial matters as forming co-operatives and workers' collectives, designing and enabling experiments in decentralized projects aimed to increase local self-reliance, building a "counter-culture" to refuse external authority, racism and patriarchy, and expanding direct action initiatives. Much attention was also given to questions of how to create and nurture connections with other groups. The need to organize beyond current boundaries and build relations with the informal associations and support services which help people survive on a daily basis was identified as especially important. As one commentator concluded: "AR planted the seeds and showed us our potential, but only energetic, effective organizing and careful community building where we live will nurture these seeds into thriving communities and a blossoming mass movement" (Solnit 1996: 3).

The New World in the Shell of the Old

Historically, anarchists have sought to create a society without government or State, free from coercive, hierarchical and authoritarian relations, in which people associate voluntarily. Anarchists emphasize freedom from imposed authorities. They envision a society based upon autonomy, self-organization and voluntary federation which they oppose to "the State as a particular body intended to maintain a compulsory scheme of legal order" (Marshall 1993: 12). Contemporary anarchists focus much of their efforts on transforming everyday life through the development of alternative social arrangements and organizations. Thus, they are not content to wait either for elite-initiated reforms or for future "post-revolutionary" utopias. If social and individual freedoms are to be expanded, the time to start is today.

In order to bring their ideas to life, anarchists create working examples. To borrow the old Wobbly phrase, they are "forming the structure of the new world in the shell of the old."[17] These experiments in living, popularly referred to as "DIY" (Do-It-Yourself), are the means by which contemporary anarchists withdraw their consent and begin contracting other relationships. DIY releases counterforces, based upon notions of autonomy and self-organization as motivating principles, against the normative political and cultural discourses of neo-liberalism. Anarchists create autonomous spaces which are not about access but about refusal of the terms of entry (e.g., nationalism, etc).

The "Do-it-Yourself" ethos has a long and rich association with anarchism. One sees it as far back as Proudhon's notions of people's banks and local currencies (see, Proudhon 1969) which have returned in the form of LETS (local exchange and trade systems). In North America, nineteenth-century anarchist communes, such as those of Benjamin Tucker, find echoes in the A-zones and squat communities of the present day.

In the recent past, Situationists, Kabouters[18] and the British punk movements have encouraged DIY activities as means to overcome alienating consumption practices and the authority and control of work. Punks turned to DIY to record and distribute music outside of the record industry.

At the forefront of contemporary DIY are the "autonomous zones" or more simply "A-Zones." "Autonomous zones" are community centres based upon anarchist principles, often providing meals , clothing and shelter for those in need. These sites, sometimes but not always squats, provide gathering places for exploring and learning about anti-authoritarian histories and traditions. Self-education is an important aspect of anarchist politics. A-Zones are important as sites of re-skilling. DIY and participatory democracy are important precisely because they encourage the processes of learning and independence necessary for self-determined communities.

A-Zones are often sites for quite diverse and complex forms of activity. The "Trumbellplex" in Detroit is an interesting example. Housed, ironically, in the abandoned home of an early-twentieth-century industrialist, the Trumbell Theatre serves as a co-operative living space, temporary shelter, food kitchen and lending library. The carriage house has been converted into a theatre site for touring anarchist and punk bands and performance troops like the "Bindlestiff Circus."[19]

Because of their concern with transcending cultural barriers, residents of A-Zones try to build linkages with residents of the neighbourhoods in which they were staying. The intention is to create autonomous free zones which may be extended as resources and conditions permit.

Communication across these diasporic communities is made possible, in part, by recent technological innovations (e.g., videocameras, internet and micro-transmitters). While remaining highly suspicious of the impacts of technology, its class-exclusivity and its possible uses as means of social control, anarchists have become proficient in wielding these technological products as tools for active resistance.

Emphasis on direct action and Do-It-Yourself has given rise to activists using camcorders in social struggle to document important events or to observe police to prove what happened on a demo or picket. Video activism serves as an important alternative to reliance upon corporate media for coverage of events or dissemination of information. Harrassment of anarchists and racist practices by police in residential communities have led to the formation of Copwatch, which utilizes video cameras to watch police and to discourage the use of force by police. The aggression displayed towards anarchists beyond the view of mainstream media at AR shows the significance of this form of documentation. That most police actions and arrests were directed against the video activists of CounterMedia, shows that the authorities also recognize the significance of the video witness.

Anarchy has also developed a busy presence on the internet. The main venue for direct exchange among anarchists is A-infos, a daily multi-language international anarchist news service produced by tireless activist groups in five countries. Also much used is Spunk Press, run by an international collective since 1992. Their catalogue contains over 1000 items, including speeches, essays and lectures by prominent anarchists—works on issues such as ecology, alternative education, anarchist poetry, anarchist art, addresses for groups and reviews of anarchist books. Work is done by volunteers, in their spare time, often with borrowed equipment.

The major means for distributing information remains the lively anarchist press. Longstanding publications include *Freedom, Fifth Estate, Anarchy* and *Kick it Over.* At the local level DIY zines such as *The Match, Anarchives, Demolition Derby* and *Agent 2771* have kept anarchist thought alive while expanding the range of anarchist politics to include new participants.

Additionally there has been a recent explosion in micro-broadcasting. Numerous illegal radio stations have sprung up in North America, such as Free Radio Berkeley.

These various practices are all part of complex networks which are transnational, transboundary and transmovement.[20] They encourage us to think about writing against the movement as movement. Movement processes involve complex networks outside of and alongside of the State (transnational and transboundary).

The Criminalization of Dissent

These "self-valourizing" activities entail a very contradictory process, which is often temporary and fleeting, especially in the face of State surveillance and direct violence. Lurking in the landscape of autonomous zones are "those who would reject the idea that people should be free to follow their feelings and express themselves through newly created styles of living" (Hetherington 1992: 96). States do not react kindly to efforts to undermine their power and authority. "As Malatesta used to say, you try to do your thing and they intervene, and then you are to blame for the fight that happens" (Paul Goodman quoted in Ward 1973: 142).

Police aggression against anarchists began during the Festival of the Oppressed. Part way through the march (as the procession moved up Milwaukee Avenue) the police began forcing demonstrators off of the sidewalk while mounted police corralled marchers into one traffic lane. Later police began to harass representatives from Countermedia. When the anarchists' police liason asked for the reasons behind increasing police aggression he was dragged from the march (Solnit 1996). This caused a tense standoff between demonstrators and police until the police line finally backed up and the procession moved forward.

Soon thereafter the Shundahai[21] van was stopped by police and five occupants, including one who had been put in the van to be cared for after having been seriously injured by a police horse, were arrested. Witnesses reported seeing the injured activist kicked by police (Sand 1996; Subways 1996). He was charged with assault. At the police station, the injured protester was interrogated by nine officers before being allowed medical attention. The van and a prop[22] it was carrying were impounded and film of the events was destroyed. Papers and a planner went missing.

Demonstrators formed a defensive line to keep the police from taking anyone else. Eyewitnesses reported numerous instances of police violence against individual protesters. Eight marchers were arrested during the Festival of the Oppressed, including the traffic safety coordinator. Several Countermedia reporters were arrested and others had film taken from them. One video camera was smashed by police (Solnit 1996). Police formed a line to keep photograhers and reporters away from the arrests. Journalists who tried to get near were threatened with arrest (Solnit 1996). Despite all of this, protesters managed to occupy the main six-way intersection in Wicker Park, staging their demonstration against corporate domination.

> We felt the day was a victory since we were able to take the street and carry out our entire march and performance in the intersection despite police arrests and provocation. The procession ended back in the park where we began. After putting down our puppets and props, we formed a circle, planned our responses to the police arrests, and closed with a dance performance. Then, people left for a vigil at the police station for those arrested. (Solnit 1996: 3)

Later, during the evening, Chicago police gathered in a parking lot outside of the two conference housing sites, the Spice Factory and the Ballroom, in preparation for a raid.[23] At approximately 8:00 p.m., uniformed police entered the Ballroom ordering everyone inside to sit down. "People repeatedly requested a search warrant, and asked for the badge numbers of the police who had removed them from their shirts and hats," (Solnit 1996: 3) but the police ignored them and continued their raid. Those who refused to sit down were pushed and one woman was kicked (Active Resistance 1996; Solnit 1996). Two people were hospitalized because of the effects of pepper spray. The Ballroom was searched[24] and radio equipment, files and phone lists were confiscated (Active Resistance 1996; Solnit 1996). At least one occupant was pepper-sprayed (Solnit 1996).

The next day, AR and CounterMedia organized "a demonstration and press conference at the 14th district police headquarters to publicize the raid and arrests, and pressure the police to release those still in jail" (Solnit 1996: 3). Representatives from AR, CounterMedia, the National Lawyers Guild, Festival of Light[25] as well as the property manager who had rented the sites for the Spice Factory and Ballroom made presentations.[26]

Sand (1996) suggests that the social control practices exhibited at the Democratic National Convention offer a glimpse into the techniques of protest management which may be deployed by authorities against future demonstrations.

> Where there was no violence, the media found no story, and therefore no message slipped out to the mainstream. Police and government authorities have clearly learned from the mistakes of the 1960s and used this knowledge effectively during the 1996 Convention to suck the public energy out of protest. Activists of the 1990s will have to take these lessons to heart and counteract them in order to make their dissent heard. (Sand 1996: 26)

Overall, Chicago police arrested sixteen participants in Active Resistance.[27] As Sand (1996: 26) notes there were no cameras present when most of the arrests occured or "when police raided the anarchists' headquarters the night of August 29."

Significantly, most of the anarchists arrested during the convention were videographers affiliated with CounterMedia. "CounterMedia, a collective of media makers who came to the DNC to document the demonstrations and protests there, trained its cameras on police during demonstrations, keeping a specific eye on potential brutality" (Sand 1996: 23). Because they were often the only ones covering the protests, they most regularly received the attentions of the Chicago Police Department who clearly did not want their actions caught on film or video. Six video-activists who were part of the CounterMedia coalition were arrested while simply recording events as they transpired. "Their cameras were confiscated and some of their film was destroyed by arresting officers" (Active Resistance 1996: 14). Earlier in the week two CounterMedia vieographers had been arrested for disorderly conduct, and only the day before police had stopped and illegally searched their mobile unit. Despite their actions during the convention, "Chicago police survived the Convention with their media image intact" (Sand 1996).

Anarchy is Order

The word "anarchy" comes from the ancient Greek word *"anarchos"*and means "without a ruler" (Woodcock 1962; Horowitz 1964; Joll 1964; Marshall 1993). While rulers, quite expectedly, claim that the end of rule will inevitably lead to a descent into chaos and turmoil, anarchists maintain that rule is unnecessary for the preservation of order. Rather than a descent into Hobbes's war of all against all, a society without government suggests to anarchists the very possibility for creative and peaceful human relations. Proudhon neatly summed up the anarchist position in his famous slogan: "Anarchy is Order."[28]

The first systematic political philosophy which could be called anarchist is usually attributed to William Godwin. For Godwin, laws discourage creative responses to social problems, firstly because they reduce human experiences to a general measure, and secondly because they consign human thought to a fixed condition, thereby impeding improvements. Godwin (1977: 120) sees coercion as an injustice, incapable of convincing or conciliating those against whom it is employed. Coercion, as expressed in law and punishment, only teaches that one should submit to force and agree to being directed not "by the convictions of your understanding, but by the basest part of your nature, the fear of personal pain, and a compulsory awe of the injustice of others" (Godwin 1977: 121-122). The road to virtue, for Godwin, lies not in submission to coercion but only in resistance to it. In place of punishment, which he regards as evidence of a profound lack of imagination, Godwin advocates removing the causes of crime (government and property) and "rousing the mind" through education.

Tolstoy, himself a pacifist anarchist, offered these reflections on laws: "[L]aws are demands to execute certain rules; and to compel some people to obey certain rules (i.e. to do what other people want of them) can only be effected by blows, by deprivation of liberty, and by murder. If there are laws, there must be the force that can compel people to obey them" (1977: 117). For Tolstoy, then, the basis of legislation is not found in such uncertain notions as rights or the "will of the people" but in the capacity to wield organized violence, in the coercive power of the State. Laws represent the capacity of those in power to use violence to effect practices profitable to them (Tolstoy 1977).

Pierre-Joseph Proudhon, the first to call his social philosophy "anarchist," argued that vice and crime, rather than being the cause of social antagonisms and poverty as popularly believed, are caused by social antagonisms and poverty (1969: 49). He considered State order to be "artificial, contradictory and ineffective," thereby engendering "oppression, poverty and crime" (1969, 53). In his view the constitution of societies under States was strictly anomalous. Furthermore, "public and international law, together with all the varieties of representative government, must likewise be false, since they are based upon the principle of individual ownership of property" (1969: 54). For Proudhon, jurisprudence, far from representing "codified reason," is nothing more than "simply a compilation of legal and official titles for robbery, that is for property" (1969: 54). Authority is incapable of serving as a proper basis for constituting social relations.[29] The citizen must be governed by reason alone, and only those "unworthy and lacking in self-respect" would accept any rule beyond their own free will (1969: 94). In place of political institutions Proudhon advocated economic organizations based upon principles of mutualism in labour and exchange, through co-operatives and "People's Banks," as means towards that end.[30] The consequences of this reorganization of social life include the limiting of constraint, the reduction of repressive methods and the convergence of individual and collective interests (1969: 92). This Proudhon calls "the state of total liberty" or anarchy, and suggests that it is the only context in which "laws" operate spontaneously without invoking command and control.[31]

Michael Bakunin, who popularized the term "anarchy" and whose work was instrumental in the early development of the anarchist movement, argues in his scattered writings that external legislation and authority "both tend toward the enslavement of society" (1953: 240). All civic and political organizations are founded upon violence exercised from the top downward as systematized exploitation. Again political law is understood as an expression of privilege. He rejects all legislation, convinced that it must turn to the advantage of powerful minorities against the interests of subjected majorities. Laws, inasmuch as they impose an external will, must be despotic in character. For Bakunin, political rights and "democratic States" are flagrant contradictions in terms. States and laws only denote power and domination, presupposing inequality. "Where all govern, no one is governed, and the State as such does not exist. Where all equally enjoy human rights, all political rights automatically are dissolved" (Bakunin 1953: 240). Bakunin distinguishes between the authority of example and knowledge, "the influence of fact," and the authority of right. While he is willing to accept the former, situationally and voluntarily, he rejects the latter unconditionally:

> When it is a question of houses, canals, or railroads, I consult the authority of the architect or engineer ... though always reserving my indisputable right of criticism and control.... Accordingly there is no fixed and constant authority, but a continual exchange of mutual, temporary, and, above all, voluntary authority and subordination. (Bakunin 1953: 253-254)

The influence of right, an official imposition, he terms a "falsehood and an oppression" which inevitably leads to absurdity (1953: 241). Like Proudhon, Bakunin envisions future social organizations as economic rather than political. He sees society as organized around free federations of producers, both rural and urban. Any coordination of efforts must be voluntary and reasoned.

Peter Kropotkin divided all laws into three main categories: protection of property, protection of persons and protection of government (Kropotkin 1970). Kropotkin saw that all laws and governments are the possession of privileged elites and serve only to maintain and enhance privilege, and he argued that most laws serve either to defend the appropriation of labour or to maintain the authority of the State. Speaking of the protection of property, Kropotkin noted that property laws are not made to guarantee producers the products of their labour but rather to justify the taking of a portion of the producer's product and placing it into the hands of a non-producer. For Kropotkin (1977: 213), it is precisely because this appropriation of labour (and its products) is a glaring injustice that "a whole arsenal of laws and a whole army of soldiers, policemen and judges are needed to maintain it." In addition, many laws serve only to keep workers in positions subordinate to their employers (Kropotkin 1970: 213). Other laws (those regarding taxes, duties, the organization of ministerial departments, the army and police) serve no other end than to "maintain, patch up, and develop the administrative machine," which is organized "almost entirely to protect the privileges of the possessing classes" (Kropotkin 1970: 214). With regard to "crimes against persons," he viewed this as the most important category because it is the reason the law enjoys any amount of consideration and because it has the most prejudices associated with it. Kropotkin's response is twofold. First, because most crimes are crimes against property their removal is predicated upon the disappearance of property itself. Second, punishment does not reduce crime. His reflections led him to conclude that not only is law useless it is actually hurtful—engendering a "depravity of mind" through obedience, and stoking "evil passions" through the performance of atrocity (Kropotkin 1970). Because punishment does not reduce the amount of crime, Kropotkin also called for the abolition of prisons. The best available response, he argued, is sympathy.

Twentieth-century anarchists have developed these readings of State/society relations in more nuanced ways. Of much significance for contemporary anarchist analysis is the work of Gustav Landauer who, more than half a century before Foucault, offered a vision of power as decentred and situationally enacted. Landauer conceptualized the State not as a fixed entity, but as specific relations between people dispersed throughout society.

> The state is a condition, a certain relationship among human beings, a mode of behavior between them; we destroy it by contracting other relationships, by behaving differently toward one another.... We are the state, and we shall continue to be the state until we have created the institutions that form a real community and society of men [sic] (Landauer, quoted in Lunn 1973: 226).

In a recent work Murray Bookchin (1982) speaks of the State as "an instilled mentality" rather than a collection of institutions. In the liberal democracies of the twentieth-century power is exercised less through displays of naked force and more through nurturance of what La Boetie called "voluntary servitude". Contemporary practices of governance lead Bookchin to characterize the State as "a hybridization of political with social institutions, of coercive with distributive functions, of highly punitive with regulatory procedures, and finally of class with administrative needs" (quoted in Marshall 1993: 22).

With the profusion of laws and regulations governing everything from smoking to the baring of breasts, the line dividing State and society has certainly blurred if not disappeared entirely. As laws and legal surveillance extend into ever-increasing realms of human behaviour everyone stands accused, subject to the judgments of state authority.

While respecting the gains won from the State through centuries of social struggle, and not wishing to see these gains unilaterally and callously removed, anarchists nonetheless refuse to follow social democrats in embracing the welfare state. For anarchists, the regulatory and supervisory mechanisms of the welfare state are especially suited to producing docile and dependent subjects. Through institutions like social work and public education, authorities extend the practices of ruling from control over bodies to influence over minds.[32] Moral regulation provides a subtle means for nurturing repression and confomity. "By undermining voluntary associations and the practice of mutual aid [the welfare state] eventually turns society into a lonely crowd buttressed by the social worker and the policeman" (Marshall 1993: 24).

Where defenders of the State appeal to its protective functions as a justification for its continued existence, anarchists respond that the coercive character of the State, as exemplified in the proliferation of regulations, police and prisons, far exceeds whatever protection it might extend (Marshall 1993). Furthermore, States are, in practice, incapable of providing equal protection for all members of society, typically protecting the interests of more priviledged members against the less fortunate. Laws which overwhelmingly emphasize property protection, the restricted and elite character of legal knowledge, guarded by law schools with their exhorbitant tuition fees and exclusionary entrance requirements, and racist overtones in the exercise of "law and order", provide anarchists with evidence enough of the injustices of State "justice". For anarchists, the State with its vast and comlex array of law, prisons, courts and armies stands not as the defender of social justice against inequality but as a primary cause of injustice and oppression.

Additionally, and this is the uniquely anarchist critique, State practices actually undermine social relations within communities, even when not exhibiting a specific bias against the less powerful. This occurs through the substitution of State networks for mutual aid networks in ever-spreading realms of human activity. It results, in relations of dependence rather than self-determination, as the external practices of the State increasingly come to be viewed as the only legitimate mechanisms for solving disputes or addressing social needs. For anarchists the "rule of law" administered through the institutions of the State is not the guarantor of freedom, but, rather, freedom's enemy, closing off alternative avenues for human interaction, creativity and community while corralling more and more people within its own bounds.

Furthermore, the State is not even efficient as a mechanism for redistributing resources. In actuality the State diverts resources from those in need and channels them into itself. "Instead of paying taxes to the State which then decides who is in need, anarchists prefer to help directly the disadvantaged by voluntary acts of giving or by participating in community organizations" (Marshall 1993: 24). Anarchists propose that the social service and welfare functions of the State can be better met by voluntary mutual aid associations, which involve the people affected and respond directly to their needs. Mutual aid at the face-to-face level is regarded as preferable to institutionalized programs or charity.

Once again, contemporary anarchists follow Landauer in understanding anarchism not as a revolutionary establishment of something new, a leap into the unknown or as a break with the present; rather, he regarded anarchism as "the actualisation and reconstitution of something that has always been present, which exists alongside the state, albeit buried and laid waste" (Landauer quoted in Ward 1973: 11). Similarly, Paul Goodman argued that "[a] free society cannot be the substitution of a 'new order' for the old order; it is the extension of spheres of free action until they make up most of social life (quoted in Ward 1973: 11). Starting from this perspective contemporary anarchists seek to develop non-authoritarian and non-hierarchical relations in the here-and-now of everyday life.

Anarchists nurture loyalties other than to States through extended networks of autonomous groupings. Through "day-to-day disavowals of state legality" anarchism exists as "a secret history of resistance" which, by force or by choice, is forever "flowing under and against state and legal authority" (Ferrell 1997: 149).

> There is an order imposed by terror, there is an order enforced by bureaucracy (with the policeman [sic] in the corridor) and there is an order which evolves spontaneously from the fact that we are gregarious animals capable of shaping our own destiny. When the first two are absent, the third, as infinitely more human and humane form of order has an opportunity to emerge. Liberty, as Proudhon said, is the mother, not the daughter of order. (Ward 1973: 37)

Enemies of anarchism typically respond to it by claiming that it rests upon a naive view of "human nature" (see Mayer 1993). The best response to such criticisms is simply to point to the diversity of anarchist views on the question of human nature. What commonality is their between Stirner's self-interested "egoist" and Kropotkin's altruistic upholder of mutual aid? Indeed, the diversity of anarchist views regarding "the individual" and its relation to "the community" may be upheld as testimony to the creativity and respect for pluralism which have sustained anarchism against enormous odds (Shantz 1997). Anarchists simply stress the capacity of humans to change themselves and the conditions in which they find themselves. "The aim is not therefore to liberate some 'essential self' by throwing off the burden of government and the State, but to develop the self in creative and voluntary relations with others" (Marshall 1993: 642-643). Social relations, freely entered, based upon tolerance, mutual aid and sympathy are expected to discourage the emergence of disputes and aid resolution where they do occur. There are no guarantees here, the emphasis is always on potential.

Conclusion

The non-authoritarian, non-hierachical and pluralistic communities envisioned by anarchists have much to offer critical thinking about power, authority and the State. As Ferrell (1997: 153) argues, anarchism serves "by standing outside the law" and through its "disavowal of legal authority and its destructive effects on social and cultural life" works "to remind us that human relations and human diversity matter—and that, in every case, they matter more than the turgid authority of regulation and law." Anarchism ensures that we are never without reminders that things can be done differently than they are. It encourages us to question ingrained assumptions and to rethink habitual practices. Anarchism "offers a clear-sighted critique of existing society and a coherent range of strategies to realize its ideal both in the present and the future" (Marshall 1993: 662). Rather than rejecting "democracy," anarchists offer visions of a participatory democracy that permeates all spheres of life (including the workplace, schools, the family and sexuality). In the spirit of Hakim Bey's *Temporary Autonomous Zones*, contemporary anarchists call for a proliferation of "free" spaces, places and practices that refuse capture within the rigidly mapped territories of States and legal authority. These "autonomous"[33] realms of thought and action emphasize inclusivity, openness and fluidity, against the temporal and spatial confinement of States.

Contemporary anarchists are also keenly aware of the dangers of majoritarian opinion in nurturing oppressive relations. Indeed, contemporary anarchism is partly a response to the dull conformity of consumer capitalism that constrains desires in the permitted realm of market circuits. As a creative response, anarchists defend pluralism and diversity in social relations encouraging experimentation in living and disdaining censorship. Not believing in the possibility of one "correct" response to questions of authority and power, anarchists encourage people to develop multiple alternatives through consideration of the specific conditions with whch they are confronted. Thus, today's anarchists identify themselves variously as punks, animal rights activists, syndicalists, social ecologists or neo-primitives "arming their desires"[34] through collage, veganism, "noise music," polysexuality and "electronic civil disobedience." As always, anarchists provide an alternative to authoritarian forms of social organization, both capitalist as well as socialist.

Perhaps, as Colin Ward (1973: 11) argues, anarchy is always here, "like a seed beneath the snow, buried under the weight of the state and its bureaucracy, capitalism and its waste, privilege and its injustices, nationalism and its suicidal loyalties." In a manner remniscent of Landauer, Ward sees anarchism not as "a speculative vision of a future society," but as "a description of a mode of human organization, rooted in the experience of everday life, which operates side by side with, and in spite of, the dominant authoritarian trends of our society" (Ward 1973: 11).

Endnotes

[1] The 1989 gathering was "Without Borders" held in San Francisco.

[2] Originally the title of Alexander Berkman's newspaper of the nineteen-teens, it has been adopted by contemporary anarchists in Minnesota for their own paper.

[3] This was the code name assumed by the assassin and terrorist Sergei Nechaev, a colleague of Bakunin's and author of the notorious *Catechism of a Revolutionary*. Nechaev was the source for Dostoevsky's character Peter Verkhovensky in *The Possessed*.

[4] One need only recall the 300 or so pages of *The German Ideology*, which Marx devoted to largely personal attacks upon the proto-anarchist Stirner, or his stinging condemnation of Proudhon in *The Poverty of Philosophy*. Of course, the most dramatic example remains Marx's sabotaging of the First International to keep it out of the hands of Bakunin and his colleagues.

[5] This characterization comes famously from Lenin (1965), *'Left-Wing' Communism, An Infantile Disorder*.

[6] See Plekhanov's (1912) confused polemic in *Anarchism and Socialism*.

[7] During the Russian Revolution, anarchists concentrated upon reconstructing society through the workers councils (Soviets) rather than through the State. In areas such as Ukraine, anarchists attempted to establish free communes. These initiatives were violently repressed as part of the consolidation of Bolshevik state power. For poignant accounts of the smashing of workers councils and the final defeat of the anarchists at Kronstadt in 1921, see Berkman (1992) and Bookchin (1986). For details of the Makhnovist movement in Ukraine, see Makhno (1995) and Voline (1954; 1955).

[8] The anarcho-syndicalist resistance during the Spanish Civil War is generally considered the high water mark of anarchism. For details of anarchist efforts in Spain, see Orwell (1986) and Dolgoff (1974)

[9] This characterization comes from Hobsbawm (1959).

[10] For a discussion of the Situationist International see Stewart Home (1996). A fine collection of SI texts in translation is provided by Ken Knabb (1981) in the *Situationist International Anthology*.

[11] See Raoul Vaneigem (1983), *The Revolution of Everyday Life.*

[12] See Guy Debord (1983), *Society of the Spectacle.*

[13] For interesting first-hand accounts of the May-June events of 1968 see René Viénet (1992), *Enragés and Situationists in the Occupation Movement, France, May '68* and Roger Gregoire and Fredy Perlman (1991), *Worker-Student Action Committees, France, May '68.*

[14] See Alberto Melucci (1980), Claus Offe (1985) and Kenneth Tucker (1991).

[15] In addition to sources cited in the text, my discussion of events surrounding Active Resistance is indebted to the eyewitness reports of AR participants Peter Graham, Laura Quilter of CounterMedia and Greg Willerer of Chicago's A-Zone.

[16] A coalition of groups including the Prairie Fire Organizing Committee, the Autonomous Zone, the Puerto Rican Cultural Center, Women's Action Coalition and the National Lawyers Guild (Subways 1996).

[17] This phrase is found in the "Preamble" to the Constitution of the Industrial Workers of the World (I.W.W.).

[18] Kabouters ("elfs") were active in Amsterdam in the late-1960s and early-1970s. See Roel van Duyn (1972), *Message of a Wise Kabouter*, an interesting mix of Kropotkin and cybernetics.

[19] "Bindlestiff" is the Wobbly name for itinerant workers who traversed the countryside following jobs. Reviving historic phraseology is typical practice for contemporary anarchists who have a deep appreciation for those who have gone before.

[20] The violation of boundaries is literal, not simply metaphoric. Contemporary anarchist networks extend, significantly, through the walls of prisons. Most anarchist publications are made available to prisoners through free subscription. Tireless work is done on behalf of prisoners by organizations such as Anarchist Black Cross (ABC), a prisoners' aid group, founded by Albert Melzer (1920-1996).

[21] The anti-nuclear Shundahai Network.

[22] The prop was a giant mock nuclear waste cask.

[23] Police had routinely cruised by the two AR buildings and repeatedly visited the sites during the week.

[24] The Spice Factory was not raided, but only because it had been evacuated and belongings had been removed by the time police arrived.

[25] A group including former Yippies who had been at the convention in 1968 who maintained a camp at Grant Park and held protests around drug legalization. They had been charged with "felony mob action" and "felony battery" after a bottle was allegedly thrown at police during the "Not on the Guest List" march.

[26] By October, 1996, charges had been dropped for all of those arrested during the Festival of the Oppressed.

[27] Coalition-building activities in local neighbourhoods were of special interest to authorities. The case of the Dunbar High School Band is particularly telling. The band, its members African-American teens, was supposed to play in the march focusing on jobs in the community and opposition to the "war on the poor." Although the music teacher was in favour of participation, police persuaded him to pull the band out of the march.

[28] The actual quote, in *What is Property?*, is this: "As man seeks justice in equality, so society seeks order in anarchy" (quoted in Berman 1972). Graffiti artists have neatly symbolized the slogan as the famous "circle-A" (@).

[29] Far from it for Proudhon. He refers to authority as "the curse of society" (1969: 94).

[30] This emphasis made Proudhon's work an important early influence in the emergence of syndicalism.

[31] Proudhon emphatically rejected communism: "[I]f society moves closer and closer toward communism instead of toward anarchy or the government of man by himself (in English: *self-government*)—then the social organization itself will be an abuse of man's [*sic*] faculties" (1969: 94).

[32] See Mariane Valverde (1994), and Mitchell Dean (1994).

[33] Discourses of autonomy serve both as a "fuel" for mobilization and as what Dallmayr (1987) terms an "antidote to co-optation."

[34] *Anarchy* magazine is identified in its subtitle as "A Journal of Desire Armed."

Bibliography

A-Zone. 1996. *Active Resistance: A Counter-Convention*. Chicago (pamphlet).

Active Resistance. 1996. "Chicago Cops Freak as Clinton Speaks—Raids and Felonies." *Love and Rage* 7(5): 14.

Bakunin, Mikhail. 1953. *The Political Philosophy of Bakunin: Scientific Anarchism*. New York: The Free Press of Glencoe.

Berkman, Alexander. 1992. *Life of an Anarchist: The Alexander Berkman Reader* (Ed. Gene Fellner). New York: Four Walls Eight Windows.

Berman, Paul (Ed.). 1972. *Quotations from the Anarchists*. New York: Praeger.

Bookchin, Murray. 1982. *The Ecology of Freedom*. Palo Alto: Cheshire Books.

———. 1986. *Post-Scarcity Anarchism*. Montreal: Black Rose Books.

Bey, Hakim. 1991. *T.A.Z.: The Temporary Autonomous Zone, Ontological Anarchy, Poetic Terrorism*. New York: Autonomedia.

Dallmayr, Fred. 1987. "Hegemony and Democracy: A Review of Laclau and Mouffe." *Philosophy and Social Criticism* 13(3): 283-296.

Dean, Mitchell. 1994. "'A Social Structure of Many Souls': Moral Regulation, Government, and Self-Formation." *Canadian Journal of Sociology* 19(2): 145-168.

Debord, Guy. 1983. *Society of the Spectacle*. Detroit: Black and Red.

Dolgoff, Sam (Ed.). 1974. *The Anarchist Collectives: Workers' Self-management in the Spanish Revolution 1936-1939*. Montreal: Black Rose Books.

Ferrell, Jeff. 1997. "Against the Law: Anarchist Criminology." *Thinking Critically About Crime* (Eds. Brian D. MacLean and Dragan Milovanovic). Vancouver: Collective Press, pp. 146-154.

Godwin, William. 1977. "On Punishment" (Ed. George Woodcock). *The Anarchist Reader*. Glasgow: Fontana, pp. 118-124.

Gregoire, Roger and Fredy Perlman. 1991. *Worker-Student Action Committees, France, May '68*. Detroit: Black and Red.

Heider, Ulrike. 1994. *Anarchism: Left, Right and Green*. San Francisco: City Lights Books.

Hetherington, Kevin. 1992. "Stonehenge and its Festival: Spaces of Consumption" (Ed. Rob Shields). *Lifestyle Shopping: The Subject of Consumption*. London: Routledge, pp. 83-98.

Hobsbawm, E. J. 1959. *Primitive Rebels: Studies in Archaic Forms of Social Movement in the 19th and 20th Centuries*. Manchester: Manchester University Press.

Home, Stewart (Ed.). 1996. *What is Situationism?: A Reader*. Edinburgh: AK Press.

Horowitz, Irving L. (Ed.). 1964. *The Anarchists*. New York: Dell.

Joll, James. 1964. *The Anarchists*. New York: Grosset and Dunlap.

Knabb, Ken. 1981. *Situationist International Anthology*. Berkeley: Bureau of Public Secrets.

Kornegger, Peggy. 1996. "Anarchism: The Feminist Connection" (Ed. Howard J. Ehrlich). *Reinventing Anarchy, Again*. Edinburgh: AK Press, pp. 156-168.

Kropotkin, Peter. 1970. "Law and Authority." *Kropotkin's Revolutionary Pamphlets: A Collection of Writings by Peter Kropotkin* (Ed. Roger N. Baldwin). New York: Dover Publications, pp. 196-218.

———. 1977. "The Uselessness of Laws." *The Anarchist Reader* (Ed. George Woodcock). Glasgow: Fontana, pp. 111-117.

Lenin, V.I. 1965. *'Left-Wing' Communism, An Infantile Disorder*. Peking: Foreign Languages Press.

Lunn, Eugene. 1973. *The Prophet of Community: The Romantic Socialism of Gustav Landauer*. Berkeley: University of California Press.

Makhno, Nestor. 1995. *The Struggle Against the State and Other Essays*. Edinburgh: AK Press.

Marcus, Greil. 1989. *Lipstick Traces: A Secret History of the Twentieth Century*

Marshall, Peter. 1993. *Demanding the Impossible: A History of Anarchism*. London: Fontana Press.

Marx, Karl. 1963. *The Poverty of Philosophy*. New York: International Publishers.

Marx, Karl and Friedrich Engels. 1970. *The German Ideology*. London: Lawrence and Wishart.

Mayer, John R. A. 1993. "A Post-Modern Look at the Tension Between Anarchy and Socialism." *History of European Ideas* 16(4-6): 591-596.

Melucci, Alberto. 1980. "The New Social Movements." *Social Science Information* 19(2): 199-226.

Offe, Claus. 1985. "New Social Movements: Challenging the Boundaries of Institutional Politics." *Social Research* 52(4): 817-868.

Orwell, George. 1986. *Homage to Catalonia*. London: Penguin Books.

Plekhanov, George. 1912. *Anarchism and Socialism*. Chicago: C. H. Kerr.

Proudhon, Pierre-Joseph. 1969. *Selected Writings of Pierre-Joseph Proudhon*. Garden City: Anchor Books.

Rinaldo, Rachel. 1996. "Anarchy in the Windy City: A Look at the Active Resistance Counter-Convention." *Love and Rage* 7(5): 10.

Sand, Jay. 1996. "Convention Activism." *Z Magazine* 9(10): 22-26.

Shantz, Jeffrey. 1997. "Listen Anarchist!: Murray Bookchin's Defence of Orthodoxy." *Alternate Routes: A Journal of Critical Social Research* 14: 69-75.

Solnit, David. 1996. "Anarchy in Chicago." *Fifth Estate* 31(2): 1-3.

Subways, Suzy. 1996. "Not on the Guest List or the Newscasts: Resistance at the Republicrats' Conventions." *Love and Rage* 7(5): 11.

Tolstoy, Leo. 1977. "The Violence of Laws." *The Anarchist Reader* (Ed. George Woodcock). Glasgow: Fontana, pp. 117-118.

Tucker, Kenneth. 1991. "How New Are the New Social Movements?" *Theory, Culture and Society* 8(2): 75-98.

Valverde, Mariana (Ed.). 1994. *Studies in Moral Regulation*. Toronto: Centre for Criminology, University of Toronto.

van Duyn, Roel. 1972. *Message of a Wise Kabouter*. London: Duckworth.

Vaneigem, Raoul. 1983. *The Revolution of Everyday Life*. London: Rebel Press.

Viénet, René. 1992. *Enragés and Situationists in the Occupation Movement, France, May '68*. New York/London: Autonomedia/Rebel.

Voline. 1954. *Nineteen-Seventeen: The Russian Revolution Betrayed*. New York: Libertarian Book Club.

———. 1955. *The Unknown Revolution (1917-1921)*. London: Freedom Press.

Ward, Colin. 1973. *Anarchy in Action*. New York: Harper Torchbooks.

Woodcock, George. 1962. *Anarchism: A History of Libertarian Ideas and Movements*. New York: World Publishing.

Governing Criminal Knowledge—'State,' Power and the Politics of Criminological Research

Reece Walters
Victoria University of Wellington
Mike Presdee
University of Sunderland

It is not only to the poets therefore that we must issue orders requiring them to portray good character in their poems or not to write at all; we must issue similar orders to all artists and craftsmen, and prevent them portraying bad character, ill-discipline, meanness or ugliness in pictures of living things, in sculpture, architecture or any work of art, and if they are unable to comply they must be forbidden to practise art among art. (Plato, *The Republic*)

Introduction

As the opening quotation to this chapter suggests, governments have regulated or silenced critical voices for thousands of years, even Plato, who has been described as something of a visionary for his times, subscribed to suppression and censorship of those ideas considered contrary to the State's best interests. We would argue that criminological knowledge is experiencing similar forms of regulation and censorship, and we aim to address several important questions in this chapter. For example, are there politics involved in

An earlier version of this paper was published in *Current Issues in Criminal Justice*. 1998 (10) (2)

the processes and production of criminological knowledge? Are there governing practices that influence the contours and outcomes of criminological research? If so, what forms do these practices take, and what impact, if any, do they have on contemporary criminological scholarship?

The study of crime and deviance is of significant political and social concern. Whether it challenges existing notions of social order or critiques government policy and practice, criminological research does not take place in a political vacuum (Jupp 1989; Hughes 1996). It is a sensitive enterprise, which often questions the role and management of the state, structures of power and governance as well as notions of social order. Whether challenging underlying and established notions of social order or confronting government policy and practice, criminological research is a genre of knowledge (Garland 1997) that may provide unwelcome views to those governments which seek confirmation of their political ideologies and agendas. Indeed criminological researchers who question existing regulatory practices in society may risk conflict with those officials and authorities that govern such practices.

Modalities of power (Foucault 1980) often seek to regulate the production and utility of knowledge. Governmental practices, contextualized within broader notions of regulation, continue to evolve and hybridize in late modernity (Foucault 1977). These emerging forms of governance (private industry, state and local authorities, regulatory bodies) are central to understanding the production and consumption of criminological research. As Hogg points out: "the production and circulation of criminological knowledge and programs are also governed practices, dependent on and relative to particular institutional, technical and normative conditions and frameworks" (Hogg 1998: 146-147).

The production of criminological knowledge may present a site of contestation and conflict. Hogg and Brown (1998) refer to the uncivil process of law and order, a mechanism by which government stifles and suppresses public debate in an attempt to regulate dissenting views of existing state policy (Hogg and Brown 1998: 1-2).

The reluctance of governments to entertain criticism or opposing views is of critical concern given the changing nature of funded research. O'Malley (1997) points out that criminological research is becoming more market driven. Broader political changes demanding a cost-effective public-sector have placed pressure on universities to be business- or even profit-oriented institutions. Criminologists are finding themselves working in environments that demand greater efficiency and output, where tenure is more difficult to obtain and where university "managers" are placing pressure on academics to engage in contract research in an attempt to promote entrepreneurialism while generating financial growth (O'Malley 1997: 270). The increasing pressure to conduct government evaluations or consultancies under contract (as other sources of funding diminish) places criminologists in a legal position of service provider to the state or client. Contractual arrangements between the two parties set a variety of boundaries around the research to be completed. These include the nature of information to be gathered, the way the research will be reported and regulations over future forms of dissemination. It is our view that these burgeoning contractual arrangements between criminologists and the state are sites for potential contestation.

We are also witnessing an unprecedented volume of private criminological research or consultancies where the researcher enters into a transaction as service provider to a designated client. These contractual arrangements continue to blossom as government and private industries seek expertise or aim to demonstrate accountability, and with them they bring a range of regulations over the scope of the research as well as legal controls over the way the research findings are reported and disseminated. The promulgation of New Right ideologies is affecting the production of new knowledges across a variety of disciplines as well as challenging the traditional role of academic institutions, although it is the governance of criminological knowledge on which this chapter will focus.

This chapter aims to analyze the ways in which 'deviant knowledge' (Brusten 1981) is often policed and/or censured by 'state' authorities. We aim to unearth those unwritten events or struggles which seem to have become 'part and parcel' in contemporary criminological endeavour yet barely receive attention in the final product (Hughes 1996). We wish to address a range of questions in this chapter. For example, to what extent do governments as a means of regulating criminological research use commercial contracts? How should academics react to governments, which threaten legal action or attempt to suppress critical findings? Will the increase in market-driven and market-funded criminological research produce more information gathering for government and less critique of government policy and practice? We are hopeful that our case study based on our experience in Australia (discussed below) may spark further debate by addressing some of these questions as well as identifying some lessons for future criminological inquiry.

Case Study

> Fight to put contract research in public realm—Criminologists risk gag for touching raw nerve with State

This headline appeared in *The Australian's* Higher Education section of February 7, 1996 (Smellie 1996a). The newspaper report described the attempted suppression by the South Australian[1] Attorney-General's Department of two papers presented at the 1996 Australian and New Zealand Society of Criminology conference. The papers, entitled "Mixing Policy and Practice with Politics: The Pitfalls of Community Crime Prevention" by Mike Presdee and Reece Walters and "Telling Stories of Crime in South Australia" by Mark Israel, were alleged by the South Australian Attorney-General's Department in correspondence sent to the conference's convenors to contain material that was potentially in breach of a contract dated 9 August 1993 between the presenters and the South Australian Government.

The Crown Solicitor for the South Australian Attorney-General assumed that the paper's contents constituted a breach of the aforementioned contract. Therefore, on the basis of viewing the titles of the said conference papers and not their contents, the crown solicitor wrote: "Remedies are available to enforce and protect the rights of the South Australian Government and it appears that as Victoria University of Wellington has arranged this conference, any such remedies may be enforceable against the University" (Correspondence dated 25 January 1996).

Earlier correspondence sent to the conference convenors only days before by the manager of the South Australian Crime Prevention Unit (including seventeen pages of Hansard and commentary) attempted to discredit the research alleged to be linked to the proposed papers stating, "I believe the above mentioned papers are based on this research [Review of the South Australian Crime Prevention Strategy], and hence I suggest it would be in the best interests of the ANZSOC [sic] Conference for you to discuss this matter with me" (Milbank 1996).

When the conference convenors did not submit to the demands of the South Australian Government, arguing "I see it neither as my role nor as my responsibility as Convenor of the above Conference to scrutinize all papers submitted to ensure their compliance with external contractual obligations" (Morris 1996), the South Australian Attorney-General's Department moved swiftly and sent legal documentation to Victoria University of Wellington, necessitating the involvement of that university's vice-chancellor.

This event marked a watershed for the conference of the Australian and New Zealand Society of Criminology; never before had a government department, let alone a foreign government, threatened legal action against presenters, the society itself (including its members) and the host university. If the vice-chancellor of Victoria University of Wellington had acceded to this request it could be argued that vice-chancellors of all universities would be responsible for the contents of all the papers presented at every conference held throughout Australia and New Zealand. As a result, vice-chancellors could be forced to act as censors in the very arena that many would consider the fount of freedom of thought. As such the actions of the South Australian Government constituted a substantial attack on academic freedom and showed clearly how the state could interfere and seek to control research processes and findings.

The convenors of the conference invited representatives of the South Australian Government to present their concerns at the conference. Initially the Attorney-General's Department in Adelaide agreed but eventually withdrew only days before the conference started. In its place the convenors held a special plenary session on academic freedom chaired by Professor Carson (vice-chancellor of Auckland University) and Professor Young (Victoria University of Wellington). The plenary session explored some of the current issues facing criminologists engaged in commercially contracted research.

In his opening address to the plenary session attended by over 150 conference delegates, Professor Carson presented the New

Zealand Education Act, which protects academic freedom and the rights of university staff to disseminate research and engage in public debate. Furthermore, Professor Carson commented:

> Academic freedom in the field of Criminology is perhaps even more problematic and more important than quite a few areas of academic endeavor because it's touching the State at a raw nerve.... Almost automatically, if we are studying crime we are messing around with some of the most powerful constructs the State has at its disposal. (Smellie 1996a)

Professor Warren Young told the plenary that criminologists should safeguard against loss of copyright and intellectual property by carefully negotiating such matters prior to signing contractual agreements. However, Professor John Braithwaite (Australian National University) took a different view. He told the plenary that social science researchers were constantly faced with governments having "carte blanche over intellectual property" and that criminologists needed to be "buccaneers" when it came to publishing their research. Braithwaite further added: "I say, 'You can try and stop me and you can probably take away the report, but that would be foolish because I will go to the press and get the report out in a much better way'" (Smellie 1996b).

Similar threats had preceded the submission of the final evaluation report, which had reviewed the South Australian Crime Prevention Strategy (see discussion below). As O'Malley (1997) has pointed out, "[E]valuation, that most technical of the operations of crime prevention, thus again proves to be highly political. Perhaps nowhere has this been more visible than in the struggles that emerged over the evaluation of the South Australian crime prevention program" (O'Malley 1997: 269). It is our intention here to present some of the details involved in the review of the South Australian Crime Prevention Strategy in order to illustrate some of the struggles which criminological researchers must engage in when they criticize state policy. In doing so, we acknowledge that not all governments are out to suppress the truth, as well as suggesting that not all academics produce good work. Yet we are concerned that the increase in contract research, concomitantly with the state's rejection of criticism in times of accountability (see Hogg and Brown 1998), are likely to produce more examples of conflict between researcher and funding bodies. What we aim to do here is to reveal something of the process, which is not evident in the end product of evaluation research. A process that highlights the sometimes intimidating mechanisms of the state when faced with critical research.

Background of the Research

In August 1993 La Trobe University (Melbourne, Australia) was contracted by the South Australian Attorney-General's Department to review that state's Crime Prevention Strategy, a Labour Party policy launched in 1989. The final report, entitled "Policies and Practices of Preventing Crime: A Review of the South Australian Crime Prevention Strategy," was authored by Mike Presdee and Reece Walters. It was submitted in draft form to the Crime Prevention Unit (CPU) in June 1994 with an agreement by the CPU to provide "feedback" to the authors within one week—this never occurred. The 300-page (approx.) draft report, containing 66 conclusions and 33 recommendations, examined *inter alia* issues such as crime prevention for Aboriginal peoples, the prospects and problems with inter-agency or partnership models, the role of the community in local crime problems, public perceptions of safety in the streets of Adelaide, the relationship between young people and police, the development and progress of 500 crime prevention programs, the impact of dry area legislation in South Australia, crime and the media and so on. In sum the report described a range of pragmatic hurdles confronting the development and implementation of localized crime prevention plans and those practices likely to produce positive outcomes (see Presdee and Walters 1994). The report included a detailed analysis of the policy development practices of the CPU, the body responsible for managing the state's crime prevention strategy. It is here that the evaluation unveils a range of political processes and sensitivities relating to government decision-making and management (see Presdee and Walters 1997).

Using cabinet papers and departmental documentation as well as extensive interview data, the evaluation pieced together the vagaries of government policy-making and managerial uncertainties that had led to community frustration and despair (Presdee and Walters 1997). The authors charted the processes of political and bureaucratic policy-making and critically concluded that the development and management of government policy had impacted significantly on the way that policy was delivered and received. This was seen as a central and therefore vital element of the research. The final report conveyed this effect by identifying the despondency of community workers and other key people involved with the crime prevention strategy. One crime prevention officer employed to deliver local crime prevention plans is quoted as saying:

> The CPU ran the professional line until they finally came clean about the strategy, that is, the CPU finally admitted their lack of knowledge and this was a first for them. They should have been up front from the outset rather than leaving communities on their own without support. (Presdee and Walters 1994: 32)

Quotations such as these, supported by the words of CPU staff describing their own managerial confusion and ill direction, appear throughout the final evaluation report (Presdee and Walters 1994: 20-60). However it was the report's ability to describe, through the use of cabinet papers, how government policy itself had been created while also revealing how public servants set about manipulating the powerful and setting their own policy agendas, that proved the most disturbing in the corridors of power. The report conjured up images of policy-making processes in its now well-known description of the "Red Dot Day" (Presdee and Walters 1994 and 1997), minutely describing how the most powerful committee ever assembled in South Australian law enforcement circles huddled around pieces of butcher's paper scattered over the floor and placed sticky red dots alongside issues they thought were important. The report concluded: "the results of this 'parlour game' approach to planning resulted in a rather predictable outcome" (Presdee and Walters 1994:54), which included the identification of corrections as the key area for crime prevention. But more than anything else, it drew aside the cloak of bureaucratic and governmental secrecy to reveal that in places of power, bureaucratic advice is sometimes driven by a flimsy process of decision-making. The evidence that gave a full description of the "emperor's clothes" was in the report for all to read.[2]

Submitting the Draft Report

Within twenty-four hours of the draft report's submission (15 June 1994), the chief executive officer of the South Australian Attorney-General's Department formally wrote to the then deputy vice-chancellor of LaTrobe University, Professor Kit Carson, requesting an urgent meeting to discuss the report's alleged breach of contract as well as a range of "management issues" relating to the evaluation. In response Professor Carson wrote directly to the Acting Attorney-General (current premier), the Hon. J. Olsen, and stated:

> I am surprised by this peremptory invitation to attend a meeting with such a goal, given that there has been no previous correspondence on these matters. I am doubly surprised that the invitation is based on an incomplete draft report, especially in view of the fact that a meeting which had been arranged between the authors and the Crime Prevention Unit to discuss the draft report was apparently cancelled by the Crime Prevention Unit at the last minute without explanation. (Carson, 24 June 1994)

Within hours of this letter reaching the acting minister's office, the chief executive officer of the Attorney-General's Department phoned Professor Carson, adopting a more "conciliatory" tone than that which was evident in his early correspondence. He followed up his phone call with a letter on the same day:

> The Attorney-General (Mr. K.T. Griffin) is anxious to resolve these matters as soon as possible. He does not however, believe it appropriate to begin to deliver voluminous written materials to each other, but prefers to address the issues around the table. (Kelly 24 June 1994)

The (over) reaction of the Attorney-General's Department to a draft evaluation report demonstrated the sensitive and defensive nature of this particular department, one which clearly did not express an anxiety to "resolve matters" but instead to threaten those connected to the research in the interests of seeing the report's content either changed or suppressed. Radzinowicz (1994) has identified these Government practices of tampering with independent research as government's "setting the agenda" ... in relation to the administrator's (and ultimately the Minister's) conception of what kind of knowledge is needed" (Radzinowicz 1994: 101).

Discussing the Draft Report

On 29 June 1994, a meeting between the Attorney General's Department (chief executive officer, crown solicitor, attorney-general's chief of staff, CPU manager) and La Trobe University was held at the attorney-general's offices in Adelaide.

Some of the details relating to this meeting are worth documenting in order to gain a sense of how this department approached the entire issue. In doing so we concur with Hughes (1996) that there are lessons to be learned for future criminological researchers by opening up and revealing the difficulties encountered when researching crime and criminal justice.

The meeting commenced with the chief executive officer of the Attorney-General's Department handing out a seven-page document outlining the various concerns with the draft report. He emphasized that it was a paper for the purpose of that particular meeting and was, therefore, not to leave the building, claiming that it was a working document. He explained that the Attorney-General's Department was still in the process of considering their response to the draft report and did not want a working paper to prejudice their position. The La Trobe University contingent (deputy vice-chancellor [research], co-authors Presdee and Walters and La Trobe University's solicitor) considered this to be totally unacceptable. The evaluation team had submitted a draft report as required and was awaiting feedback in order to finalize its work. Instead, senior state officials were alleging breach of contract and convening urgent meetings and then denying the researchers the opportunity to take away the government's concerns and carefully consider them.

La Trobe University representatives were invited to take a few minutes to read seven pages of script and then return the document after giving their response. The document included broad statements about areas not covered in the report and a number of alleged factual inaccuracies. During La Trobe University's reading time, the chief executive officer of the Attorney-General's Department interrupted to discuss an alleged breach of confidentiality—something which he had raised in early correspondence but had withdrawn from this meeting's agenda. He accused one of the researchers of breaching confidentiality clauses in the contract by granting the chief executive officer of South Australian Aboriginal Affairs access to preliminary research findings within the previous week. The current meeting had been in session less than fifteen minutes and this attack (complete with legal threats) was clearly outside the boundaries of the agenda, yet the opportunity to threaten and plant seeds of legal challenge were seized upon. Members of the La Trobe University contingent expressed their discontent with this action and motioned towards the door suggesting that if the tactics mentioned above were to persist then the matter would be best settled in the courtroom. The chief executive officer explained that he had been misunderstood; he was simply trying to clarify a matter involving confidentiality clauses.

The meeting lasted ninety minutes and involved the Attorney-General's Department highlighting what it considered deficiencies in the evaluation report. LaTrobe University representatives listened to the feedback choosing not to enter into lengthy discussion. Given that LaTrobe University representatives were not permitted to take away the written concerns and consider them at length, they deemed inappropriate to have to defend allegations on the run, without time to consult.

The meeting concluded with the Attorney-General's Department agreeing to provide a detailed account (which the review team could have access to) of all alleged factual inaccuracies in the report and alleged breaches of contract. The deadline for submitting the final report was re-negotiated from 30 June 1994 to 15 July 1994. This meeting had been a crude attempt by the Crown Solicitor to frighten the report's authors and by doing so alter its findings. It was an intimidating structure that could have worked because of its sheer brutality, but in this case, because the authors united around the integrity of their findings, it failed.

The period between the meeting mentioned above and the deadline for the final report (notably sixteen days) was also a time closely monitored by the state. The researchers were requested to amend "factual inaccuracies" in their draft report, but their access to information and government personnel was highly regulated. All communication from the researchers was directed to the manager of the CPU. For almost a year, the researchers had been liaising daily with all members of the CPU, yet without reason the Attorney-General's Department insisted that all queries be directed to the CPU's manager, other CPU staff became unreachable during this period. Moreover, all requests by the researchers for additional information were required to be put in writing. In other words, gaining access to information became "highly procedurized and personalized" (Hughes 1996: 69) as a means of controlling external inquiry (Lee 1993).

The final report was submitted on the due date and the Attorney-General's Department remained silent for four weeks. On 22 August 1994, the evaluation report was tabled in the South Australian Parliament, whereupon allegations of breach of contract were made by the Attorney-General. Press statements were released by the Attorney-General and media interviews held with public servants all attempting to discredit the report. While LaTrobe University had spent four weeks after the submission of the final report continuously writing to the South Australian Attorney-General's Department requesting payment and receiving no reply, it is now clear that the Attorney-General's Department was orchestrating a plan to release the report and have it receive as much bad press as possible.

Despite the report's authors calling for public debate on its contents, there has been none to date. The South Australian Attorney-General (Trevor Griffin), who inherited the strategy from the previous Labour government, has described the report as not providing a "comprehensive process and outcome evaluation of the Crime Prevention Strategy as expected. It provided little analysis of crime prevention issues … " (Griffin 1995:10).

The previous Attorney-General in South Australia (Chris Sumner) referred to it as an "ideological waste of time" (Penberthy 1994). Irrespective of the Attorney-General heeding some of the recommendations contained in the report, his department has remained adamant that the document constitutes a contractual breach and, therefore, has refused to settle the outstanding amount of $72,358 owing to LaTrobe University. It is understood that La Trobe

University has not pursued the amount for reasons pertaining to legal costs. However, legal advice given to La Trobe University suggests that the report does not breach the contract between the two parties and the South Australian government is legally obliged to pay (Topsom 1995). Yet a state of deadlock has arisen since.

A question must be asked. If (as legal opinion suggests) this evaluation is not in breach of contract and has delivered its report on time, why is a state government refusing to settle? By not settling for alleged contractual reasons, the Attorney-General's Department can continue to discredit the value of the report. But again, why do this when the report contains much information for future crime prevention policies? Because the report reveals and challenges the ambiguous processes and practices of the public servants responsible for the development and implementation of the South Australian Crime Prevention Strategy. How can one report provoke such response? Why does the South Australian Attorney-General's Department continually attempt to muzzle the dissemination of a report's content that they claim was a failure, a waste of time and tells them nothing about crime prevention? We argue that evaluation reports, which produce the "wrong answers", are always susceptible to official and/or legal ramifications from funding sources.

Criminological research has the potential to unearth government decision-making and the resultant policies. These discoveries often reveal more about government processes of discretionary power than the subject of review. As the South Australian Attorney-General has said, his government's attempt to suppress the report were "protecting the state's interests" (Smellie 1996b).

General Discussion

All that we have described in micro-detail above shows state mobilization of power as part of the process of the policing of knowledge (Brusten 1981). We don't believe the above case study is a one-off incident. We see it as a useful starting point for exploring wider themes about contract research and academic freedom, or as Chomsky urges, "to seek out an audience that matters ... a community of common concern in which one hopes to participate" (1996:61). We also aim to raise questions about the changing nature of criminological research, which includes the growth of private consultancies, and explore the possible sites of tension that may arise from these new forms of knowledge production.

As mentioned, we would argue that our case study is not uncommon. It included most of the features consistent with contractual research including rigorous researcher and commissioner protocols, monthly reporting and management meetings with government officials, detailed discussions of research methods both prior to and during their implementation, as well as the submission of two written interim reports. We argue that our case study provides an illustration of the state policing knowledge, notably that which challenges government decision-making. This policing has given rise to a long struggle between researchers and those who hold power, over what counts as knowledge and truth (Stenson and Cowell 1991; May 1993). As Foucault has identified, the "art of governing" or "to govern" not only involves the protection of principality or territory but also the governing of "things", the day-to-day events (such as research and process of management) that influence, or are capable of influencing, the economy of the state (Foucault 1978: 89-91).

Evaluation work itself necessarily involves the production of new knowledges and truths about specific social policies that have emanated from within the deepest layers of the political processes. Attempts by bureaucrats to reduce evaluation to simply the scientific administration of things, is an attempt to disguise the true research nature of such work and its ability to produce new knowledges about policy making and policy practices. The resulting social policies are no more than the 'offspring' of political processes themselves and as a result come laden with the political struggles and issues of the day. Evaluation of such policies often unearths this true relationship between politics and policy which is why servants of the state may seek to control the production, distribution and consumption of emerging new knowledges about their world of policy making and practice. When researchers create new criminological understandings of these processes through their evaluative work; when they have succeeded against all odds in truly evaluating policies, then those in power may seek to control totally the distribution and consumption of these new knowledges and question the production process itself.

We see it as our duty as researchers to inform other criminologists of the existing strategies of state bureaucracies as they seek to appropriate research, in order for criminologists as a group to recognize the powerful mechanisms of control by which state agencies seek to capture and hold onto research. Researching and publishing sensitive areas of social science is always susceptible to government rebuke and official challenge (Lee 1993). However, criminologists have a responsibility to engage in public debate and publish their work (Jupp 1989).

First, we must recognize that there will always be demands by the state for operational research while discarding critical research as unscientific. This false dichotomy becomes the first point of struggle for researchers who find their work emptied of true content from the very beginning. This dichotomy is often incorporated into the process of everyday control mechanisms practised by the state in order to systematically tamper with the truth and the processes of the production of knowledge. The research contract itself reflects this process of control as the state may seek to determine the research instruments themselves, restrict the publication of results and attempt to appropriate all that is produced including ideas and analyses, all being contractually owned by the state, to be discarded or censored at will. Here the research contract becomes no more than the legalization of state interference and is always the first formal mechanism of the oppression of the truth. As Cullingworth identified three decades ago, government contracts often make up this oppression of the truth: "[T]he freedom of the social researcher— and hence the scientific nature of his work—is largely illusory if he is entirely constrained by terms of reference laid down by a public authority ... and by deadlines set by a financial timetable" (Cullingworth 1969: 13). Also, Radzinowicz has expressed concern about the state of criminological research, particularly the "attitudes of authorities to the freedom of access to information and the freedom to interpret and publish findings" which he considers are "prerequisites for any really incisive and honest research" (Radzinowicz 1994: 103).

Moreover, as Manfred Brusten has pointed out, as well as the formal sanction of restrictive contracts there are many informal sanctions used by the state to influence the processes of distribution and consumption of critical research work. These include, giving researchers a bad reputation while constructing a negative image of that type of researcher, making administrative difficulties, making the researchers wait and repeat their demands many times before reacting, putting pressure on the heads of departments in which the researcher is working to exert influence on the subordinate researcher, suspecting the researcher of activities that might lead to formal prosecution and suspecting 'secret information' in the files of the researcher (Brusten 1981).

All these strategies were brought to bear in the case we have described above and as such acts as another episode in the long history of attempted suppression of deviant knowledge. There are in the end only two fail-safe strategies to avoid getting into conflict with state bureaucracies. The first is to do research in which they are not interested; the second is to do research that they think is either harmless or the most valuable to them. All else may trigger both the formal and informal procedures by which the defensive social controls of criminological endeavours takes place (Brusten 1981).

Conclusion

As the title of this book suggests, we see the interrogation of social justice issues as a key component of criminological research. We are concerned that criminological research is becoming less and less critical. Instead we are seeing the continual emergence of administrative, uncritical and politically safe research. Academic research must reflect a commitment to intellectual authority and to our obligation as critic and conscience of society (Haskell 1996). Yet, the increase in contract research, which legally binds academics to provide information to clients or stakeholders, is capable of restricting academic freedom. Research, which moves beyond the boundaries of the state contract, (which are becoming increasingly more detailed with complex clauses about confidentiality, copyright and intellectual property), are likely to draw the sort of challenges that we have described above.

The lesson to be learned in the above research was that in the end the South Australian State apparatus was unable to maintain control outside its domain and was unable to mobilize state power Australia wide. We believe that criminologists must maintain intellectual property and academic freedom when they undertake contract research. This, however, may jeopardize the winning of a contract, yet it is important for universities to market their uniqueness, one that provides independence, diversity and critique. Attempts to convert academic departments into profitable entities or business units must co-exist with a commitment to uphold academe as a place of freedom of thought. Researchers who uphold this tradition, and challenge government policy, are likely to encounter the struggles we have identified above. While we endorse mechanisms and protocols that are likely to limit tension between state agencies and researchers, in many ways tensions are unavoidable in a political climate that promotes government sensitivities to all forms of criticisms. We argue that it is important for criminologists to publish their work, to engage in public debate and to allow their research to be scrutinized. If academic criminological research is to become nothing more than information gathering for government policy, which is not prepared to critique the role of the state for fear of losing future contracts, then we argue that we reduce ourselves to co-conspirators in the policing of knowledge.

Endnotes

[1] South Australia is one of eight states and territories (or provinces) in Australia. It has a population of 1.2 million people.

[2] We use the expression "for all to read" yet the final evaluation report, "Policies and Practices of Preventing Crime: A Review of the South Australian Crime Prevention Strategy," was never published. In late 1994 the Crime Prevention Unit released it to relevant people who contacted the Attorney-General. Even after its tabling in Parliament there were restrictions over access. According to the manager of the CPU speaking on South Australian radio in January 1996, the report can now be obtained by members of the general public at a cost of $1 per page—the report is 304 pages in length, so we must, therefore, question the extent to which it is truly a public document.

Bibliography

Brusten, M. 1981. "State control of information in the field of deviance and social control," *Working Papers in European Criminology 2*.

Carson, W.G. 1994. Written correspondence to the Hon. J. Olsen, Acting Attorney-General. 24 June 1994.

Chomsky, N. 1996. *Power and Prospects. Reflections on Human Nature and the Social Order.* St Leonards: Allen and Unwin.

Cullingworth, J. 1969. *The Politics of Research. An Inaugural Lecture Delivered in the University of Birmingham on 6th March 1969.* Birmingham: University of Birmingham.

Foucault, M. 1977. *Discipline and Punish, The Birth of the Prison.* London: Allen Lane.

Foucault, M. 1978. "Governmentality." In Burchell, G. and Gordon, C. (Eds.), *The Foucault Effect. studies in Governmental Rationality.* Mepstead: WheatsheafHemel. Pp. 1-21.

Foucault, M. 1980. "Two Lectures." In Gordon, C. (Ed.), *Power/Knowledge.* Brighton: Harvester Press. Pp. 79-96

Garland, D. 1997. "Of Crimes and Criminals: The Development of Criminology in Britain." In Maguire, M., Morgan, R. and Reiner, R. (Eds.), *The Oxford Handbook of Criminology.* Second Edition. Oxford: Clarendon Press. Pp. 11-57.

Griffin, T. 1995. "The Role Of Crime Prevention In Modern Australia." *Crime in Australia. The First National Outlook Symposium. Canberra,* 5 & 6 June 1995. Canberra: The Australian Institute of Criminology. Pp. 1-12.

Haskell, T. 1996. "Justifying the Rights of Academic Freedom in the era of 'Power/Knowledge'." In Menand, L. (Ed.), *The Future of Academic Freedom.* Chicago: The University of Chicago Press.

Hogg, R. 1998. "Crime, Criminology and Government." In Walton, P. and Young, J. (Eds.), *The New Criminology Revisited.* London: Macmillan Press Ltd.

Hogg, R. and Brown, D. 1998. *Rethinking Law and Order.* Annandale: Pluto Press. Pp. 143-162.

Hughes, G. 1996. "The Politics of Criminological Research." In Sapsford, R. (Ed.), *Researching Crime and Criminal Justice.* London: Sage Publications. Pp. 57-106.

Jupp, V. 1989. *Methods of Criminological Research.* London: Allen and Unwin.

Kelly, K. 1994. Chief Executive Officer, South Australian Attorney-General's Department. Written correspondence to Professor Carson. 24 June 1994.

Lee, R. 1993. *Doing Research on Sensitive Topics.* London: Sage Publications.

May, T. 1993. *Social Research.* London: Sage Publications.

Milbank, S. 1996. Manager, South Australian Crime Prevention Unit, Attorney-General's Department. Written correspondence, reference AGD 1368\92,15 January 1996.

Morris, A. 1996. "ANZSOC Conference Program." Facsimile correspondence dated 15 January 1996.

O'Malley, P. 1997. "The Politics of Crime Prevention." In O'Malley, P. and Sutton, A. (Eds.), *Crime Prevention in Australia. Issues In Policy and Research.* Sydney: The Federation Press. Pp. 255-274.

Penberthy, D. 1994. "Pledge on Funding to Fight Crime," *The Adelaide Advertiser*, p.10. *22* December 1994.

Presdee, M. and Walters, R. 1994. *Policies and Practices of Preventing Crime: A Review of the South Australian Crime Prevention Strategy.* Melbourne: National Centre For Socio-Legal Studies.

Presdee, M. and Walters, R. 1997. "Policies, Politics, Practices: Crime Prevention in South Australia." In O'Malley, P. and Sutton, A. (Eds.), *Crime Prevention in Australia. Issues In Policy and Research.* Sydney: The Federation Press. Pp. 200-216.

Radzinowicz, L. 1994. "Reflections on the State of Criminology," *British Journal of Criminology.* Vol. 34. no. 2. Pp. 99-104.

Smellie, P. 1996a. "Fight to Put Contract Research in Public Realm— Criminologists Risk Gag for 'Touching Raw Nerve of States'." *The Australian*, p.23. 7 February 1996.

Smellie, P. 1996b. "State Bids to Censor Crime Policy Report." *The Australian*, p.4. 31 January 1996.

South Australian Attorney-General's Department. 1996. Crown Solicitor's Office, Commercial and Finance Section. Written correspondence, reference COMF\RMF.O2:mm. 25 January 1996.

Stenson, K. and Cowell, D. (Eds.). 1991. *The Politics of Crime Control.* London: Sage Publications.

Topsom, R. 1994. Deputy vice-chancellor, La Trobe University, Contract Research and Technology. Written correspondence to Mr. Kym Kelly, Chief Executive Officer, South Australian Attorney-General's Department. 11 July 1994.

Questioning the Confines of Criminology: Can Feminism Thrive within the Discipline?

Deborah Plechner
University of California, Riverside

Introduction

Recently, there have been several thorough reviews of feminist criminological research and theorizing published (e.g., Daly and Chesney-Lind 1996; Rafter and Heidensohn 1997; Simpson 1996). This, in and of itself, is a testament to the growing importance of this field and the continuing contribution that feminists are making to the study of crime, punishment, law and social control. It is now possible to speak of a feminist criminology that has transcended national boundaries, although the contours of this "international" project are somewhat fuzzy. Meda Chesney-Lind, in the foreword to this newest collection of global feminist perpsectives (Rafter and Heidensohn 1997) writes of its significance:

> This edited collection, like the conversations and conferences (notably the Mont Gabriel Conference on Women, Law and Social Control) that gave it birth, is making intellectual history. Suddenly, women are daring to speak about crime and social control in ways that place women at the centre rather than the periphery of the inquiry. (xii)

However, feminists—Meda Chesney-Lind included—are still grappling with the fundamental question of what their impact has been within the traditional sphere of criminology, and whether a truly feminist criminology is theoretically possible (see Carlen 1996; Daly 1994; Smart 1996, 1995). The following quote describes a dilemma felt by many feminists attempting to work within the field of criminology. Although feminism has had a significant impact on academic thought, there is a growing sense of the inability of feminism to have any transformative impact within the discipline of criminology:

> We write as feminists interested in problems of crime and justice and find that we lead a double life. As feminists, we grapple with the many strands of feminist thought and activism, educate ourselves and others about the impact of gender relations on social life, and ponder our role as academics in a social movement. As criminologists, we grapple with the field's many theoretical and policy strands, educate ourselves and others on the conditions and social processes that make crime normal and deviant, and ponder the state's role in creating and reducing crime. All the while we wonder if it is possible to reconcile these double lives. (Kathleen Daly and Meda Chesney-Lind 1996: 341)

In order to assess the question of feminism's impact on criminological thought, the stage must first be set by outlining both the history of feminist thought and some of the substantive contributions of feminists working to understand the nature of women's punishment, offending and the relationship between the two.

Briefly I will outline the history and current contours of feminist criminology by tracing its development from the early 1960s onward through the writings of some of its leading figures—Dorie Klein, Meda Chesney-Lind, Pat Carlen, James Messerschmidt and Carol Smart. As the inclusion of feminist insights into the discipline of criminology is based in the history of feminism itself, I will also briefly sketch the contours of feminism as a movement during the last century. Then my essay will move on to the crucial question now being debated by feminists working squarely within the discipline, as well as those who consider themselves more on the margins of the traditional field of criminological inquiry—what has the impact of feminism been within the discipline?

In considering this question I will draw from the work of the above-mentioned scholars, and also focus on three substantive issues that have been highlighted by many feminist theorists and researchers: 1) the link between women's victimization and offending behaviour; 2) the role of the state in controlling violence against women; and 3) the dilemmas brought about by a liberal feminist strategy of social change. Finally, in light of the previous discussion, I will consider the issues facing feminist criminologists, and the field as a whole, in the future. In the end it is suggested that feminists must join forces across disciplines, especially in the fields of jurisprudence and criminology, if we ever hope to bring about meaningful change in our systems of law and justice.

A Brief History of Feminism

Feminism is both a set of theories about women's oppression and a set of strategies for social change. As a world view and a social movement, feminism is both analytical and empirical. Feminism contains a diversity of perspectives and agendas, but there are common elements uniting the various strands of feminist thought and distinguishing it as a whole (Daly and Chesney-Lind 1996).

These elements include the idea that gender is not a natural fact but a complex social, historical and cultural product; gender is related to, but not simply derived from, biological sex differences between men and women. In addition, feminists acknowledge that gender relations order social life in fundamental ways, with men's social and political-economic dominance over women being an organizing principle of social life. And feminism includes the idea that systems of knowledge reflect men's views of the natural and social world (Daly and Chesney-Lind 1996).

Feminism has the important task of critiquing existing theories for the way in which they represent men's experiences as central and normal. But feminism seeks to go beyond mere critique by contemplating what theories would look like if women's experiences were central in their construction. Feminist analysis draws from feminist theory and research, problematizes gender and concerns itself with empowering women (Bartlett and Kennedy 1991; Daly and Chesney-Lind 1996; Simpson 1996).

The "first wave" of feminism occurred in the early nineteenth century as women struggled politically to secure the right to vote, to own property as married women and to gain access to birth control.

Scholars and activists in this phase of feminism challenged the ideology of separate spheres, which emerged with industrialization and dictated that the public world of paid work was appropriate only for men, thus relegating women to the private (and uncompensated) domain of the home (Bartlett and Kennedy 1991; Kemp 1994).

Yet in challenging the inequities of gender relations, first-wave feminists paradoxically upheld and strengthened the related ideology of the cult of domesticity. They promoted an image of women as inherently different from men, morally superior and responsible for the virtuousness of the family, community and nation. First-wave feminists faced the challenges of mobilizing a mass-based movement based on the claim of women's unity while at the same time attempting to acknowledge the diversity of women and uphold individual freedom. These challenges have not eluded feminism in its more modern guises (Cott 1987; Daly and Chesney-Lind 1996; Kessler-Harris and Sacks 1987).

The "second wave" of feminists emerged in the 1960s and denounced the domestic sphere as oppressive to women. The intended goal of feminists during the 1960s and 1970s was the legal equality of women with men. Feminists challenged gender-based laws and legal practices premised on the notion of separate spheres and fought for the legal application of the equal rights doctrine (Daly and Chesney-Lind 1996; Smith 1993). Liberal feminists achieved many successes in their efforts to reform specific laws and challenge the underlying assumptions about the nature of women embedded in legal practice. But by the mid 1980s, feminists were beginning to question the efficacy of the liberal strategy of legal equality for bringing significant change to women's lives. Feminist legal theorists, in particular, were forced to acknowledge the weaknesses of a strategy of legal reform and began to explore the complex ways in which law serves to strengthen the roots of gender hierarchy despite its guarantee of equality (Bartlett and Kennedy 1991; Smith 1993).

Feminist criminology, like feminist jurisprudence, emerged in the early 1970s and was initially wedded to a liberal approach, but the trajectories and dimensions of these two schools of feminist thought have differed over the last two decades, in addition to their differing ability to influence their more traditional "parent" disciplines. Nicole Rafter and Frances Heidensohn argue that late-twentieth-century mainstream criminology was the most masculine of all the social sciences. Well into the 1970s, criminologists felt thoroughly justified in ignoring women because men committed the vast majority of crimes, and men constituted over 90% of all prisoners. Even labelling theorists and critical criminologists, "the self-appointed progressives of the 1960s and 1970s, ignored women" (Rafter and Heindensohn 1997: 5). Political science was forced to acknowledge women because they could vote. History, as a discipline, while perhaps not welcoming women's history, could not deny it. And law— another highly gendered field—also paid more attention to women because they constituted more than a tiny fraction of potential cases (ibid.: 4-5).

Feminist jurisprudence was more adept at establishing legitimacy as an academic area of study because scholars of legal theory are often also practitioners of the law. Feminist legal theorists are overwhelmingly concerned with how the law operates as a patriarchal institution, yet as legal activists they hold out the promise of utilizing the law to effect change for women (Bartlett and Kennedy 1991; Vago 1994). Criminology is different than jurisprudence in that it studies the causes of crime and has traditionally focused on individual-level explanations of criminality. The subject of women's criminality has typically been ignored. In cases when women have been included in theories of crime, they have either been added on as adjuncts or have been treated in ways that uphold mythical and stereotypical notions of women's biological and psychological nature, particularly by stressing the depravity and pathology of the female offender. The neglect and distortion of women's experiences in criminological theory and research necessitated a thorough (and ongoing) feminist critique of the discipline (Curran and Renzetti 1994; Muncie et al. 1996; Shoemaker 1996; Sommers 1995).

Early Feminist Criminology

The Early Pioneers

The need for critique was met by three pioneers—Bertrand (1969), Heidensohn (1968) and Klein (1973)—involved as academics in the study of criminology (Rafter and Heidensohn 1997). The noted omission of women from general theories of crime by Bertrand (1969) and Heidensohn (1968) has been characterized as "[the] awakening of criminology from its androcentric slumber" (Daly and Chesney-Lind 1996: 344). Early feminist critiques of criminology focused on the intellectual sexism in theories of female crime[1] and the institutional sexism in the juvenile and criminal justice systems (Daly and Chesney-Lind 1996). Dorie Klein was one of the earliest criminologists to point out that theorists such as Freud, Thomas and Lombroso saw women's criminality as a deviation (often of a sexualized nature) from the universalized and ahistorical (and asexual) ideal of white upper-class femininity (1973).

Klein argued that these earlier theories, and later theories rooted in sex-role explanations of male and female behaviour, had created two distinct classes of women: good "normal" (feminine) women versus bad criminal (and masculine) women. In doing so, these theories had promoted individualistic remedies for women's deviance ranging from sterilization to psychoanalysis. These remedies always stopped short of social change, namely because the theories consistently ignored any economic, social or political factors in their explanatory schemes. Not surprisingly then, theorists up to this time had also ignored the problems of poor and minority women (Klein 1973; Sommers 1995).

Feminist criminology continued to develop in America over the next decade. Early in the 1970s, Meda Chesney-Lind began to focus on the treatment young women received from the juvenile justice system, dispelling the then-popular idea that girls and women were treated with leniency and chivalry by judges and law enforcement officials. Chesney-Lind argued that girls' wrongdoing was overwhelmingly sexualized and that females received much stricter sanctions than boys committing the same offences. Further, Chesney-Lind argued that there was an historical (and worldwide, cf. 1985) sexist double standard in the administration of juvenile justice linked to the legal doctrine of *parens patriae* embedded in the juvenile court since its inception. The court acted to maintain traditional patriarchal family norms by requiring greater obedience and chastity from females (Chesney-Lind 1973; 1977; 1992). Just as the second wave of feminist scholarship was beginning to make inroads into criminological thought, two books emerged which essentially derailed the momentum of a feminist critique by attempting to link female criminality with the women's movement (Daly and Chesney-Lind 1996).[2]

Feminism Takes the Blame: Adler and Simon

Rita Simon's *Women and Crime* (1975) and Freda Adler's *Sisters in Crime* (1975) both echoed the central theme that women's crime had begun to change in quality and quantity as a result of increased criminal opportunities for women (Curran and Renzetti 1994). These theories were both variants of a traditional (and as Klein had argued, sexist) criminological explanation of male criminality, namely Cloward's and Ohlin's opportunity theory (1960). For Adler, the women's movement had directly resulted in women acting more like men—violent, greedy and crime-prone. Simon saw a subtler connection; for her, the specific increase in women's property crime was the result of women's increased opportunities in the workplace.

These two works provoked a great deal of controversy about the relationships between women's position in society and their resulting criminal and non-criminal opportunities. More importantly though, for feminist criminologists and feminists in general, it was a wake-up call that problematized the heretofore guiding assumption that legal and social equality would result in women's emancipation, and it suggested that criminology was somewhat impervious to feminist insights (Curran and Renzetti 1994; Daly and Chesney-Lind 1996; Shoemaker 1996; Sommers 1995).

Carol Smart to the Defence:
Feminist Criminology Awakens in Britain

Carol Smart has long been a leading feminist scholar in both the fields of criminology and jurisprudence. Her 1976 publication *Women, Crime and Criminology* is heralded as the starting point for feminist criminological studies in Britain. Like Chesney-Lind and Klein, Smart devoted great energy to exposing current attitudes about female crime by detailing the historically biased and negligent treatment of the female offender and the "wider moral, political, economic and sexual spheres which influence women's status and position in society" (1976: 185) in traditional theory. Smart provided one of the most rigorous feminist critiques of existing theory and a detailed historical account of the treatment of female offenders in Britain's prisons (Scraton and Chadwick 1996; Zedner 1991). In addition to this, Smart loudly decried criminology's neglect of women as criminals and of women as victims of crime (Sommers 1995).

In 1979 Smart published an explicit rejoinder to the work of Adler and Simon criticizing their analyses for relying on scant evidence[3] of the increase in women's crime to bolster their theories and for presenting a simplistic view of female emancipation as breaking down the social order (Sommers 1995). Here, Smart was clearly within the mainstream criminological (and positive) tradition of challenging the empirical trends in female criminality that Adler and Simon had described (Daly and Chesney-Lind 1996). At this point in time, feminists were still operating within a liberal tradition or framework and had not yet begun to debate the limits of feminist appeals to the law to uphold equality for all. But it was not long before feminists, with Smart and other critical voices leading the way, began to collectively ponder the efficacy of a liberal strategy of change in light of several setbacks.

The Problems with Liberal Feminism

During the 1980s and early 1990s, Chesney-Lind began to identify and critique some of the dilemmas posed by a liberal feminist approach to social change. In continuing to focus on the plight of women and girls within the criminal and juvenile justice systems, Chesney-Lind stressed that both criminology as a science and these systems of justice had failed to acknowledge the link between female victimization and future criminal behaviour (1985, 1989). She further developed an historical analysis of the rise of the juvenile justice system that highlighted the role of first-wave feminists and the disparagement that their successes had visited on the lives of young girls. Because the underlying sentiment of the early reform movement, and the resulting juvenile court, was the protection of moral (feminine) purity, young girls were disproportionately institutionalized for immorality and waywardness (Chesney-Lind and Sheldon 1992).

But more importantly, recent feminist efforts to reduce this historical disparity, which culminated in the passage of the Juvenile Justice and Delinquency Prevention Act of 1974, had also failed. This legislation was meant to reduce the numbers of all youth institutionalized, but, since the early 1980s, the number of girls housed in public facilities has steadily begun to climb. Young black and Hispanic women are now more likely to be detained for status offences than in the past, and an ever-increasing number of young women are being held in adult jails (Chesney-Lind 1992).

Chesney-Lind has most recently focused on the rising incarceration rates of women (Chesney-Lind, Rockhill, Marker and Reyes 1994). Although feminist criminologists have been critical of the liberal approach to social change, the increasing number of women in prison is a direct result of sentencing reforms based on the equal treatment model in law. Reforms meant to reduce class and racial disparity in the sentencing of men have resulted in far longer and more severe sentences for women (Daly and Chesney-Lind 1996). In particular, Chesney-Lind characterizes the war on drugs, and its accompanying policies of determinate sentencing, as a war on women. She stresses that the majority of the women in prison in California (renowned for the severity of its sentencing reforms) are women of colour who have suffered some type of physical or sexual abuse during their lifetime. The women being incarcerated today are also overwhelmingly mothers (Bloom et al. 1994). An application of the equality doctrine to the conditions of imprisoned women neglects their specific health needs and ignores their relationship with their children (Daly and Chesney-Lind 1996).

The Shift to Radical Feminism

Chesney-Lind's work overall exhibits a subtle shift from an explicitly liberal feminist position concerned with legal equality to a more radical feminist position, which emphasizes the structured domination of women by men in patriarchal society and how formal systems of social control further contribute to, and distort, women's victimization. Although she and Daly (1996) acknowledge that one weakness of a liberal feminist approach is its failure to account for race and class differences in women's experiences, a radical feminist approach is open to the same critique. Dorie Klein, in an afterward to her ground-breaking critique of criminological theory, stresses that because criminological research and theory on women continue to focus on their experiences as they compare with men, they uphold the distinction between maleness as normal and femaleness as the special case. And further, this distinction ignores key race and class differences among women (Daly and Chesney-Lind 1996).

Pat Carlen has discussed this tendency as exhibited in her own study of female offenders *Women, Crime and Poverty* (1988). In a later article, in which she argues for a poststructuralist perspective, she points out that in her search for a generalizable theory of women's criminality, based on traditional control theory, she privileged class and "erased the effects of racism on black women's criminal careers" (Carlen 1996: 139). For Sommers (1995), Carlen's neglect of how race, class and gender interacted among the women studied is the direct result of her discrediting her chosen qualitative methodology. Carlen ignored the rich ethnographic descriptiveness of her material, instead forcing poverty as her thesis, and failing to clarify the actual role of poverty in the women's lawbreaking careers. Sylvie Frigon, in a review of Carlen's book, criticized her work on a more fundamental level for relying on a mainstream criminological theory "created from and for a masculine understanding" (1990: 228). Frigon credits Carlen for attempting to give the women in the study a space in which to express their voices, but, like Sommers, she feels that Carlen nevertheless constructed and organized their experiences and perhaps silenced other aspects of their lawbreaking.

James Messerschmidt (1993) has been critical of a feminist criminology that privileges either class or gender as systems of oppression, and which ignores the crucial link between human structure and agency. Feminist criminology has yet to examine the complex links among race, class and gender, instead focusing exclusively on gender and its impact only on women: "In short, when it comes to men and masculinity, the discipline of criminology is, quite simply, inept" (ibid.: 15). Messerschmidt critiques feminist criminology for relying on antiquated sex-role theory to discuss the influence of gender on men and boys. Crime by men is more than an extension of their sex-role; for Messerschmidt, men's crimes are "social practice[s] invoked as resources, when other resources are unavailable, for accomplishing masculinity" (ibid.: 85). Messerschmidt is critical of radical feminism and its inroads into criminology for essentializing, and distorting, not only the nature of women but also that of men. And he critiques feminist criminologists for failing to account methodologically, and theoretically, for the interdependency of social structure and social action, a phenomenon he terms "structured action."

Messerschmidt relates his own trajectory of theoretical development as the rejection of radical feminism in favour of a socialist feminism, which explores how systems of production and reproduction interact and pattern legitimate and illegitimate conduct. Eventually he came to acknowledge that socialist feminism spoke unwittingly from a race-specific position, therefore obliterating the history and existence of racial minorities. His own version of a feminist criminology recognizes three specific social structures that underpin relations between men and women—the gender division of labour, gender relations of power and sexuality (1993).

Messerschmidt has a well-developed analysis of how the efforts of first-wave feminists to fight against prostitution led to the creation of the female teenage sexual delinquent (1987; 1993). For Messerschmidt, history teaches that the state has the potential to respond to feminist concerns, but also has "an institutionalized bias towards protecting the gendered status quo" (1993: 173-174). Because the state regulates gender relations in society as a whole, and tends to align itself with antifeminist forces, "it is not simply a vessel into which any group can pour content and meaning" (1993: 173). State processes are themselves composed of gendered practices, and different varieties of masculinity (and femininity) are institutionalized through the practices of state personnel.

Two decades later, feminists are still grappling with some of the original concerns that inspired their first foray into criminology, but their work has also raised new questions and issues of importance. Messerschmidt (1997), Klein (1997) and Chesney-Lind (1993; 1998) continue to reflect on, and question, the limits of liberal strategies of change and how state processes contribute to the continuing construction and reinforcement of unequal class, race and gender relations. But all three prominent scholars are also re-directing our conceptualization of the problems encountered in efforts for social change by incorporating postmodern insights into their work on gender and crime. Feminist criminological studies have become more sophisticated, extending their range and depth, developing new methods and recognizing diverse standpoints (Rafter and Heidensohn 1997). The crucial question to ask at this point is how has this body of work affected mainstream criminology?

Feminist Criminology in the 1990s

The Limits of Critique—from Liberalism to Postmodernism

By and large, the most consequential work of feminist criminologists has been their thorough critique of existing theories of criminality (Muncie et al. 1996; Sommers 1995). For Daly and Chesney-Lind, the problems that precipitated these early critiques are still relevant today; namely, the applicability of general theories of crime to women and the failure of theories to address the gendered nature of crime (1996). For Klein, the necessary first step of the feminist critique was to challenge the traditional assumptions about women and to redirect the search for the causes of women's behaviour to their circumstances and experiences. But the necessary next step for feminists is go beyond mere critique and to explore whether science and law are more profoundly masculine and racially biased than critiques from within the discipline can account for. Klein argues that just like twenty years ago, criminology is implicitly about men, and feminist criminology is implicitly about women. Sexuality is the primary focus of analyses of women, and, hence, is represented as a uniquely female concern (1996).

Klein goes so far as to argue that crime, the very empirical reality upon which the discipline is based, has no natural and universal status. Recognizing the tautological nature of this category of actions defined as crime, Klein stresses that feminist criminologists must analyze the roots of law and the penal system while not abandoning the possibility of "alternative visions of justice" (1996: 184). She admits, after two decades of avowed effort, the limited ability of feminist criminology to denormalize maleness and depathologize femaleness within the traditional discipline. But Dorie Klein does not suggest that the project that she helped to initiate should be abandoned; she holds out an implicit faith in the ability of feminist criminology to transcend these limitations. It is on this point alone that her critique of feminist criminology stands in marked contrast to that presented most recently by Carol Smart (1996).

Utilizing Sandra Harding's typology of feminist thought (cf. 1986), Smart considers the trajectory of feminist thought within criminology and traditional jurisprudence. For Harding, feminist work is grounded in one of three "feminist epistemological discourses, and each has its own set of problems" (1986: 28). Feminist thought, in its many guises, has transformed itself from feminist empiricism to a feminist standpoint and, in some cases, incorporates postmodern insights. But according to Smart, feminist criminology cannot partake in this larger transformation because it is so rooted in empiricism.

Smart argues that studies comparing the situation of women with men preserve men as the unproblematic standard. In addition, liberation theories of women's criminality, and the women's equality now evidenced in the rising incarceration rates of women and women "equally" serving on chain gangs, are a direct result of feminist empiricism (1996). For Smart, feminist criminology is problematic because it is primarily "feminist empiricism;" it critiques science for ignoring women and "facilitates the study of female offenders to fill in the gaps in existing knowledge" (1996: 458), but, in the end, it does nothing to challenge empiricism.

A feminist standpoint, or "standpoint feminism" as Harding (1986: 25) calls it, represents the experiences of women reflexively engaged in political and intellectual struggle. Standpoint feminism is more prevalent in feminist jurisprudence than in feminist criminology, where it features only in specific areas of study such as rape, sexual assault and wife abuse (1986).

Carlen also identifies these areas of study as ones which have benefited from a standpoint analysis that links these problems to patriarchal domination (1996). And she argues that feminist thought must now go beyond the tendency to privilege and universalize the experiences of women. But she criticizes Smart for her anti-criminology stance. Smart is guilty of what Carlen calls an anti-policy, or "theorist" tendency, and goes too far in calling for the de-construction of criminology (1996).

For Smart (1996) the entire project known as feminist criminology is problematic because it remains fettered by a modern world view, which assumes that positivism can establish verifiable knowledge or truth. Modernity is now associated with some of the most deep-seated intellectual problems of our time, including racism, sexism and Eurocentredness. Feminist postmodernism is the necessary antidote to the epistemological and political problems generated by modern modes of thought and organization. According to Smart, feminist postmodernism began with the demise of sisterhood and of Marxism in light of the recognition that women were not all white and middle-class. Feminist postmodernism is now a political practice that refuses to engage, and seeks to deconstruct, conceptually essentialistic categories such as women, crime, law and criminology (1996).

Postmodernism has had a significant impact within feminist jurisprudence. There is now an acknowledgment of the need for theories that reflect the particularity and the generality of women's experiences (Schneider 1992). Postmodernism is credited with creating an awareness of the diversity and contextuality of human experience that precludes the possibility of any one truth or reality. But its reliance on the methods of deconstuctionism has led some to comment that postmodernism encourages a debilitating scepticism (Smith 1993). It is this scepticism and the related tendency towards disassociation, from real women's experiences and from real feminist struggles, which is the most consistent criticism of postmodern arguments such as Smart's (Carlen 1996; Sommers 1995).

The Impact of Feminist Thought within Criminology

Despite the deconstructive inclinations of Smart, and her questioning of the political desirability and theoretical possibility of a feminist criminology (1990), there is an undeniable body of literature that is contributing to a feminist understanding of women's involvement in criminal activity and in criminal justice systems—as victims and offenders. Study after study has argued that women's crimes, in comparison to men's, are crimes of the powerless, and that the response to women's lawbreaking is framed by typifications of femininity and womanhood, thus abetting women's oppression (Carlen 1994). Feminists within the discipline have prioritized issues of the appropriate methodology, and the adequacy of existing and emerging theories of crime in explaining women's lawbreaking.[4]

Yet when it comes to assessing their impact within the traditional field of criminology, feminists are divided in their answers (Rafter and Heidensohn 1997). For Kathleen Daly and Meda Chesney-Lind the impact has been negligible. They argue that with the exception of feminist treatments of rape and intimate violence, criminology remains impervious to feminism's influence (1996). Nicole Rafter and Frances Heidensohn agree, stating: "It is true that whereas feminists began their criminological critique with the neglect of women as offenders, their greatest achievement has been in developing new theories about and policies for women (and children) as victims" (1997: 7). Yet they disagree as to the overall pessimistic picture that Daly and Chesney-Lind paint concerning feminism's influence.

They point to the assessment made by British sociologist Pat Carlen (1990) who notes several feminist achievements including:

- putting women on the criminological map;
- critiquing criminology's essentialized and sexualized view of women;
- promoting justice campaigns for victims (male and female);

- challenging the preoccupation with women as offenders; and
- investigating the potential of a feminist jurisprudence and a feminist criminology.

Rafter and Heidensohn also argue that if we compare the influence of feminism on criminology with that of critical or "new" criminology, we can clearly see the profound impact of feminism on criminological thought. Although feminist and critical or "new" criminology are overtly political; both present a new vision of equality and social justice; and both object to official criminology's claims to neutrality and objectivity, only feminism has had a lasting influence outside the academy by influencing criminal justice policies (1997: 7-8).

Feminists have questioned some of the basic concepts of the discipline and have reinvigorated others. While much of their work is empirical, feminists have replaced a "threadbare positivism" with new methodologies that emphasize the importance of the researcher's standpoint. In addition, feminists have developed a new criminological agenda that includes child abuse, domestic violence, fear of crime and the connection between women's victimization and women's offending. Feminists are also gleaning insights from the work of feminist legal scholars and are beginning to challenge prevalent notions of justice and legal neutrality (Rafter and Hiedensohn 1997: 8). These recent challenges and developments reflect the trajectory of feminist thought from a liberal to a more radical and, now in some cases, a postmodern approach to the issues of crime and punishment. In order to more clearly illustrate these developments, and to address the future of feminist criminology, it is helpful to focus on three substantive areas that have developed from feminist inquiry—the extent of women's victimization and the link between women's victimization and offending, the role of the state in controlling violence against women, and the ability to bring about social change by relying on legal remedies.

The Extent of Women's Victimization and the Link to Women's Offending

Chesney-Lind devoted much of her efforts during the 1970s to documenting the often neglected link between girls' victimization and their treatment within the juvenile justice system. During the 1980s and early 1990s, Chesney-Lind continued to highlight the plight of women and girls within the criminal and juvenile justice systems, stressing that both criminology as a science and these systems of justice had failed to acknowledge the link between female victimization and future criminal behaviour (1989). Today, as Kathleen Daly and Meda Chesney-Lind point out: "the more one reads the literature on victimization—the physical and sexual abuse of children, women, and men—the more difficult it becomes to separate victimization from offending, especially in the case of women" (1996: 350). In their review of the literature on women's physical and sexual abuse by women they identify several major themes and findings.

- Rape and violence—especially between intimates—are far more prevalent than previously known.
- Police, court officials, juries and members of the general public do not take victims of rape or violence seriously, especially when victim-offender relations involve intimates or friends.
- Myths about rape and intimate violence abound. They appear in the work of criminologists, in criminal justice practices and in the minds of the general public.
- Whereas female victims feel stigma and shame, male offenders often do not view their behaviour as wrong.
- Strategies for change include empowering women via protest activities, shelters and legal advocacy; and changing men's behaviour via counselling, presumptive arrests for domestic violence and more active prosecution and tougher sanctions for rape.

For Dorie Klein, the "blurring" of offender and victim definitions is one of the strongest challenges, present and future, that the work of feminists has offered to mainstream criminology. The consistent finding that emanates from feminist work on female offenders is the "prominence of their histories of victimization" (1997: 84). For Klein (1997) this finding challenges criminology's overriding concern with the pathology of individual offenders, and it also calls into question recent attempts to demonize offenders, such as the media's portrayal of the new violent female gang member (cf. Chesney-Lind 1993).

Recent reviews of the literature concerning girls in gangs reveal that for these girls, and for female delinquents in general, the experience of being a victim or witnessing victimization within their home is a common one. In addition, girls in gangs have also witnessed a great deal of indirect violence in their immediate environments, and this impacts their decision to join the gang (see Campbell 1993; Shelden et al. 1996). A recent *Los Angeles Times* series on girls and the juvenile justice system, entitled "Girl Trouble: America's Overlooked Crime Problem," reported national estimates that 50% to 70% of all girls in the juvenile justice system are sexually, physically or emotionally abused. In addition, according to official FBI statistics, 57% of juvenile runaways are females. In 1994 of the 678,500 girls who were arrested in the U.S., three-quarters were guilty of violating a status offence (such as truancy, violating curfew, incorrigibility or running away from home). This suggests that girls are often penalized by the juvenile justice system for trying to escape abusive situations in their homes and communities (Mehren 1996).

In short, rampant abuse clearly plays a part in girls' delinquency. The extent of women's victimization is clearly underestimated and therefore hampers our ability to fully understand the relationship between women's victimization and offending behaviour, although there is no denying the empirical evidence that a relationship exists. Feminist efforts to understand this link have led them to question the role of the state in controlling violence against women and the ways in which actions on the part of our formal legal system might further contribute to women's victimization.

Questioning the Role of the State

Kathleen Daly and Meda Chesney-Lind pose one of the key questions now facing feminists: "What role, then, should the state play in controlling men's violence and protecting women from such violence?" (1996: 352). State criminal laws for the arrest and prosecution of spouse abuse and rape have changed a great deal recently (Davis and Smith 1995). Civil remedies such as the temporary restraining order to protect battered women are also more widely available than before. As Daly and Chesney-Lind point out, these legal changes are a symbolic victory for many feminists, yet their effect on changing police and court practices seems far less impressive.

Both scholars see hope in the promise of presumptive arrest as a method of reducing intimate violence, based on the results of Sherman and Berk's 1984 study in Minneapolis that arrest did deter future assaults. Yet they also acknowledge that presumptive arrest is a short-sighted solution to a problem that is ultimately connected to the structured inequality between men and women. Further, a strategy of presumptive arrest policy "offers women short-term protection and retributive justice, but it is part of a more general incarceral 'solution' to crime that has arisen in the last decade" (Daly and Chesney-Lind 1996: 353).

Some feminists argue that any state intervention is better than none, because in the absence of intervention the message received by the larger public is that men's violence against women is condoned by the state. But there are noted disadvantages to state intervention. Feminists are now beginning to examine the likelihood of mandatory arrest policies leading to the arrest of women or to their incarceration for failure to comply with prosecutorial efforts against their batterers. Further, it is argued that this policy upholds a theoretical view of women as victims and denies them any agency in their appeal to the legal system for help (Klein 1997; Dixon 1995). As Daly and Chesney-Lind stress, it remains to be seen what long-term effects these policies will have on women's lives (1997).

As feminists grapple with the ramifications of legal efforts to stem violence against women, they are also questioning the many ways that this violence and its legal remedies are mired in a therapeutic, or medical, construction of the problem. The construction of violence against women as a medical problem is consistent with some longstanding views of women as physically and psychologically deviant. It is this view of women's bodies as deviant which has been institutionalized in mainstream criminological theory and continues to thwart feminist efforts at change, within and outside of the discipline (Frigon 1995). The medicalization of the problem also has an influence on how laws and well-meaning legal efforts at eliminating violence are enacted and further construct the problem.

The Construction of Violence Against Women as a Medical Problem

Prior to the 1960s, there was an explicit denial of the issue of violence against women in academic, legal and social discourse. During the 1970s, violence against women became visible, but conceptualizations of the problem contributed to the primacy of a therapeutic approach aimed at resolving interpersonal conflict within the family. The 1975 study by Gelles and Straus, which found that violence among intimates was sex-symmetrical, and the ensuing debate among feminists over these findings had a huge impact in terms of public policy (see Gelles and Strauss 1979). The public discourse surrounding violence in the home shifted the definition of the problem from one of woman abuse to one of family abuse.

It was 1979 when the new categories of battered spouse and battered woman were added to the International Classification of Diseases: Clinical Modification Scheme, which is a list compiled by the US National Center for Health Statistics that catalogues all known diseases. The initial creation of these two new categories was hailed as a breakthrough by many therapists and some activists. At this point in time, some professional therapists did stress issues of structural inequality and male domination as factors in domestic violence. But any remnants of this perspective have now been fully replaced by discourses that emphasize the personal pathology of battered women and the need for individual treatment—of battered women and of the men who cause them injury. Battered women are now seen as having unique personality disorders. They are considered to be masochistic, deviant and in need of therapy (Dobash and Dobash 1992).

The rise of the therapeutic society is traced back to the same early-twentieth-century social purity movement that was influential in creating the early reformatories and juvenile justice system. Social welfare workers (mostly women) sought legitimacy as a professional group by embracing the therapeutic and psychiatric ideals then beginning to emerge. They shifted their focus away from aiding the poor by addressing the structural conditions that produced slums in the first place and began to focus on poverty as a personal problem, treatable through scientific—psychiatric and psychological—interventions. Up until the 1950s, therapy was seen as necessary for those on the margins of American life—the poor, the mentally ill and, of course, criminals. But the therapeutic society was firmly established in American life when professionals began to encompass "everyday anxieties, failures, frustrations and setbacks" as personal problems requiring therapeutic solutions (Dobash and Dobash 1992: 219). As Dobash and Dobash note, there are serious consequences to the envelopment of the problem of domestic violence within the language and strategies of our therapeutic society:

> Through this process, the vision of the movement and the potential for social change associated with making the private public and political are seriously eroded. The more women are seen as clients in need of therapy rather than people in need of alternatives and choices, the less the movement challenges prevailing conceptions of the problem. The processes associated with clienthood strip the relationship between women and activists as well as the movement of a wider political vision. (1992: 234)

Sylvie Frigon and Dorie Klein both share the above concerns. Frigon has noted that the use of battered women's syndrome (BWS), now a recognized medical condition, as a legal defence in cases where woman are violent towards abusive partners, has both positive and negative implications for all women. Despite its successful use in some cases of spousal homicide, there are many more cases where the use of BWS as a legal defence has not secured acquittals (Klein 1997). Klein notes that in many cases the use of BWS can and does work against those women who do not conform to the syndrome's definition by appearing "stereotypically traumatized" (ibid.: 85).

Further, the need to rely on BWS as a legal defence strategy points to the fact that traditional legal defences are not viable for women and that only when doctors and psychiatrists verify women's experiences of abuse are these experiences taken seriously in a legal forum and otherwise. Frigon is especially critical of these medicalized legal defences, such as BWS and PMS, or pre-menstrual syndrome, which has been used as a defence in cases of maternal-infant killings. For Frigon, the definition and legal acceptance of these syndromes are only brief instances in the historical trend to view women's bodies as deviant and in need of regulation (1997).

Once again, feminist efforts for legal and social change in relation to the problem of violence against women are having unintended consequences because of these historical views. But it is not just the possible diffusion of the legitimacy of feminist claims for political and economic change that is so worrisome. It is also the horrific treatment that women have suffered as a result of the growth of the medical, and related, therapeutic model of social problems and of society. What is ultimately most troubling for Frigon is the long history of viewing and treating women's bodies as dangerous, pathological and in need of confinement exhibited in medical, legal, and criminological discourses (1997).

Women have been subject to social control within the medical realm with much more frequency than men, and with a wider variety of methods. As Sylvie Frigon notes:

> Through prison, psychiatry, the institution of marriage, medicine, tranquilizers, electro-convulsive therapy, 'premenstrual syndrome', gynaecological surgery and laws [ ] society pathologizes and criminalizes women's bodies and women's minds. (1995: 22)

For Thomas Szasz (1983, 1987) there is no doubting the coercive nature of psychiatry and the institutions designed as settings in which to treat the mentally ill. Szasz argues that psychiatry, while premised on the "myth of mental illness," is really a reflection of society's growing discomfort with social misfits and the state's increasing ability to use medicine as the guise for more sophisticated means of social control (Szasz 1983).

In the past, those who deviated from societal norms were seen as witches; today, those who deviate are seen as mentally ill (Scheffe 1975). The psychiatric, psychological and therapeutic treatment of women is consistent with the historical image of women as witches (Frigon 1995). In their review of the history women's punishment, Burford and Shulman argue:

> It is impossible to record the history of female punishment without reference to witchcraft since those accused of this crime were chiefly women. However much society managed to control its female members through law or custom there remained an underlying suspicion and fear that the weaker vessel was corrupt and open to the blandishments of the Devil, and might by demonic power overturn the authority of Church and State. (1992: 201)

Woman has embodied madness for over two thousand years and continues to do so. The historically dominant images of women as mad, and of women as witches, were extended in early biological theories of women's criminality. These early theories were later fused with racist anti-immigrant sentiments in the eugenics movement (Frigon

1995). The crucial roles of medicine, criminology and the state in condoning violence against women, particularly poor minority women, are exemplified in the twentieth-century eugenics movement.

The Forced Sterilization of Women of Colour

One result of the eugenics movement and its underlying view of women as pathologically deviant was the policy of forced sterilization enacted in many states in the early 1920s. In this way, the fusion of crime, poverty and race identified in the early part of the century by Katz (1995) was manifested in disturbing social policy. During this period, Henry H. Goddard argued that those immigrants considered morons, according the early versions of the IQ test, were a dangerous and criminal threat to society. The answer was the segregation and sterilization of supposedly feebleminded immigrants (Curran and Renzetti 1994).

Despite the egregious nature of such actions on the part of the state, there is evidence that the policy of sterilizing women of colour persists to this day. Patricia Williams, a scholar of law, has written about the evidence of this current-day policy that she uncovered while working at the Western Center on Law and Poverty. In a 1984 study released by the Division of Reproductive Health (a branch of the Center for Health Promotion within the Centers for Disease Control and Prevention) she learned that as of 1982, 49% of Puerto Rican women between the ages of 15 and 44 had been sterilized. She also came across a fact sheet published by the Women of All Red Nations Collective of Minneapolis, Minnesota, which stated that in 1988 almost 50% of all Native American women of childbearing age had been sterilized (1992).

These reports are consistent with the autobiographical story of Mary Crow Dog, a member of the Lakota tribe, who recounts her sister's forced sterilization (the doctors took her womb out without permission while she was undergoing a Caesarean birth) and the hysterectomy performed on her mother, also without permission. According to Crow Dog, forced sterilizations were performed on thousands of Indian and Chicano women by Bureau of Indian Affairs doctors (1990). As Williams notes, one serious problem in getting a sense of the frequency of this procedure is that the CDC data on sterilization procedures are gathered by the National Hospital Discharge Survey and do not cover federal hospitals or penitentiaries (1992).

The ongoing state policy of the forced sterilization of women of colour amounts to violence against women, and originates, in part, from early-twentieth-century fears about the criminogenic (and diseased) nature of immigrant groups. The therapeutic society described by Dobash and Dobash (1992) is both reflective of, and contributive to, a continuing focus on criminality and poverty as individual or family-level pathologies. Now, violence against women and violence among youth are being declared diseases by federal agencies and have been incorporated within a medical discourse. Note that one implication of the way that the problems of violence are now being framed is that men are conspicuously absent as a focal point in these discussions.

Certainly, any efforts to reduce violence and to prevent its occurrence in the first place are useful, but the full ramifications of violence now being defined as a public health problem remain to be seen. The problem is that we simply don't know what the impact of this new focus will be. The relationships between feminism, the state and criminology are poorly understood. What is most problematic about the subsuming of violence, especially violence against women, within the public health approach is that criminologists fail to critically reflect on its occurrence. Similarly, the role of the state in perpetuating violence against women is obscured and continues to be reflected primarily as a benign or, at most, protective factor in alleviating the problem. Yet some feminists have gone even further and argue that not only has the state perpetrated violence against women in the past, such as is the case with sterilization practices, but that the state continues to trivialize and, thus, allow violence against women. Hence, the violence women experience is conceptualized by some to be a political crime. For Susan Caulfield and Nancy Wonders violence against women is clearly a state crime. This is evidenced by specific instances of state-enacted violence such as sterilization and the fact that, in general, the state actively chooses "not to intervene or limit serious harms if they are directed primarily toward women" (1993: 80-81).

Dorie Klein is also critical of the state's role in addressing violence against women. While she argues that there has been significant progress in both the public acknowledgments of the problem and services available to female victims, she draws attention to many state policies that are troublesome. In the United States the increasing focus on incarceration above all else, combined with a punitive approach to drug use, have "created unprecedented public sectors of policing and imprisonment that criminalize increasing numbers of the most vulnerable women and their family members, fail to address women's safety concerns, and move us farther away from a [feminist] vision of justice" (1997: 81). Klein also draws attention to recent policy initiatives, such as efforts to stigmatize teenage pregnancy, increase the surveillance of suspected child abuse and eliminate welfare and public health benefits, that have the potential to further harm these same groups of women (1997).

While liberal feminism attempted to enact social change through appeals to the state, it is clear that there are many positive and negative consequences and implications of this strategy. In light of the previous arguments, it is clear that feminist criminologists are contributing to a thorough re-thinking of the role of the state in acknowledging and reducing women's victimization. The potential role of the state in reducing and exacerbating women's victimization is only one of the theoretical and practical questions that feminist criminologists will be grappling with in the future.

The Future of Feminist Criminology

According to Rafter and Heidensohn there are three major issues or questions that will be of particular importance to feminist criminologists in the years ahead (1997: 10-11). These issues include considering how feminists are going to address the essentialism that limits much of the current work on crime and justice. Relatedly, feminists must address whether a feminist criminology is possible, or only a contradiction in terms? And finally, Rafter and Heidensohn stress that in assessing the future of feminist work on crime and punishment we must contemplate the extent to which "criminology and crime control policies [are] implicated in the construction of hierarchies based on gender, race, class and sexuality" (1997: 11). This final issue boils down to the consideration of feminism's ability to bring about more equal and just forms of social organization and to transform criminological and scientific thought in the process. Briefly, I will examine each of these issues and add my own suggestions to the mix as to the future impact of feminist criminology.

How will Feminists Deal with the Essentialism of Current Work on Crime and Justice?

There are several ways in which feminist criminologists, in their eagerness to point out the historical neglect of women in traditional criminology, have essentialized the experiences of women. Stressing the commonality of women's experiences may be the first step in a field of study so riddled with the neglect of women, but eventually feminists must address the way that emphasizing what women share denies the crucial differences among women and their experiences. As Rafter and Heidensohn point out, in an era of globalization, feminist criminologists working in the United States and in Western Europe must concede their contribution to criminology's ethnocentrism. This is especially crucial because women in other parts of the world often face more serious crime and justice problems, including genital mutilation and widespread sexual slavery (1997). Sally Simpson also laments the neglect of racial differences among women within feminist criminology and urges feminists to move beyond the "add race and stir" mentality that has predominated any examination of differences up to this point. She suggests that there may be key differences in the causes, frequency and nature of offending for women of different races (1996: 331-332).

Feminist scholars of law, specifically women of colour, have developed one of the most thorough critiques of essentialism within feminist thought. Marlee Kline (1993) argues that race is crucial to dominant perceptions of women's goodness or badness, especially on the part of the state. Angela Harris stresses that race is critical to any analysis of women's victimization or criminalization (1990). Both Harris and Patricia Hill Collins (1993) have explored the complex ways that the experience of rape has differed for women of colour. Rape and other forms of sexual violence against black women were not historically punished as crimes. Both the threat of rape, in the absence of any legal protection, and rape itself have been continuous features of the social control of black women. As Elizabeth Schneider notes, legal efforts to aid battered women have not yet addressed the reality that the criminal justice system is not protective of women of colour and women immigrants (1992). Feminist theorizing within criminology that uncritically starts from official definitions of deviance and victimization will remain essentialistic and will continue to echo age-old distortions of the salience of race, class and gender to our experiences and sense of identity.

A related point (but one which is often neglected in feminist reviews) is that in stressing the commonality of women, and thereby neglecting race, class, age and other differences among women, feminist criminologists have also neglected or essentialized men's experiences. For Smart, one of the biggest failures of feminist criminology is its inability to focus on masculinity: "Precisely because standpoint feminism has arisen from a grassroots concern to protect women and to reveal the victimization of women, it has not been sympathetic to the study of masculinity" (1996: 461). Lynne Segal has argued that there are crucial connections between crime, especially violent crime, and the ways in which masculinities are constructed in terms of heterosexual power (1996). Maureen Cain has argued that gender is an inherently relational concept and that we must re-introduce men into feminist studies of crime, law and criminal justice institutions, especially in light of the fact that most police, judges and lawyers remain men. The traditional question in criminology concerning gender has been why women do not offend, but feminists must push for new understandings of "what in the social construction of maleness is so profoundly criminogenic" (1996: 471). The traditional framing of this question also suggests that men's criminality, especially among men of certain racial and class backgrounds, is accepted and normalized by mainstream theories and research (Cain 1996).

Messerschmidt's work illustrates the importance of viewing gender not just as an aspect of personality but as an aspect of collective processes and institutions. He analyzes how the police construct various masculinities as agents of state power, and stresses that the state is not a monolith but is made up of actors engaged in gendered (and raced and classed) practices which change over time (1993). His work stresses the importance of studying the complexity of race, class and gender as structured action and the inevitable failure of strategies of social and legal change which fail to recognize the collective and socially constituted aspects of power.

Both Messerschmidt (1997) and Klein (1997), among many others, are critical of feminist criminology for its seemingly singular focus on the experiences of white women. In addition, both criticize the field for failing to account for the complex interaction of race, gender and class in women's everyday lives. Yet both are hopeful that feminists can move beyond these criticisms towards creating new conceptualizations of the relationships between structure and agency and between race, class and gender. Notwithstanding their criticisms and concerns, they remain hopeful as to the ability of feminist criminology to transcend its intellectual lineage.

But the future potential of feminist criminology, both intellectually and practically in its ability to bring about meaningful social change, is far from being taken for granted.

Is a Feminist Criminology Possible?

As Rafter and Heidensohn note, the perception of a "fundamental incompatibility" between feminism and criminology first surfaced forcefully in England (see Cain 1986, 1996). The newest collection of international feminist perspectives echoes the concerns of Carol Smart (1996) that criminology is an "intellectual vortex" (457) because it remains confined by a modern world view that assumes that positivism can establish verifiable knowledge or truth. For Smart, criminology is hopelessly masculinist and continues to distort women's experiences. Both criminology and the legal system continue to frame women's experiences in ways which limit the ability (or the desirability) of legal reforms to empower women. The images of the criminal woman, the raped woman, the prostitute, the sexed woman and the unruly mother still dominate legal and criminological discussions of women's lives (1995).

For Smart, feminist criminology must adapt a postmodern epistemology and practice that will have the effect of turning the question "What does feminism have to offer criminology?" on its modern head, transforming it into the question "What does criminology have to contribute to feminism?" (1996: 462). According to Rafter and Heidensohn:

> Over and over in these chapters we observe a search for what Pitch calls a new "site", a berth within the academy that will nurture investigations of gender, crime, and social control. In all likelihood, we will have to continue creating that site for ourselves. (1997: 10)

Maureen Cain concurs, arguing for a "transgressive feminist criminology" which starts from "outside criminological discourse"

(1996: 467). But it remains to be seen whether feminism can be both transgressive and criminological. Sylvia Frigon states the dilemma succinctly:

> Criminology can be a conceptual, traditional straight jacket from which we need to distance ourselves to a certain extent. I am not arguing for the abolition of criminology, but for a more flexible discipline which would allow us to borrow from other disciplines (sociology of law, health, education …), other perspectives (feminism …), and take on a broader view of gender, social control, deviance, and the state which can go well beyond the conventional object of criminology, 'crime'. One also needs to challenge criminology, as a discipline for it is not unproblematic. (1990: 228)

Can a Feminist Criminology Contribute to Social Change?

Feminist criminologists have made great strides in illuminating the neglect of women in mainstream criminology and in trying to address this neglect. There is certainly a need for more empirical work centred in women's experiences. One challenge for feminist criminologists is to continue to document women's histories within the criminal justice system, while paying greater attention to their agency, and to the particular influences of race, class and gender on their histories. For many feminist criminologists, remaining dedicated to social change for women entails a continuing commitment to filling in the empirical gaps that persist in criminology concerning women's lives. There is still a great need to document the ideological, political and economic conditions surrounding women's lawbreaking and their careers through formal institutions of control such as prisons and psychiatric hospitals (Cain 1996; Carlen 1996; Chesney-Lind and Shelden 1992; Daly 1994). But there appear to be limits to the potential for social change emanating from a purely empirical challenge to current systems of power and social control.

Many of the criticisms directed at feminist criminology to date—its essentialism, its focus on women as victims, its neglect of gender as a relational concept—seem to stem from the fact that feminists are still trying to insert women's issues into a field historically concerned with (and dominated by) men. And feminists are starting to question criminology's reluctance to engage feminism in light of analyses that highlight the historically troubling relationship between criminology and feminism.

There are several historical examples of the complex and poorly understood relationships between the state, criminology and feminism. First-wave feminists were crucial, along with criminologists, in the establishment of the juvenile justice system and stricter age-of-consent laws because they sought to protect young women from the sexual voraciousness of men. But their efforts led to the increased repression and coercion of young women because of their limited ability to shape how the justice system operated (despite their own participation), and because they were unaware of the gender, class and racial biases underlying their campaigns (Odem 1995). The efforts of second-wave feminists, fighting for women to have legal access to the same opportunities as men, were distorted and sidetracked by a new strain of criminological thought which argued that the women's movement was responsible for an increase in women's crime.

Chesney-Lind stresses the disastrous and unintended consequences of the 1974 Juvenile Justice and Delinquency Prevention Act, and of recent sentencing "equality" for women in an era of overcrowded prisons and long mandatory sentences. She is now working tirelessly to expose the extreme amount of distortion surrounding current media portrayals of female gang members. For Chesney-Lind, this distortion and the extreme amount of attention being given to this supposed "new female offender" are eerily reminiscent of the attack on women's equality suggested by the work of Adler and Simon in the early 1970s. Once again, the opportunities and ties to work and family that have consistently been portrayed as integrative and conformity-producing factors for men in criminological thought, are being blamed for creating more worrisome strains of female deviants (Chesney-Lind 1998; Sommers 1995).

The above dilemmas and the recurring portrayal of women's efforts for equality as criminogenic throw serious question on the role of criminology in constructing and enforcing inequality. The analyses of these dilemmas and trends resonate with postmodern concerns that criminology, as a science intent on explaining and controlling the actions of individuals, is part of the refinement and expansion of knowledge, power and social control associated with the modern age (Foucault 1977; Rafter and Heidensohn 1997). Feminism may be able to address some of its empirical shortcomings. But it must also begin to focus on the larger theoretical issues surrounding the historical exclusion and distortion of women in criminology, and the way that feminist concerns get transformed, with unintended legal and political consequences, in their interaction with criminological knowledge.

There are so many elements of women's experience which remain outside the confines of criminological thought that any attempt to bring feminism into criminology may create further distortion of the historical extent and nature of women's social control. And there is no theoretical vantage point, within criminology, to examine the historical connections and interplay between feminism, the state and law, including legal and criminal justice systems, and criminology itself. As Carol Smart has recently stated: "The thing that criminology cannot do is deconstruct crime. It cannot locate rape or child sexual abuse in the domain of sexuality or theft in the domain of economic activity or drug use in the domain of health" (1996: 458). Smart's work provides a model for feminist criminologists in both her attempt to understand the complex process of social change and in her efforts to theoretically bridge the disciplinary bounds of criminology and jurisprudence.

The criticisms levelled at Carol Smart's call for feminism to abandon criminology and to realize the limited emancipatory potential of law have much to do with her decidedly postmodern stance (1995). Postmodernism stresses the fragmentation of modern life, it rejects essentialism and it emphasizes the deconstruction of systems of power and knowledge, as opposed to their utilization for social change. Smart's appeal to postmodernism has left her vulnerable to critique from activists concerned with bettering women's lives now, instead of deconstructing modernity. But in the end, it is this type of theoretical effort that may hold promise for a feminist criminology that can move beyond critique and which can place its own efforts in some type of historical, political and legal context. Feminists have much to gain from engaging in dialogue with each other, across disciplines, rather than beating on the door for admittance into traditionally male-centred areas of study.

By remaining reflexive, feminism will continue to have an impact within criminology and within other traditionally male-centred disciplines. The fragmentation of modern academic disciplines is inevitable, and desirable, from a postmodern stance:

> The only problem with the fragmentation of criminology is criminologists who fret about it. Problems arise when

> criminologists essentialize the field within their preferred
> template of political and/or academic correctness.... The
> only viable *academic* sensibility is to encourage people to
> let their minds wander, to travel intellectually across the
> boundaries and frontiers and perhaps never return to them.
> (Ericson and Carriere 1996: 512-15)

Feminists must strive to build bridges across academic disciplines, including criminology, instead of operating specifically within one or another traditional field. For Klein: "There have been rich exhanges between scholars, journalists, advocates, activists, practioners and policymakers around women's criminal justice issues, and there need to be far more" (1997: 86).

In particular, feminist scholars of law and feminist criminologists have much to gain from enhanced communication and collaboration. Feminists studying jurisprudence have focused on the nature of law and the problems with relying on legal change for social change by appealing to either women's sameness with men or difference from them. Postmodern thought has inspired feminists studying law to question the very desirability of a strategy of legal change and to historically examine the dilemmas arising from feminist attempts to appeal to the state for justice and equality. There is also a more developed critique of the dangers of essentialism—race, class, gender and otherwise—in both theory and practice emanating from feminist scholars of law, especially from women of colour.

Feminist efforts to understand the history of women's criminal punishment and offending could enrich the feminist study of law, in particular by highlighting the often ignored circumstances preceding women's entanglements with the state. If feminists are to remain dedicated to social change they will have to move beyond the study of just criminal law, or law. Ultimately feminists must begin to explore and explain the historical continuity and discontinuity of men's and women's social control, and the myriad ways that power gets reproduced and enacted along class, race and gender lines. For Smart, feminists must stop seeing legal struggles as the preeminent source of change and recognize that law operates in contradictory ways (1989). Although feminism has often been criticized for being cacophonous, its diversity may be the antidote to the modern vestiges of strictly bounded academic disciplines and unrelenting social inequality.

It is clear that feminist criminology, in spite of, and yet partly owing to, its conflicts and contradictions, will continue to flourish and contribute to our understanding of crime, punishment and social control. Feminists working in various disciplines related to the study of these issues—history, jurisprudence, criminology, punishment—will hopefully continue to communicate with each other in ways that contribute to new theoretical understandings and new avenues for social change. For Dorie Klein, one of the greatest promises of feminist criminology is its potential for reimagining justice: "Within the academy, disillusionment with the traditional paradigms of retribution, rehabilitation and deterrence has spurred a search for alternative models" (1997: 87). Feminists in a diversity of settings are now beginning to engage in cross-national discussions of what these alternative visions of justice might look like and how they could be implemented.

It bodes well for traditional criminology to take notice of the diverse global and interdisciplinary climate of feminist study:

> The long-term health of Western criminology as both an academic specialty and a tool for social improvement may well lie in its willingness to open its boundaries to feminist analyses, postmodernist ideas and interdisciplinary endeavours (Rafter 1990).

If criminology continues to marginalize and ignore feminist insights it will suffer from its own rigidity in the long run. Feminists are clearly here for the duration, and the question of feminism's impact within criminology may well become irrelevant in the future if criminology remains isolated from the changes and developments occurring around it:

> In some countries criminology may be able to assimilate (at least partially) the new currents flowing around it; elsewhere it is likely to remain a rock in the stream, impervious to change. In either case, feminist work on crime and social control will probably continue unabated, for its primary aim has always been to improve not criminology but people's lives. (Rafter and Heidensohn 1997: 6)

Endnotes

[1] See Dorie Klein (1973) and Carol Smart (1976) for a comprehensive discussion of the problems and hidden assumptions in traditional theories of crime prior to the 1970s.

[2] Rafter and Heidensohn (1997) lump together the work of Adler (1975) and Simon (1975) referring to their collective works as "evidence of a feminist criminological agenda" (5). However, this period in the development of feminist criminology was fraught with controversy, as indicated in my discussion, and in other reviews (see Simpson 1996). I believe that the critical self-reflection and the debates caused by the publication of Adler's and Simon's works are still relevant to current feminist concerns about the possibility of a feminist criminology.

[3] Smart (1979) argued that Simon and Adler had relied on misrepresentative percentage increases in the numbers of women indicted for violent crimes. For example, official statistics for England and Wales for the time period 1965-1975 reveal a 500% increase in the occurrence of murder by women. But, this percentage inflates the picture because the increase is based on the absolute figure of one woman indicted in 1965 compared with five women indicted in 1975. Smart also constructed ratios of the percentage of males versus females found guilty of criminal offences and compared them over time. In 1930, the ratio of male to female convictions was 89%/11%. In 1975 the ratio was similar at 85%/15%.

[4] See Sally Simpson (1996) and Kathleen Daly and Chesney-Lind (1996) for recent summaries of feminist criminological research and theory. Although neither work claims to be a thorough review of the literature, they both outline the contours of the field.

Bibliography

Adler, F. 1975. *Sisters in Crime: The Rise of the New Female Criminal*. New York: McGraw-Hill.

Bartlett, K. T. and R. Kennedy (Eds.). 1991. *Feminist Legal Theory: Readings in Law and Gender*. Boulder: Westview Press.

Bertrand, M. A. 1969. "Self-image and Delinquency: A Contribution to the Study of Female Criminality and Women's Image." *Acta Criminologia: Etudes sur la Conduite Antisociale* 2: 71-144.

Bloom, B., Chesney-Lind, M. and B. Owen. 1994. *Women in California Prisons: Hidden Victims of the War on Drugs*. San Francisco, CA: Center on Juvenile and Criminal Justice.

Burford, E.J. and S. Shulman. 1992. *Of Bridles and Burnings: The Punishment of Women*. New York: St. Martin's Press.

Cain, M. 1996. "Towards Transgression: New Directions in Feminist Criminology." In *Criminological Perspectives: A Reader*, J. Muncie, E. McLaughlin and M. Langan (Eds.): 466-474. Thousand Oaks, CA: Sage.

Cain, M. 1986. "Realism, Feminism, Methodology, and Law." *International Journal of the Sociology of Law* 14: 255-267.

Campbell, A. 1993. *Men, Women and Aggression*. New York: Basic Books.

Carlen, P. 1996. "Criminal Women and Criminal Justice: The Limits to, and Potential of, Feminist and Left Realist Perspectives." In *Criminological Perspectives: A Reader*, J. Muncie, E. McLaughlin and M. Langan (Eds.): 475-483. Thousand Oaks, CA: Sage.

Carlen, P. 1990. "Women, Crime, Feminism, and Realism." *Social Justice* 17(4): 100-123.

Carlen, P. 1988. *Women, Crime and Poverty*. Milton Keynes: Open University.

Caulfield, S. L. and N. W. Wonders. 1993. "Personal AND Political: Violence Against Women and the Role of the State." In *Political Crime in Contemporary America: A Critical Approach*, Kenneth D. Tunnell (Ed.): 79-100. New York: Garland.

Chesney-Lind, M. March 9th, 1998. *Girls. Gangs and Violence: Anatomy of a Backlash*. Presentation at Robert Presley Center for Crime and Justice Studies: University of California, Riverside.

Chesney-Lind, M. 1997. Preface to *International Feminist Perspectives in Criminology: Engendering A Discipline*. Nicole Rafter and Frances Heidensohn (Eds.). Philadelphia: Open University Press.

Chesney-Lind, M. 1993. "Girls, Gangs and Violence: Anatomy of a Backlash." *Humanity and Society* 17(3): 321-344.

Chesney-Lind, M. 1992. "Women's Prisons: Putting the Brakes on the Building Binge." *Corrections Today* 54(6): 30-34.

Chesney-Lind, M. and R. G. Shelden. 1992. *Girls, Delinquency and Juvenile Justice*. Belmont, CA: Wadsworth.

Chesney-Lind, M. 1989. "Girls' Crime and Woman's Place: Toward a Feminist Model of Female Delinquency." *Crime and Delinquency* 35(1): 5-29.

Chesney-Lind, M. 1985-1986. "Sexist Juvenile Justice: A Continuing International Problem." *Resources for Feminist Research/Documentation sur la Recherche Feministe* 14(4): 7-9.

Chesney-Lind, M. 1977. "Judicial Paternalism and the Female Status Offender: Training Women to Know Their Place." *Crime and Delinquency* 23(2): 121-130.

Chesney-Lind, M. 1973. "Judicial Enforcement of the Female Sex Role: The Family Court and the Female Delinquent." *Issues in Criminology* 8(2): 51-69.

Chesney-Lind, M., Rockhill, A., Marker, N. and H. Reyes. 1994. "Gangs and Delinquency: Exploring Police Estimates of Gang Membership." *Crime, Law and Social Change* 21(3): 201-228.

Cloward, R. A. and L. E. Ohlin. 1960. *Delinquency and Opportunity*. New York: Free Press.

Collins, P. H. 1993. "The Sexual Politics of Black Womanhood." In *Violence Against Women: The Bloody Footprints*, P. B. Bart and E. G. Moran (Eds.): 85-104. Newbury Park, CA: Sage.

Cott, N. 1987. *The Grounding of Modern Feminism*. New Haven: Yale University Press.

Crow Dog, M. and R. Erdoes. 1990. *Lakota Woman*. New York: Harper Perennial.

Curran, D. J. and C. M. Renzetti. 1994. *Theories of Crime*. Boston: Allyn and Bacon.

Daly, K. 1994. "Gender and Punishment Disparity." In *Inequality, Crime and Social Control*, G. S. Bridges and M. A. Myers (Eds.): 117-133. San Francisco: Westview Press.

Daly, K. and M. Chesney-Lind. 1996. "Feminism and Criminology." In *Readings in Contemporary Criminological Theory*, P. Cordella and L. Siegel (Eds.): 340-363. Boston: Northeastern University Press.

Davis, R.C. and B. Smith. 1995. "Domestic Violence Reforms: Empty Promises or Fulfilled Expectations?" *Crime and Delinquency* 41(4): 541-556.

Dixon, J. 1995. "The Nexus of Sex, Spousal Violence, and the State. Review Essay." *Law and Society Review*, 29(2): 359-376.

Dobash, R. E. and R. P. Dobash. 1992. *"Women, Violence and Social Change."* New York: Routledge.

Ericson, R. and Carriere, K. 1996. "The Fragmentation of Criminology." In *Criminological Perspectives: A Reader*, J. Muncie, E. McLaughlin and M. Langan (Eds.): 508-515. Thousand Oaks, CA: Sage.

Foucault, M. 1977. *Discipline and Punish, The Birth of the Prison*. Translated by Alan Sheridan. New York: Pantheon.

Frigon, S. 1997. "A Gallery of Portraits: Women and the Embodiment of Difference, Deviance, and Resistance." In *Post-Critical Criminology*, Thomas O'Reilly-Fleming (Ed.): 78-110. Scarborough, Ontario: Prentice-Hall Canada.

Frigon, S. 1995. "A Genealogy of Women's Madness." In *Gender and Crime*, R. E. Dobash, R. P. Dobash and L. Noaks (Eds.): 20-48. Cardiff: University of Wales Press.

Frigon, S. 1990. "Review of P. Carlen, *Women, Crime and Poverty*." *International Journal of the Sociology of Law*, 18(2): 225-229.

Gelles, R. J. and M. Straus. 1979. "Determinants of Violence in the Family: Toward a Theoretical Integration." In *Contemporary Theories About the Family*, W. Burr, R. Hill, F. I. Nye, and I. Reiss (Eds.): 549-81. New York: Free Press.

Harding, S. 1986. *The Science Question in Feminism*. Ithaca, NY: Cornell University Press.

Harris, A. P. 1990. "Race and Essentialism in Feminist Legal Theory." *Stanford Law Review*, 42: 581-616.

Heidensohn, F. M. 1968. "The Deviance of Women: A Critique and an Enquiry." *British Journal of Sociology* 19(2): 160-175.

Katz, M. B. 1995. *Improving Poor People: The Welfare State, the "Underclass," and Urban Schools as History*. Princeton, NJ: Princeton University Press.

Kemp, A. A. 1994. *Women's Work: Degraded and Devalued*. Englewood Cliffs, NJ: Prentice-Hall.

Kessler-Harris, A. and K. B. Sacks. 1987. "The Demise of Domesticity in America." In *Women, Households, and the Economy*, L. Beneria and C. R. Stimpson (Eds.): 65-84. New Brunswick, NJ: Rutgers University Press.

Klein, D. 1997. "An Agenda for Reading and Writing about Women, Crime and Justice." *Social Pathology* 3(2): 81-91.

Klein, D. 1996. "The Etiology of Female Crime." In *Criminological Perspectives: A Reader*, J. Muncie, E. McLaughlin and M. Langan (Eds.): 160-186. Thousand Oaks, CA: Sage.

Klein, D. 1973. "The Etiology of Female Crime: A Review of the Literature." *Issues in Criminology* 8: 3-30.

Kline, M. 1993. "Race, Racism, and Feminist Legal Theory." In *Feminist Legal Theory: Foundations*, K. Weisberg (Ed.): 371-382. Philadelphia: Temple University Press.

Mehren, Elizabeth. "Girl Trouble: America's Overlooked Crime Problem" (part of series "Girl Trouble: America's Overlooked Crime Problem"). *Jagged Justice*. Tuesday, July 9, 1996. *Los Angeles Times* E: 2-3.

Messerschmidt, J. W. 1997. "From Patriarchy to Gender: Feminist Theory, Criminology and the Challenge of Diversity." In *International Feminist Perspectives In Criminology: Engendering A Discipline*: 167-188. Nicole Rafter and Frances Heidensohn (Eds.). Philadelphia: Open University Press.

Messerschmidt, J. W. with foreword by R. W. Connell. 1993. *Masculinities and Crime: Critique and Reconceptualization of Theory*. Boston Way, Maryland: Rowman and Littlefield Publishers, Inc.

Messerschmidt, J. W. 1987. "Feminism, Criminology and the Rise of the Female Sex 'Delinquent', 1880-1930." *Contemporary Crises*, 11(3): 243-263.

Muncie, J., McLaughlin E. and M. Langan (Eds.). 1996. *Criminological Perspectives: A Reader*. Thousand Oaks, CA: Sage.

Odem, M. E. 1995. *Delinquent Daughters: Protecting and Policing Adolescent Female Sexuality in the United States, 1885-1920*. Chapel Hill, NC: The University of North Carolina Press.

Rafter, N. and F. Heidensohn (Eds.). 1997. "Introduction: The Development of Feminist Perspectives on Crime." In *International Feminist Perspectives In Criminology: Engendering A Discipline*: 1-14. Philadelphia: Open University Press.

Rafter, N. 1990. "The Social Construction of Crime and Crime Control." *Journal of Research in Crime and Delinquency* 27(4): 376-389.

Scheffe, T. J. (Ed.). 1975. "On Reason and Sanity: Some Political Implications of Psychiatric Thought." In *Labeling Madness*: 12-21. Englewood Cliffs, NJ: Prentice-Hall.

Schneider, E. M. 1992. "Particularity and Generality: Challenges in Feminist Theory and Practice in Work on Woman-Abuse." *New York University Law Review*, 67: 520-568.

Scraton, P. and K. Chadwick. 1996. "The Theoretical and Political Priorities of Critical Criminology." In *Criminological Perspectives: A Reader*, J. Muncie, E. McLaughlin and M. Langan (Eds.): 284-298. Thousand Oaks, CA: Sage.

Segal, L. 1996. "Explaining Male Violence." In *Criminological Perspectives: A Reader*, J. Muncie, E. McLaughlin and M. Langan (Eds.): 187-202. Thousand Oaks, CA: Sage.

Segal, L. 1990. *Slow Motion: Changing Masculinities, Changing Men*. London: Virago.

Shelden, R. G., S. K. Tracy and W. B. Brown. 1996. "Girls and Gangs: A Review of Recent Research." *Juvenile and Family Court Journal* 47(1): 21-39.

Sherman, L. A. and Berk, R.A. 1984. "The Specific Deterrent Effects of Arrest for Domestic Violence." *American Sociological Review* 49(2): 261-292.

Shoemaker, D. J. 1996. *Theories of Delinquency: An Examination of Explanations of Delinquent Behavior*, third edition. New York: Oxford University Press.

Simon, R. J. 1975. *Women and Crime*. Lexington, MA: Lexington Books.

Simpson, S. S. 1996. "Feminist Theory, Crime, and Justice." In *Readings in Contemporary Criminological Theory*, P. Cordella and L. Siegel (Eds.): 319-339. Boston: Northeastern University Press.

Smart, C. 1996. "Feminist Approaches to Criminology or Postmodern Woman Meets Atavistic Man." In *Criminological Perspectives: A Reader*, J. Muncie, E. McLaughlin and M. Langan (Eds.): 453-465. Thousand Oaks, CA: Sage.

Smart, C. 1995. *Law, Crime and Sexuality: Essays In Feminism*. London: Sage.

Smart, C. 1990. "Law's Power, the Sexed Body, and Feminist Discourse." *Journal of Law and Society*, 17(2): 194-210.

Smart, C. 1989. *Feminism and the Power of Law.* New York: Routledge.

Smart, C. 1979. "The New Female Criminal: Reality or Myth?" *British Journal of Criminology*, 19(1): 50-59.

Smart, C. 1976. *Women, Crime and Criminology: A Feminist Critique.* Boston: Routledge and Kegan Paul.

Smith, P. (Ed.). 1993. *Feminist Jurisprudence.* New York: Oxford University Press.

Sommers, E. K. 1995. *Voices from Within: Women Who Have Broken the Law.* Toronto: University of Toronto Press.

Szasz, T. 1987. *Insanity: The Idea and Its Consequences.* New York: Wiley.

Szasz, Thomas. 1984. *The Therapeutic State: Psychiatry in the Mirror of Current Events.* New York: Prometheus Books.

Vago, S. 1994. *Law and Society*, fourth edition. Englewood Cliffs, NJ: Prentice-Hall.

Williams, P. J. 1992. "On Being the Object of Property." In *The Alchemy of Race and Rights*: 216-236. Boston: Harvard University Press.

Zedner, L. 1991. "Women, Crime, and Penal Responses: A Historical Account." *Crime and Justice: A Review of the Research*, 14: 307-361.

Crimes of Violence: An Examination of the Identification of Women as "Violent" Offenders in the Canadian Criminal Justice System

Colleen Anne Dell
Carleton University

This paper is an examination of the relationship between identity and criminality in Canada. It explores the application of the violent offender label to women charged with or convicted of a violent crime. It is critical of the dominant perspectives of women involved with violent offences as either victims or unnatural/evil. These perspectives lend support to prevailing stereotypes of violent women as either helpless or mad, which is suggested to be a desired result of the operation of a form of capitalist patriarchy. Socialist feminist theory is proposed as a preliminary point of examination. It offers a structural explanation of the material and ideological maintenance of the harmful stereotypes. Examples within the Canadian criminal justice system of material maintenance and examples within the Canadian media of ideological maintenance of the stereotypes are provided. The paper concludes with two proposed research directions.

This research was supported by a doctoral fellowship from the Social Sciences and Humanities Research Council of Canada and a Carleton University scholarship for graduate studies. Sincere gratitude is expressed to both.

Introduction

> Critique is a prerequisite for the formulation of an alternative
> perspective. (Smart 1976:xv)

Since the beginning of the 1990s, increased attention has been
allotted to female violence in Canada. Specifically within the past
few years, it has escalated at an alarming rate. It initiated around the
time of the 1995 trial of Karla Homolka[1] and has since filtered into
various realms, such as Patricia Pearson's 1997 publicly favoured
book, *When She Was Bad*.

Ironic, however, is that as public awareness of the female violent
offender has increased, the rate of female adult and youth police
reported and court processed violent offences has decreased (Dell
and Boe 1998; Dell and Boe 1997). In fact, official statistics suggest
that the rate of violent crime in Canada has declined since the early
1990s (Boe 1997). Why, then, has an inordinate degree of attention
been placed on the female violent offender in Canada?

This paper proposes that the violent female offender identity is a
deliberate social construction. Two dominant stereotypes of violent
female offenders exist: as innately unnatural or evil and as a helpless
victim. Taking socialist feminist theory as an introductory point of
explanation, and drawing on theoretical and empirical literature and
current examples in the Canadian criminal justice system, these
stereotypes, or identities, are argued to be a desired result of the
operation of a form of capitalist patriarchy.[2] Using socialist feminist
theory, specifically the unified systems variant, as the starting point
to address this claim, it is explained that the ruling class in capitalist
patriarchy must maintain the marginalization of women's productive
and reproductive labour to perpetuate its own powerful position. It is
proposed that the increase of female emancipation in recent years in
Canada is viewed as a threat to this form of capitalist patriarchy. The
ruling class represses female emancipation through the promotion
and sustenance of a powerless female character structure (e.g., women
are encouraged to be weak, passive, complacent and nonviolent).
The violent female offender does not fit this condoned patriarchal
image. Powerless, violent female offender stereotypes have therefore
been developed as a means of oppression. This denies power to all
women because the violent female offender stereotype is portrayed

as the condemned prototype against which the socially oppressive and condoned feminine character structure is compared.

This paper addresses four examples of the perpetuation of the female violent offender identity in Canada: (1) the 1994 conduct of the emergency response team in the Kingston Prison for Women; (2) the initiation of Judge Rutushney's review of Canadian women who claim to have killed their partners in self-defence; (3) use of the Offender Intake Assessment with federal female inmates by the Correctional Service of Canada; and (4) the media coverage of the crises in the new federal female institutions.

In the concluding section, the imperativeness of producing critical knowledge to challenge and demystify the fallacious violent female offender identity in Canada is examined. To conclude, two research directions are proposed.

Socialist Feminism: A Brief History

In the 1970s, socialist feminism surfaced as a paradigm in feminist thought and strategy (Philipson and Hansen 1990:3). It essentially emerged in response to the political fragmentation within the women's liberation movement.[3] And it was due to political dissent that socialist feminism basically ceased as a movement and adopted a theoretical orientation (Segal 1987:44; Froines 1992:126). With the marked decline in public forums for debate outside the university, academia came to play a significant role in the continuation and agenda of socialist feminism (Philipson and Hansen 1990). Near the close of the 1980s though, the voice of socialist feminism was "remarkably silent in popular feminist debate" (Segal 1987:44). This remains true a decade later. However, although limited, exciting and commendable work is currently done in the field (i.e., Comack 1993; Danner 1996).

Capitalist Patriarchy, the Gender Division of Labour and Power

There are several variants of socialist feminist theory, diverging in focus and origin.[4] Following the early period in socialist feminist theorizing, which was dominated by efforts to relate Marxism to women's paid and unpaid labour, concern shifted in the mid 1970s to specifying the theoretical links between a concept used widely by radical feminists and women liberationists—patriarchy—and Marx's theory of capitalism. It was no longer the theoretical aim of socialist feminism to fit women into Marxist categories, but rather, it was to transform and unite the two separate theoretical traditions. One stage in the development of socialist feminist thought was unified systems theory, which emerged in response to criticisms of its predecessor, dual systems theory.[5]

Unified systems theory sets out to "describe and explain all forms of social oppression, using knowledge of class ... hierarchies as a base from which to explore systems of oppression centring not only on class, but also on gender" (Lengermann and Niebrugge-Brantley 1988:426-27). This theory views class (capitalism) and gender (patriarchy) structures as inextricably intertwined. It analyzes capitalism and patriarchy together through the use of one concept: capitalist patriarchy. This form of capitalist patriarchy "emphasizes the existing mutual dependence of the capitalist class structure and male supremacy" (Eisenstein 1979). The concept of capitalist patriarchy is a starting point for examining the development and perpetuation of the violent female offender identity in Canada.

This socialist feminist perspective centres on the structure of patriarchal society and the operation of its capitalist institutions as controlling forces in the lives of women. It claims production (capitalism) and reproduction (patriarchy) comprise the foundation of society which uniformly facilitates female oppression and male domination (Comack 1992). Relations of production are defined as the creation of economic necessities, such as food, shelter and clothing, between producers and non-producers in a society (Jary and Jary 1991). Capitalism is an economic system in which the means of production and distribution are for the most part privately owned and operate for private profit (Evans 1995). The relations of reproduction include "the need to reproduce, obtain sexual release, experience affection, socialize the young, and [maintain] daily life" (Messerschmidt 1986:28). Patriarchy is defined here as a system whereby males achieve and maintain social, cultural and economic dominance over females. It is predicated on an understanding of gender relations as inequalities of power (Evans 1995).

The central concept of the unified systems theory is the gender division of labour. With the advent of capitalism in Canada, women were allocated the role of the reserve army of labour (Martin 1986). Tong (1989) explains that

[b]ecause a large reserve of unemployed workers is necessary to keep wages low and to meet unanticipated demands for increased supplies of goods and services, capitalism has both implicit and explicit criteria for determining who shall constitute its primary, employed workforce and who shall act as its secondary, unemployed workforce. For a variety of reasons, not the least being a well-entrenched gender division of labour, capitalism's criteria identified men as "primary" work force material and women as "secondary" work force material. Because women were needed at home in a way that men were not—or so patriarchy concluded—men were more free to work outside the home than women were. (184)

The reserve army of labour marginalizes women's productive and reproductive labour. The marginalization of women is an essential component of capitalism.

To understand the relations of production (capitalism) and reproduction (patriarchy), one must examine their inter-relation of power (Eisenstein 1979:21). The unified systems theory is interested in understanding the system of power derived from capitalist patriarchy. In industrial Canadian society, the interconnected nature of the power of patriarchy and capitalism results in specific patterns of social involvement.

Focussing on the system of production and the gender division of labour, an upper class exists (men) that has a ruling and exploitative relationship with the working class (women). The upper class possesses power in Canadian society. Messerschmidt explains:

What maintains this class rule are both repressive and ideological institutions of the "superstructure". The capitalist class is served by, and so controls, at least indirectly, the means of organized violence represented by the state—the military and criminal justice system. Through its preeminent influence on the state, the capitalist class is able to repress behaviors that challenge the status quo. Other institutions, like the educational system and the mainstream media, expound an ideology supporting the status quo. Overall, then, the relations of production under capitalism have both material and ideological dimensions. (1986:32)

Focussing on the system of reproduction and the gender division of labour, patriarchal relations are essentially power relations with men exercising control over women by appropriating their labour power and controlling their sexuality (Messerschmidt 1986:34). In fact, Messerschmidt points out that

> ... men control the economic, religious, political and military systems of power in society. Women's exclusion from these positions is fundamentally parallel to their regulation of primary responsibility for reproductive labour. This exclusion is a major reason why women are relatively powerless to centrally change ... the sexual division of labor. (1986:34)

Since the ruling class is primarily comprised of men, behaviours that call into question patriarchy are repressed. As well, institutions of the state,[6] such as the mainstream media, uphold the patriarchal ideology of the ruling class. Relations of reproduction under patriarchy, like relations of production, have both material and ideological dimensions (Messerschmidt 1986:34).

Overall, the systems of production (capitalism) and reproduction (patriarchy), from a unified systems theory perspective, unite in their oppression of women. Together they maintain the gender division of labour and thus, ensure the marginalization of women. This is done in the interest of the ruling class to preserve its position of power in this form of capitalist patriarchy. In 1979, Eisenstein, a unified systems theorist, claimed society was uniformly plagued by a capitalist class structure and a hierarchal sexual structuring. I have suggested this remains true today and will present an ensuing ramification: the development of two oppressive violent female offender identities to perpetuate the oppression of Canadian women.

A Socialist Feminist Explanation of the Development and Perpetuation of the Female violent Offender Identity

Acknowledging the location of power in this form of patriarchal capitalism provides a basis for understanding why female violent offender identities are created and perpetuated in Canadian society. In 1976 Carol Smart stated:

> [i]n the past female criminality has not been thought to constitute a significant threat to the social order and even in the present, with the increases in the rates of offenses committed by women, criminologists and policy-makers are slow to re-evaluate the notion that female offenders are little more than insignificant irritants to the smooth running of law and order. (2)

Twenty-two years later, a development has occurred from Smart's position: women are perceived as a threat to the social order (capitalist patriarchy). I suggest that the label of violent female offender is used in Canada to restrict female emancipation. In the past three decades, women's escalating power has been both challenged and sanctioned as a threat to the patriarchal structure of capitalism (Messerschmidt 1986; Wolf 1991). In the interest of maintaining capitalist patriarchy, constraints exist on women to ensure they do not acquire a degree of power that will upset the gender division of labour and existing social order: ruling class dominance. A primary technique is the promotion and sustenance of the female character structure. Women and girls are encouraged to be passive, weak, complacent, dependent and nonviolent (Steffensmeier and Allan 1996:477). Concrete examples of the overwhelming acceptance of this position can be effortlessly located throughout Canadian society in advertisements,[7] public attitude,[8] television programs, pornography, cartoons, etc. (Wolf 1991).

The violent female offender identity exudes characteristics associated with the masculine character structure—strength, aggression, independence, autonomy, boldness and violence. These characteristics do not fit the condoned patriarchal image of the Canadian female. Lloyd describes the violent female as "not living up" to her socially prescribed oppressive female role (1995:36). In fact, the violent female challenges the condoned female and male character structures in this form of capitalist patriarchy. She dismisses portions of the female character structure and adopts characteristics of the male structure. In doing this, the violent female dismisses the powerless values of capitalist patriarchy (female characteristics) and adopts the dominant ones (male characteristics) (Messerschmidt 1986:40).

I propose that oppressive violent female offender stereotypes have been developed as the condemned prototype against which the socially oppressive and condoned feminine character structure is compared. This has been done in the interest of the ruling class because when women transcend the gendered image of the "female," it is a direct challenge to the current structure of capitalist patriarchy. Breaking the law becomes secondary to the violent female breaking from her feminine stereotype. Stereotyping violent women as unnatural and as helpless victims maintains and perpetuates power differences in society: the dominance of men and the oppression of women. Let us now turn to Canadian theoretical literature and empirical research on female violent offenders that supports this position.

Female Violent Lawbreakers in the Literature

In a comprehensive review of Canadian and American literature,[9] Shaw concluded there has been an absence of theoretical and empirical interest in violence by women[10] (1995a:5). This is supported by Faith (1993:97) and the research cited in Shaw (1995b).[11] In review of the literature from a theoretical[12] and empirical perspective, there is both an intelligible absence of scholarship and much of the writing that does exist contributes to the creation and maintenance of oppressive stereotypes of the violent female offender. Before examining this claim, violence is defined.

A. Defining Violence

The Criminal Code of Canada classifications of violent crime include

> ... assaults ranging from less serious offences as threats to use violence, or pushing or shoving, through to serious attacks which result in physical injury; sexual assaults; robbery which may involve a threat to use force, display of a weapon, use of a weapon and actual physical force; abduction; infanticide, attempted murder, murder and manslaughter. (Shaw 1995a:8)

Criminal Code classifications are not questioned here because the aim is to examine the application of the violent offender label (or lack of it) to women charged with or convicted of a violent crime. The existing Criminal Code definition and its classifications of violent crime are inherently related to the masculine character structure and, therefore, are reflective of the powerful values of capitalist patriarchy discussed in this paper. As explained, the ruling class negatively stereotypes women who commit violent crimes as unnatural and helpless victims rather than as violent. To attribute the characteristics related to a violent crime in capitalist patriarchy to women would provide them with the characteristic power attached to men. The stereotyping of female violent offenders as unnatural and as helpless victims promotes the dominant position of the ruling class in society. We are able to see that "[t]he capitalist class is served by, and so controls, at least indirectly, [a] means of organized violence represented by the state …—the criminal justice system" (Messerschmidt 1986:32). Indeed, critical attention (such as that located in the literature on women's use of violence in self-defence[13]) is needed in addressing the Canadian Criminal Code definition of violent crime, but that surpasses the scope of this paper.

B. Theoretical Explanations of Female Violent Lawbreakers

Violent female offender stereotypes in the theoretical and empirical literature perpetuate the oppression of women in several ways: (1) theories and studies present the violent female as unnatural, inherently controlled and as an aberration to the true feminine female; (2) theories present the violent woman as a victim—as helpless and powerless; and (3) studies ignore the violent female offender and oversimplify her crime. The literature on violent female offenders, in sum, assists in the maintenance of the operation of capitalist patriarchy by presenting oppressive and powerless stereotypes of the violent female offender and by neglecting to question the enduring stereotypes.

I) Individual Explanations

Traditional theories of female crime adhere to sexist stereotypes of women, treat women as other and perceive women and their crimes as single conceptual categories.[14] These theories are dominated by the individual pathology perspective that is based in biological,[15] psychological[16] and societal (view women as socially sick)[17] explanations. The legacy of the individual perspective is evident in contemporary theories of female violent crime (Lloyd 1995:xvi; Smart 1976:16). For example, women's conduct has been over-medicalized and explained by pre-menstrual syndrome,[18] mental illness,[19] and heredity.[20]

Though individual theories of women's violent lawbreaking introduced women into criminological explanations, it remains questionable whether the negative attention has proven to be a greater detriment than no attention. Individual based explanations stereotype women as unnatural for displaying traits of the masculine character structure (e.g., violence). As argued above, this maintains ruling class dominance: women are prevented from acquiring characteristics of a masculine (powerful) identity because it would challenge our existing form of capitalist patriarchy.

A second way individual explanations maintain this form of capitalist patriarchy is they do not present women's violent criminal conduct as a consequence of their volition, but rather due to their hormones, mental illness, etc. Viewing women's conduct as inherently determined denies women autonomy—a characteristic of the masculine character structure.

A shift from individual based explanations to the acknowledgment of societal influences in women's violent crime surfaced in the late 1960s with role theory.[21] Role theory focused on differential socialization, differential illegitimate opportunity structures and differential social reaction (Smart 1976:68). Role theory, however, ignored the larger picture: it neglected to question why women were assigned specific roles (Sommers 1995:18).

ii) Societal Explanations: Emancipation and Opportunity Theories

Societal accounts of female criminality similarly emerged in the late 1960s with the advent of feminist theory and feminist criminology. Heidensohn's (1968) work initiated focus on the social domination of women and its relation to crime. The first theory to acquire large-scale attention was Adler's emancipation/masculinity thesis (1975), and to a lesser extent Simon's occupational/opportunity thesis (1975). Both proposed that as women's roles became less structured, they had increased opportunity to deviate from their traditional roles and commit criminal acts conventionally committed by men (Smart 1976:70-76). Adler proposed the increase in women's crime, especially violent crime, was a direct result of the women's liberation movement. This sparked great debate within the tradition and although Adler's work was widely discredited, the myth of the liberated woman continues to surface in contemporary work.[22]

Collaterally, Faith claims "[t]he attention that came to her [Adler's] work assured a place for issues on women and crime on the criminological agenda" (1993:68). To illustrate, more than twenty years have passed since the emancipation and opportunity theories were introduced, and as Lloyd (1995:50) points out " ... where are all these new liberated female criminals?" Emancipation has not been shown to have contributed to an increase in women's involvement in violent crime.[23] For the past several decades in Canada, women have firmly comprised 12% of the total violations against a person (Shaw 1995b:188; Faith 1993). [24] Thus, the gender equality hypothesis can be refuted.[25]

In 1976, Smart proposed that the emancipation and occupational theories were an attempt to scientifically legitimize women's inferior social position (76). This remains true today. Lloyd states:

> This ... myth is proving durable precisely because it provides yet another stick with which to attack women who are working to improve the position of women in our society. It's a new ... way of blocking that improvement, a new way of keeping women in line. (1995:52)

The emancipation and opportunity theories implicitly critique any change in women's social position and challenge any attempt of women to gain power. Chesney-Lind states:

> [i]t is time to recognize clearly the notion of the liberated female crook as nothing more than another in a century-long series of ... attempts to keep women subordinate to men by threatening those who aspire for equality with the images of the witch, the bitch and the whore. (1980:29)

The emancipation and opportunity theories inherently suggest that women breaking from the confines of their traditional female character structures are unnatural because they are attempting to be male. These theories explicitly attempt to confine women to their powerless role in capitalist patriarchy. This, once again, upholds the ruling class interest of maintaining the gender division of labour: women are denied powerful (masculine) characteristics.

iii) Victimology

The victimology school of thought is rooted in the work of Elias (1986). With feminist criminology's increasing focus on the "larger picture" in the 1980s, it acknowledged the role of the victim in society. This overwhelmingly resulted in a view of women's violent conduct as a response to their victimization in an abusive situation or a past abusive experience (Shaw 1995b:120). Two examples are the theory and legal defence use of the battered woman syndrome[26][27] and the thoroughly publicized Canadian criminal justice system's review (by Judge Rutushny) of the cases of 98 women who claimed to have killed their partners in self-defence. At the time of the review, Rutushny stated of it that it " … is valuable … because it helps us … understand why these killings happened and whether abuse led to it" (*The Winnipeg Sun* 1996:3). The message filtered to the public was that female killers were wrongfully convicted because they acted in self-defence to an abusive partner. Today, particularly in Canada, the focus of feminist criminology remains largely on women as victims of domestic violence (Shaw 1995b:115-121; Walklate 1995:343).

Theories emerging from victimological concerns have served to place our understanding of violent female lawbreakers in a macro context, but they have overwhelmingly treated women as powerless victims within it. This has contributed to the stereotype of the female violent offender as a helpless victim.[28] This identity portrays women as incapable of self-initiated violence and therefore devoid of the masculine characteristic of autonomy (a characteristic of power in capitalist patriarchy). Additionally, by portraying women as merely reacting to men's violence, it oversimplifies their crime (Shaw 1995b:121).

From the initial individual pathological explanation of female violent offenders to the introduction of the emancipation and opportunity theories and feminist criminology's focus on women as helpless victims, little advancement has been made in explaining female violent lawbreakers. Feminist criminological theory, similar to traditional criminological theory, is guilty of not allotting adequate attention to women who commit violent crimes (e.g., Messerschmidt 1986). The form of capitalist patriarchy discussed in this paper is upheld by neglecting to address the violent female offender because it allows existing oppressive stereotypes to be perpetuated. The same criticism is made of the empirical research.

C. Empirical Accounts of Female Violent Lawbreakers

(I) Official Statistics

Official statistics are one means of measuring the amount of violent crime committed by women. According to Canadian statistics, very few women commit violent crimes (Lloyd 1995:36; Schur 1983:214). As revealed, in 1994 women comprised 12% of all people charged with a violent crime. Court statistics further demonstrate that when women are charged with a violent crime it is likely to be a minor assault and the majority of women receive a non-custodial sentence (Dell and Boe 1998; Lloyd 1995:56; Shaw 1995a:8).

Even though official statistics are widely cited as indicators of violent behaviour, there are extensive concerns with their use. These include: (1) police and court convictions are renditions of societal reactions and are therefore not accurate indicators of behaviour; (2) an undetermined amount of crime goes undetected and is therefore not accounted for (see Chesney-Lind and Sheldon 1992); (3) some crime that is reported goes unrecorded (see Hood and Sparks 1970:35); (4) categories of crime (including violent) are vaguely defined and variously recorded (see McCleary et al. 1982; Silverman and Teveen 1980); and (5) methods of computing vary and are often used inappropriately.[29]

Official statistics alone cannot be used to draw conclusions about the extent of women's violent conduct (or any conduct for that matter). They can be used, however, to examine the labelling of women (or lack of it) as violent. In essence, official statistics partially represent the response of official agencies of social control to female violence. For example, Lloyd (1995) and Shaw (1995a) concluded in their respective studies that the majority of women charged with a violent crime received a non-custodial sentence and women's involvement in violent crime has remained at a low rate over the past two decades in Canada (Shaw 1995b:188; Faith 1993).

These examples support my position that the ruling class in capitalist patriarchy, through state institutionalized means (the criminal justice system and its official labelling of women as violent), oppresses women to maintain its dominant class position. I have argued that it is in the interest of the ruling class not to define women as violent (that would attribute powerful masculine characteristics to them), but rather to deny their violent crimes of power by stereotyping the offenders as unnatural or victims. The empirical research on violent women offenders provides further evidence of this.

(ii) Empirical Research

Shaw made the following claim in her comprehensive review of the literature on violence by women:

> The lack of basic information about women who commit violent offences is a particular problem in Canada although it has been noted elsewhere ... .In Canada there are no national court statistics or in-depth studies which would allow us to look at the issue of violence by women in any detailed way. There exists only a handful of studies which have attempted to approach the issue. (1995b:120)

Since the publication of Shaw's report the situation has not improved.

Canadian studies of violent women offenders have primarily focused on women who have killed (e.g., Jones 1991; Pearson 1997; Priest 1994). This is also true in the United States (Shaw 1995b:120). Shaw (1995b:116) states the studies range from

> ... statistical accounts of women who kill (Silverman and Kennedy 1993); historical and descriptive accounts (Jones 1980; Carrigan 1991); feminist analysis of the impact of the Battered Wife Syndrome (Comack 1993; Noonan 1993); journalistic 'moral tales' of women accused of murder (Priest 1992), to more recently, accounts which try to contextualize representations of such women. (Walford 1987; Birch 1993)

The focus of the studies that do exist on violent women is generally presented as out of curiosity and intrigue, and the women are mainly depicted as aberrations to the "true feminine female" (Lloyd 1995). The majority of studies rely on individual pathology explanations (similar to the individual theories of women's violent crime). They primarily focus on the: (1) altruistic, (2) physical, (3) domestic, and (4) substance abuse nature of women's violent conduct. I address each in order.

The first prominent Canadian study of female violence focused on women who killed; it was conducted in 1974 by Rosenblatt and Greenland. They examined the circumstances of homicide and wounding cases and concluded women's violent crimes were altruistic. Because so few studies exist in Canada, Rosenblatt's and Greenland's study has been routinely cited and its findings generally left unquestioned. Unfortunately, the study is neither generalizable to the population it studied nor to the women serving federal sentences today[30] (Shaw 1995a).

Another landmark study on female violence that had influence in Canada was conducted by Ward and Ward (1969) in the US. They concluded that women killed men when men were at their physically weakest (e.g., asleep or ill) (Shaw 1995a:17). Numerous other studies have relied on physiological explanations, such as Wolfgang (1958) who reported women used minor physical strength to commit murder, Felson (1996) who concluded physical power was an important factor is explaining the decision to engage in violence, and Daly and Wilson (1988) who used an evolutionary perspective and difference in "fitness variance" (biological determination) in their study of violent female offenders.

The third theme, specifically of studies on women who have killed, is that their victims are emotionally close to them: husbands, lovers, relatives, and children.[31] Both the crimes and their explanations have a domesticated overtone.

And the final theme of studies on violent women is the establishment of a connection between women's violence and substance abuse. Recent studies by Brownstein et al. (1994) and Robertson et al. (1987) concluded the use of alcohol and illicit drugs were strongly correlated to women's violent conduct.

Three principal criticisms of studies on female violent offenders are proposed: (1) they oversimplify women's violent conduct, (2) they rampantly focus on women who have killed, and (3) there is an absence of research on female violent offenders. I will explain how each is grounded in the perpetuation of an oppressive female violent offender identity.

First, the studies are overly simplistic—they propose a single explanatory factor (either altruistic, physical, domestic, substance abuse) for female violent crime. Though limited counter-research exists in the area, a 1989 study of federally sentenced women in Canada, part of the Federally Sentenced Women Initiative, concluded a type of violent crime committed by women and a type of female violent offender do not exist. Similarly, a study of female violent offenders by Shaw (1995b) concluded that all women were not found to act violently in response to a violent situation (e.g., domestic abuse) (see Table I). The studies of female violent conduct (excluding Shaw 1989, 1995b) cited in this section rudimentarily typify the female offender to causally explain her violent conduct with one explanatory factor. Overly simplistic explanations deny women autonomy. Once again, we can see how refusing to equate the powerful characteristic of violent crime (autonomy) with the female violent offender serves an oppressive function. The perpetuation of the harmful stereotype of the female violent offender serves to maintain the dominance of the ruling class in the form of capitalist patriarchy discussed in this paper.

A second criticism is that the studies onerously focus on the act of killing. The sensationalization attached to murder in itself endorses a negative identity to the female offender as evil or unnatural.[32] As

---

Table 1: Circumstances of the crime for a population of eighty-five federal female inmates convicted of murder or manslaughter (Shaw 1995b: 122)

1. "Battered woman" kills a spouse or common-law husband.
2. Woman kills an acquaintance following sexual advances.
3. Woman kills in a complex situation (e.g., following extensive alcohol consumption or drug use).
4. Woman commits a passionate crime—kills a lover or lover's partner.
5. Woman kills a client or acquaintance for money or drugs (e.g., John or drug supplier).
6. Woman kills in the course of a robbery.
7. Woman kills a child due to depression, accident, vengeance, etc.

Faith states: "murder stories, when focussed on the deed, take on the quality of monster tales" (1993:97). Left untouched are the circumstances and nature of the crimes. The act of killing is misleading without an understanding of the context (Lloyd 1995:xviii).

And third, there is an absence of studies on violent women offenders. Limited research (and therefore knowledge) has significantly contributed to the perpetuation of oppressive stereotypes of the female violent offender. Also, because few studies exist, those that do are presented and accepted as truth due to the absence of counter-evidence (e.g., Rosenblatt and Greenland 1974). In the next section I will expand on the ramifications of the lack of research in Canada.

The Canadian Experience

To this point I have examined how criminological theories and studies, as well as their absence, have contributed to the creation and perpetuation of harmful female violent offender identities. I have argued how these identities, in the interest of capitalist patriarchy, operate to disempower women. Adhering to the outlined variant of socialist feminism, I further suggested that through the relations of production and reproduction, our current form of capitalist patriarchy (ruling class power) is maintained in two ways: material and ideological control. This section provides examples within: (1) the Canadian criminal justice system (as an institution of the ruling class) of the material maintenance of the stereotype of the violent woman offender as evil or unnatural and, (2) the media (as an institution of the ruling class) of the ideological maintenance of the same stereotypes.[33] These examples support the view that, as Lloyd states, " ... the system operates against such deviant women because the system itself is deeply embedded in a very traditional and conservative part of the society on whose behalf it operates" (1995:193).

A. Material Control

The operation of the Canadian criminal justice system, in its support of the interest of the ruling class, condones the material control of female violent offenders through physical violence. An horrific Canadian example was the treatment of female offenders as evil on April 26 and 27, 1994, at the Prison for Women (P4W) in Kingston, Ontario. The Kingston Penitentiary Emergency Response Team (riot team) was called into the institution to "extract" "rebellious"[34] prisoners from their cells following two days of "rebellious" conduct (Marron 1996:125). A video was taken of the actions of the riot team with the female offenders and it revealed "shocking images of female prisoners being stripped naked, shackled, prodded with batons and forcibly removed from their cells by male guards in riot suites and helmets" (Marron 1996:124). To illustrate:

> A Native woman who had been stripped while she was apparently half-asleep looked disoriented and totally humiliated, as she was forced to back up against a wall with a transparent plastic riot shield against the front of her naked body. Another naked woman kneeled with hands behind her head, motionless as if in a yoga position, asking in vain for a gown, while a chain was fastened around her waist and two guards stood in front of her with their batons raised like erect penises. But perhaps the most disturbing images were of a woman protesting and struggling as two men pinned her, face-down on the floor, and helped a female guard rip her clothes and tear them from her body. (Marron 1996:124)

This disturbing image depicts the treatment of women prisoners as evil when in fact their conduct was later not deemed as such (see Arbour 1996). The Arbour Report (1996) suggested it was not even necessary for the emergency response team to be called in to P4W for the rebellious conduct of the female inmates. In my view, the only revolt was the women's rebellion against the socially sanctioned patriarchal stereotype of femininity. Essentially, the violent women were treated similar to the theoretical and empirical literature's portrayal of the violent female offender as unnatural and an aberration to the true feminine female. On April 26 and 27, 1994, women at P4W had their power and autonomy stripped from them both physically and as prisoners within Canada's capitalist patriarchal system.

It is interesting to note a personal experience of public support for the material control of female violent offenders. In the days following the public release of the video depicting the deplorable actions of the riot team at P4W (February 25, 1995) I was employed as the executive director of the Elizabeth Fry Society of Manitoba (an agency committed to assisting women in conflict with the law). During this time I responded to numerous public and media perceptions that the women deserved what they got because they are violent women and that there is something wrong with the violent women, they are not feminine.

A second example of the material control of female offenders by the Canadian criminal justice system is the current incarceration of women in makeshift sections of male institutions (e.g., Prince Albert, Saskatchewan and in the Special Handling Unit in Quebec) and the proposed placement of high-security-level females in 1997 into the Kingston male institution. With the scheduled closing of P4W (supposedly the end of 1997 [35]) the twenty-two maximum security offenders of B range were to be transferred to the male institution. The majority of women scheduled to be transferred, as well as those currently in sections of male institutions in Canada, were not classified as maximum security because of the crimes they had committed or because they posed a threat to society, but rather "because of their tendency to suicide or self-injury—a typical response to sex abuse in childhood" (Driedger 1997). By relocating the high security or evil and unnatural women into male institutions, the Canadian criminal justice system had proposed, and currently does, treat them as aberrations to the true feminine female. The women are punished, in what I view as one of the worst ways possible, for being a maximum security offender, and thus for being an unfeminine female. Marron remarks that

> [u]ntil the 1930s, female offenders were housed in a series of different makeshift sections of men's prisons. The Prison for Women in Kingston, now universally known as P4W, was opened in 1934 to correct that situation. But it was plagued with problems from the very beginning. (1996:126)

I propose that the Canadian criminal justice system is reverting back to its shameful beginnings with the placement of women, once again, into makeshift sections of male institutions.[36]

A third example of material control of female offenders, in this case specifically by the Correctional Service of Canada (CSC), is CSC's implementation of the Offender Intake Assessment (OIA). The OIA instrument is used to collect and analyze information on over 200 risk and needs indicators to determine criminal risk, offender needs and security classification (Blanchette 1997).

With the introduction of the OIA in 1994 as part of all federal offenders institutional intake process, there had been hesitancy toward using it with female offenders. This was primarily because it was designed for and tested on a strictly male population. Initially, the OIA was not viewed as necessary for female offenders. However, with the recent CSC restructuring (the creation of five new regional institutions) and the problems surrounding the transfer of females to the new facilities (in particular the crises at the Edmonton Institution for Women—inmate murder, staff assault, walk always), the OIA was (re-)introduced as the essential tool to classify female offenders with regard to their institutional placement and security classification (minimum, medium or maximum). Simply, the OIA has been deemed by CSC as a means to identify female violent offenders.

However, the applicability of the institutional intake risk/needs scoring system for females is questionable. As stated, a main criticism is that the OIA is a male based tool or measuring rod. That is, the OIA design is based on a tradition of androcentric correctional practices and criminological literature reviews. Equally serious, the OIA has only been validated against male offender populations and therefore it is invalid to directly transfer it to asses female offender populations.

To illustrate, female offenders were excluded from consideration in the creation of the Community Risk/Needs Management Scale (CRNMS), which the institutional OIA is based on. The first evaluation of the CRNMS took place in 1989 and it was confined to a strictly male population (Motiuk 1989). Four years later, Motiuk and Brown (1993) included females in their study of the validity of offender needs identification and analysis of community corrections in the Ontario region, but the female sample was extremely small (31 females; 573 males). Recently, Blanchette (1997) conducted a study that focused exclusively on the risk and needs ratings of medium and maximum sentenced federal female offenders and concluded trend differences. The criticism remains that females are treated as correctional afterthoughts because a male based tool is used for the assessment and the applicability of the tool is not questioned.

Undeniably, there is need for specific research on the risk/needs scoring system for female offenders. And, until that occurs, the current OIA instrument is used to classify the risk and need levels, and determine the security classification, of violent and non-violent female offenders. Basically, the OIA is a state instituted tool that can be used as a means to achieve its goal—the classification of female offenders as violent or a security risk.

B. Ideological Control

This paper has presented the female violent offender identity as a deliberate construction to assist in maintaining the current form of capitalist patriarchy. It was suggested that the stereotype of the female violent offender as unnatural is perpetuated in the theoretical and empirical literature (as well as in the absence of it) and through material control. How is it, though, that the violent female offender identity is overwhelmingly accepted and maintained among the Canadian public? How is it that members of the Canadian public supported the horrific treatment of the female inmates at P4W by the emergency response team? The primary medium is the media.

The mainstream media, as a capitalist patriarchal institution, daily expounds an ideology supporting the status quo (Messerschmidt 1986:32; Schwartz and DeKeseredy 1993:259-260). This includes the ideology that violent female offenders are unnatural. An example is the excessive media attention surrounding the creation of the Edmonton federal female institution. Public concern over the placement of the prison for women in the city was fuelled by the media. Excessive media attention centred on where the institution for the "mad and crazy" women was to be placed. For example, prior to securing a location, headlines in the *Edmonton Journal* read "Where To Place Evil Women" (February 8 1995), and "I Don't Want Them in My Back Yard" (February 12 1995). Eventually, the prison was built in an industrial section of the city, symbolically on the fringe of the community.

Media attention supporting the stereotype of the violent female lawbreaker as an aberration to the true feminine female resurfaced with renewed vigour when several women walked away[37] from the Edmonton institution. The incident was followed by a media blitz, with the portrayal of women as inherently dangerous (when in fact they were not) and as having escaped (when in fact they simply climbed a three-foot chain-link fence and walked away). (If after being confined for ten years, and there was a sure means to walk out, could you say that you would resist the temptation?) The headlines of the *Edmonton Journal* read "Three Dangerous Women Escape" (March 17 1996) and "Beware: Violent Femmes on the Loose" (March 16 1996).

When the women were caught, video footage and newspaper pictures graphically focussed on one woman who swore and spat at the camera. All the women were depicted, once again, as evil. There are regular walk aways at male institutions across Canada as well as at psychiatric facilities, however, few receive the type of media attention the violent women at the Edmonton institution did. Some may claim that because the institution was new and initially raised concern in the community, such media reaction was to be expected. The question I raise is who initiated concern over the safety of the community? Who created and supplied the community with the image of the violent and evil woman offender? And, who neglected to inform the public that the women who walked away were not classified as maximum security risks? The media.

The examples provided of the material and ideological control of the female violent offender stereotype as unnatural support my argument that the Canadian criminal justice system treats and views the female violent offender as an aberration to the true feminine female. As stated, the Canadian criminal justice system, as an institution of the state (which upholds the interests of the ruling class), through both material and ideological forms, works to maintain our current form of capitalist patriarchy. Once again, we are able to see that the interconnected systems of production (capitalism) and reproduction (patriarchy), from a unified systems theory perspective, marginalize women so that the gender division of labour is maintained and thus the ruling class is ensured its powerful position in capitalist patriarchy.

I have suggested throughout this paper that the oppressive violent female offender identities are premeditated creations by the ruling class (supported through institutions of the state) and maintain our form of capitalist patriarchy. I also suggested that the stereotypes are created and maintained because the increasing attempted emancipation by women in Canadian society is viewed as a threat to the current form of capitalist patriarchy. I view it as inevitable that increased social measures will be enacted to ensure women, in general, are kept in an oppressed position in comparison to men. To address and combat this, the next section provides two suggestions for precursory research.

Suggestions for Further Reading

I have presented in this paper evidence to support that the theoretical literature and empirical research on violent female offenders is, at best, inadequate. Not only is there an absence of research, but the majority of that which exists perpetuates an oppressive violent female offender identity as unnatural and as a helpless victim. As revealed, these stereotypes are determinantal to the position of all women in the form of capitalist patriarchy discussed. For this reason, the stereotypes of the female violent offender must be critiqued and dispelled (Shaw 1995b; Faith 1993). Two introductory research directions are suggested: (1) reliable quantitative and qualitative research, and (2) concentration on the effect of variables such as race, class and age on the application of the female violent label to women charged with or convicted of a violent crime.

First and foremost, as expressed, research must be conducted on women violent lawbreakers. The absence of research has served as a detriment because the stereotypes have not been questioned and thus have been upheld and applied (e.g., riot team incident at P4W and the media's negative representation of the women who walked away from the Edmonton Prison for Women). Both adequate quantitative and qualitative research are required. Satisfactory quantitative research is absent in the area of female violent crime. To attain an understanding of the extent of violent crime committed by women, it is suggested that a large-scale self-report study be conducted. This type of study is necessary to first, and foremost, acquire an accurate account of the extent of violent crime committed by women in Canada. As well, a self-report study that varied across such boundaries as ethnicity and class would provide a glimpse into the effect of individual characteristics. It is necessary that all women are not treated as a totality (as the existing research does).[38] A self-report study could further provide an introductory understanding of the context and nature of women's violent crime.

I suggest that once a preliminary understanding of the extent and context of female violent crime is established, it would be useful to conduct in-depth qualitative studies. An open-ended interview approach would allow for further examination of findings revealed in self-report studies and would also facilitate the exploration of unidentified areas of female "violent crime". In fact, I view it as imperative because female violence has not been examined in any depth in Canada (Shaw 1995b:120). To accomplish this, we must provide the forum for women to share their experiences. Sommers illustrates that

> [w]omen in conflict with the law have their own ideas about why and how they become lawbreakers. They've lived through the experience of lawbreaking, and they know about it. They have survived the wrenching situations in which they were moved to act in ways that they sometimes angrily justify and sometimes profoundly regret. They have struggled with the social systems and structures that turn them from lawbreakers into criminals. They face the reality of who they are as individuals every time they look into the mirror. (1995:3)

Women's voices must be captured because within them lies the knowledge we are currently lacking in Canada.

Ethnographic studies are also a fruitful qualitative approach to understanding female violent conduct. Again, addressing my second suggestion of accounting for the effect of variables such as race, class and age, it would be valuable to conduct an ethnographic study in the prairie region of Canada to examine the over-representation of First Nations women in the criminal justice system for violent offences (Marron 1996:134) and the high incidence of violence, characteristic of many First Nations communities (York 1992). To illustrate, the main street of Winnipeg, Manitoba, which is one of the highest poverty ridden and Aboriginally populated sections of Canada, would be an ideal research location to examine these factors.

Both adequately designed quantitative and qualitative studies would be able to account for the amount and context of female violent conduct in Canada. The findings would, invariably, challenge the existing oppressive stereotypes of the female violent offender. Based on my argument in this paper that the ruling class in our Canadian form of capitalist patriarchy has created and maintains oppressive stereotypes of the female violent offender to oppress women in general, I ask this question: How can the treatment of women in society improve if we do not address the construction of the harmful violent female offender stereotypes through progressive and critical research? Ideally, I have conveyed the importance of this.

Endnotes

[1] Karla Homolka was sentenced in Canada for her involvement in the murders of Lesley Erin Mahaffy and Kristen Dawn French.

[2] Capitalist patriarchy is defined on page 112.

[3] The women's liberation movement formed in the early 1950s in response to the lack of attention allotted to the needs of women within the larger civil rights, anti-war and student movements.

[4] See Gottlieb (1989), Jaggar (1988), Lengermann and Niebrugge-Brantley (1988) and Tong (1989).

[5] Dual systems theory initiated attention on women's experience in relation to domestic work and the fact that it served men and capital. It recognized that women's experience could no longer be accounted for by solely focussing on their role in the reproduction of labour power. This marked a move away from the primacy of Marxism with its basis in the economic sphere. Dual systems theory afforded primacy to neither capitalism nor patriarchy, instead the system was seen as comprised of two systems or structures (Messerschmidt 1986). Dual system theorists maintained that "patriarchy and capitalism [were] distinct forms of social relations and distinct sets of interest, which, when they intersect[ed], oppress[ed] women in particularly egregious ways" (Tong 1989:175).

[6] The state is the apparatus of rule or government within a particular territory. It is a social system that is subject to a particular rule or domination. In this form of capitalist patriarchy, the ruling class has great influence on the operation of the state (Jary and Jary 1991:623).

[7] In March, 1998 Fisher Price introduced its new line of all male action heros (e.g., fireman) in a television commercial. It promotes the viewer to deduce that girls are not the "action heros" but rather they are the mythical "damsels in distress." Similarly, two 1988 Warehouse One (a Canadian clothing company) t-shirts read "D & G: Dumb and Gorgeous" and "Caution Blonde Thinking."

[8] A 1998 Ottawa, Ontario, licence plate reads "chvlry."

[9] Shaw's review covered the disciplines of psychology, psychiatry, sociology, criminology, social work and education. It focused on the most recent published articles. To examine the range of materials available it covered 1984-1994.

The CD ROM databases included the *Social Science Index*, *Sociofile*, *Psychlit*, *Eric*, *Uncover*, *Canadian Business* and *Current Affairs*. Library searches were conducted at five universities and the library of the Ministry of the Solicitor General, Ottawa.

The US sources included the NCJRS database, the Information Center for the National Institute of Justice, Fay Knopp and the Safer Society

Program, Russ Immarigeon Criminal Justice Writer, Sharon Smolick and the Bedford Hills Correctional Facility, New York (Shaw 1995b: Appendix A).

10 Note that the Canadian Criminal Code classification of violent crime is not indicative of violent conduct. For further explanation see page 116: defining violence.

11 See Krug (1989), Simpson (1991), Morris and Wilczynski (1993), Dougherty (1993), Campbell (1993) and Shaw (1995a).

12 This includes explanations that focus on societal factors and individual factors as the source of female violent crime.

13 See Thomas (1994).

14 See Klein (1973), Morris (1988), Scraton (1990) and Smart (1976).

15 See Cowie et al. (1968) and Lombroso and Ferrero (1895).

16 See Gibbens (1957), Glover (1969) and Greenwald (1958).

17 See Konopka (1966) and Thomas (1923).

18 See Kendall (1991) and Ussher (1992).

19 See Maden et al. (1994), Ogle et al. (1995) Singer et al. (1995) and Walklate (1995).

20 See Lloyd (1995).

21 See Heidensohn (1968) and Hoffman-Bustamante (1973).

22 See Robertson et al. (1987).

23 See Messerschmidt (1986), Steffensmeier (1996:469) and Robertson et al. (1987:754).

24 Refer to page 123 for the problems associated with the use of official statistics as a measurement of the amount of violent crime committed by women.

25 Note that women's participation in petty economic crimes has steadily increased (e.g., shoplifting and theft and fraud under $1000). Studies have concluded, however, that this is a consequence of economic marginalization and not emancipation (Carlen 1988; Dell 1996; Johnson and Rodgers 1993; Steffensmeier 1996).

26 See Allen (1987:82), Comack (1993) and Marron (1996:126).

27 "Leonore Walker suggests a three phase cycle [of the battered woman syndrome] which begins with an escalation of tension, followed by an explosive violent episode and a subsequent period of calm and reconciliation. She uses the psychological concept of 'learned helplessness' to argue that, over time, battered women feel that they cannot prevent violence" (Kelly 1993:64).

28 There are theories of wife abuse that do not appropriate autonomy (power) from women (see Lenton 1995). However, a greater proportion currently do.

29 For example, some have used males and females as the base for computing rates of rape (Hagan 1984).

30 The study "was based on a sample of twenty-two women psychiatric patients retained under a Warrant of the Lieutenant Governor for murder, attempted murder or wounding, and just four federally sentenced women at the federal penitentiary in Kingston" (Shaw 1995b:121).

31 See Mann (1996), Ward, Jackson and Ward (1969) and Wolfgang (1958).

32 It is important to note that there is increasing attention and a growing literature that sensationalizes female youth violence and violent gang participation (see Krantrowitz and Leslie (1993) and Sommers and Baskin (1994)).

33 I have limited my focus in this section to the violent woman offender identity as unnatural and evil. However, both material and ideological examples exist of the portrayal of women involved with violent offences as victims. For example, the state's initiation of Judge Rutushny's review of women who claim to have killed their partners in self-defence and the media and legal portrayal of Carla Homolka as a battered wife.

34 In Judge Arbour's review of the incident she concluded the rebellious acts were not, in fact, rebellious. She stated the women's conduct did not pose a threat to the safety of the institution or its occupants (1996).

35 A recent court decision, initiated by the fewer than twenty women who remain at P4W and the Canadian Association of Elizabeth Fry Societies in response to the placement of the women into the male Kingston institution, mandated the prison to remain operational for an additional four to five years.

36 Six new federal female institutions have been built across Canada in the last five years. However, after the institutions were built it was decided that they were not equipped to incarcerate maximum security offenders.

37 An inmate at a correctional institute is defined as having walked away when there are no physical barriers preventing the inmate from doing so. When there are physical barriers (such as a barbed wire fence) the inmate is defined as having escaped.

38 I recognize that I treated women as totalities in this paper—but the basis of my argument, being that it is a preliminary examination, is not impeded by doing so.

Bibliography

Adler, F. 1975. *Sisters in Crime: The Rise of the New Female Criminal.* New York: McGraw Hill.

Allen, H. 1987. *Justice Unbalanced: Gender, Psychiatry and Judicial Decisions.* Milton Eynes: Open University Press.

Arbour, L. 1996. *Commission of Inquiry into Certain Events at the Prison for Women in Kingston (Canada)*. Ottawa: Public Works and Government Services Canada.

Barrett, M. and M. McIntosh. 1985. "Ethnocentrism and Socialist-Feminist Theory." In *Feminist Review*, No. 20. pp. 22-47.

Birch, H. 1993. *Moving Targets: Women, Murder and Representation*. London: Virago Press.

Blanchette, K. 1997. *An Examination of Medium- and Maximum-Security Federally-Sentenced Female Offenders*. Correctional Service Canada. R-55.

Blanchette, K and L. Motiuk. 1997. *Maximum-Security Female and Male Federal Offenders: A Comparison*. Correctional Service Canada. R-53.

Boe, R. 1997. *Review of the Offender Population Forecast: Models, Data and Requirements—with Provincial Forecasts for 1998 to 2007*. Ottawa: Correctional Services of Canada. R-59.

Boritch, H. 1997. *Fallen Women. Female Crime and Criminal Justice in Canada*. Ontario: ITP Nelson.

Brownstein, H., B. Spunt, P. Goldstein, M. Fendrich and S. Langley. 1994. "Alcohol and Homicide: Interviews with Prison Inmates." *Journal of Drug Issues* Winter/Spring 1994, Vol. 24. No. 1-2, pp. 143-164.

Bryson, V. 1992. *Feminist Political Theory. An Introduction*. New York, NY: Paragon House.

Campbell, A. 1993. *Men, Women and Agression*. New York, NY: Basic Books.

Campbell, A. 1991. *The Girls in the Gang*. Massachusetts: Blackwell.

Campbell, A., S. Mancer and B. Gorman. 1993. "Sex and Social Representations of Aggression: A Communal Agenetic Analysis." In *Aggressive Behaviour*, Vol. 19. No. 2. pp. 125-136.

Carlen, P. 1988. *Women, Crime and Poverty*. England: Open University Press.

Carrigan, D.O. 1991. *Crime and Punishment in Canada, A History*. Toronto: McClelland & Stewart Inc.

Chesney-Lind, M. 1980. "Rediscovering Lilith: Misogyny and the New Female Criminal." In C. T. Griffith and M. Nance (Eds.), *The Female Offender: Selected Papers From an International Symposium*. Vancouver: Criminology Research Centre, Simon Fraser University.

Chesney-Lind M. and R. Sheldon. 1992. *Girls, Delinquency and Juvenile Justice*. California: Brooks/Cole Publishers.

Comack, E. 1993. *Women Offenders' Experience with Physical and Sexual Abuse: A Preliminary Report*. Winnipeg: University of Manitoba.

Comack, E. 1992. "Women and Crime." In Rick Linden (Ed.), *Criminology*: pp. 127-162. Ontario: Harcourt Brace Jovanovich Canada Inc.

Conroy, M. 1980. "Sex-Role Concepts Among Federal Female Offenders." In C. Griffiths and M. Nance (Eds.), *The Female Offender: Selected Papers*

From an International Symposium: pp. 257-269. Burnaby: Criminology Research Centre of Simon Fraser University.

Cowie, J., V. Cowie and E. Slater. 1968. *Delinquency in Girls*. London: Heinemann.

Crump, J. 1995. *Literature Review on Women's Anger and Other Emotions*. Ottawa: Correctional Services of Canada.

Daly, M. and M. Wilson. 1988. *Homicide*. New York: Aldine de Gruyter.

Danner, Mona J. E. 1996. "Gender Inequality and Criminalization: A Socialist Feminist Perspective on the Legal Social Control of Women."In Martin D. Swartz and Dragan Milovanovic (Eds.), *Race, Gender, and Class in Criminology*: pp. 29-48. New York: Garland Publishing Inc.

Danner, M. J. E. 1991. "Socialist Feminism: A Brief Introduction." In B. MacLean and D. Milovanovich (Eds.), *New Directions in Critical Criminology*: pp. 51-54. Vancouver: Hignell Printing Ltd.

Dell, C. A. October, 1996. *Offending Women: Gender and Sentencing. An Analysis of the Criminal Justice Processing of Blue- and White-Collar Theft and Fraud Offenders*. Winnipeg: The University of Manitoba Master of Arts Thesis.

Dell, C. A. and R. Boe. 1998. *Adult Female Offenders: Recent Trends*. Ottawa: Correctional Service Canada. B-23.

Dell, C. A. and R. Boe. 1997. *Female Young Offenders: Recent Trends*. Ottawa: Correctional Services of Canada. B-21.

Dobash, R., R. Dobash and L. Noaks (Eds.). 1995. *Gender and Crime*. Cardiff: University of Wales Press.

Dougherty, J. 1993. "Women's Violence Against their Children: A Feminist Perspective." In *Women and Criminal Justice* 4(2): 91-114.

Driedger, S. February 1997. "Shutdown at P4W. Women are Being Moved Into Men's Prisons." Maclains Magazine.

Eisenstein, Z. 1979. *Capitalist Patriarchy and the Case for Socialist Feminism*. New York: Monthly Review Press.

Elias, R. 1986. *The Politics of Victimization: Victims, Victimology and Human Rights*. New York: Oxford Press.

Elizabeth Fry Society of Manitoba. 1996. *Annual General Meeting Report*. (ed). C. A. Dell.

Evans, J. 1995. *Feminist Theory Today*. London: SAGE Publications.

Faith, K. 1993. *Unruly Faith*. Vancouver: Press Gang Publishers.

Felson, R. 1996. "Big People Hit Little People: Sex Differences in Physical Power and Interpersonal Violence." *Criminology* Vol.34. No.3. pp. 433-453.

Froines, A. 1992. "Renewing Socialist Feminism." *Socialist Review* Vol 22. No. 2. pp. 125- 131.

Gibbens, T.C.H. 1957. "Juvenile Delinquency." *British Journal of Delinquency* Vol. 8. No. 3.

Glover, E. 1969. *The Psychopathology of Prostitution*. London: ISTD Publication.

Gottlieb, R. 1989. *An Anthology of Western Marxism. From Lucas and Gramsci to Socialist-Feminism*. New York: Oxford University Press.

Greenwald, H. 1958. *The Call Girl*. New York: Ballantine Books.

Hagan, J. 1984. *The Disreputable Pleasures. Crime and Deviance in Canada* 2nd Edition. Toronto: McGraw-Hill Ryerson.

Heide, W. 1975. "Feminism and the 'Fallen Woman'." In *The Female Offender*, pp. 77-81. London: Sage Publications.

Heidensohn, F. 1968. *Crime and Society*. London: Macmillian.

Hoff, L. 1991. *Battered Women as Survivors*. New York: Routledge.

Hoffman-Bustamante, D. 1973. "The Nature of Female Criminality." In *Issues in Criminology* 8: 117-136.

Hood, R. and R. Sparks. 1970. *Key Issues in Criminology*. New York: McGraw-Hill.

Jaggar, A. 1988. *Feminist Politics and Human Nature*. Sussex: Rowman & Littlefield Publishers, Inc.

Jary, D. and J. Jary. 1991. *Dictionary of Sociology*. Great Britain: Harper Collins Publishers.

Johnson, H. 1987. "Getting the Facts Straight: A Statistical Overview." In E. Adelberg and C. Currie (Eds.). *Too Few to Count*. Press Gang Publishers. Pp. 23-46.

Jones, A. 1980. *Women Who Kill*. New York, NY: Holt, Rinehart and Winston

Jones, F. 1991. *Murderous Women*. Toronto: Key Porter Books Ltd.

Kelly, L. 1988. *Surviving Sexual Violence*. Minneapolis: University of Minnesota Press.

Kendall, K. 1991. "The Politics of Premenstrual Syndrome: Implications for Feminist Justice." *The Journal of Human Justice*. Vol. 2. No. 2. (Spring) pp. 77-98.

Klein, D. 1973. "The Etiology of Women's Crime: A Review of the Literature." *Issues in Criminology* Vol. 8 (Fall) pp. 3-30.

Knelman, J. 1998. *Twisting in the Wind. The Murderess and the English Press*. Toronto: University of Toronto Press.

Konopka, G. 1966. *The Adolescent Girl in Conflict*. New Jersey: Prentice-Hall.

Krantrowitz, B. and C. Leslie. August 2, 1993. "Wild in the Streets." *NewsWeek* Vol. 22. No. 5. pp. 40-47.

Krug, R.S. 1989. "Adult Male Report of Childhood Sexual Abuse by Mothers: Case Descriptions, Motivations and Long-Term Consequences." In *Child Abuse and Neglect* 12: 111-119.

Lengermann, P. and J. Niebrugge-Brantley. 1988. "Contemporary Feminist Theory." In G. Ritzer (Ed.), *Sociological Theory*. New York: Alfred A. Knopf.

Lenton, R. 1995. "Feminist Versus Interpersonal Power Theories of Wife Abuse Revisited." *Canadian Journal of Criminology* Vol. 37. No. 4. (October) pp. 567-574.

Lloyd, A. 1995. *Doubly Deviant, Doubly Damned. Society's Treatment of Violent Women*. England: Penguin Books.

Lombroso, C. and W. Ferrero. 1895. *The Female Offender*. London: Fisher Unwin.

Maden, A., M. Swinton and J. Gunn. 1994. "A Criminological and Psychiatric Survey of Women Serving a Prison Sentence." *British Journal of Criminology* Vol. 34. No. 2. (Spring) pp. 172-191.

Mann, C. R. 1996. *When Women Kill*. New York: State University of New York Press.

Maroney, H. J. and M. Luxton. 1996. "Gender at Work: Canadian Feminist Political Economy Since 1988." In W. Clement (Ed.). *Understanding Canada: Building on the New Canadian Political Eocnomy*, pp. 85-117. Kingston: McGill-Queen's University Press.

Marron, K. 1996. *The Slammer. The Crisis in Canada's Prison System*. Toronto: Doubleday Canada Limited.

Martin, G. 1986. *Socialist Feminism: The First Decade*. Washington: Freedom Socialist Publications.

McCleary, R., B. Nienstedt and J. Erven. 1982. "Uniform Crime Reports as Organizational Outcomes: Three Time Series Quasi-Experiments." *Social Problems* Vol. 29. No. 4. pp. 361-372.

Messerschmidt, J. 1986. *Capitalism, Patriarchy and Crime*. New Jersey: Rowman and Littlefield.

Moore, M., S. Estrich, D. McGillis, and W. Spelman. 1984. *Dangerous Offenders. The Elusive Target of Justice*. Massachusetts: Harvard University Press.

Morgen, S. 1990. "Conceptualizing and Changing Consciousness: Socialist Feminist Perspectives." In K. V. Hansen and I. J. Philipson (Eds.), *Women, Class and the Feminist Imagination: A Socialist Feminist Reader*: pp. 277-291. Philadelphia: Temple University Press.

Morris, A. 1988. "Sex and Sentencing." *The Criminal Law Review*: pp. 163-171.

Morris, A. and A. Wilczynski. 1994. "Rocking the Cradle: Mothers who Kill their Children." In H. Birch (Ed.). *Moving Targets: Women, Murder and Representation*. London: Virago Press. Pp. 198-232.

Motiuk, L.L. 1989. "Identifying and Assessing Needs of Offenders under Community Supervision: The Conditional Release Supervision Standards

Project." A paper presented at the First Annual Corrections Research Forum, Quebec City.

Motiuk, L.L. and S.L. Brown. 1993. *The Validity of Offender Needs Identification and Analysis in Community Corrections.* Ottawa: Correctional Service of Canada. R-34.

Muszynski, A. 1991. "What is Patriarchy?" In J. Vorst et al. (Eds.), *Race, Class, Gender: Bonds and Barriers*: pp. 65-87. Toronto: Gage Educational Publishing Company.

Naffine, N. 1987. *Female Crime: The Construction of Women in Criminology.* Sydney: Allen and Unwin.

Ogle, R., D. Maier-Katkin and T. Bernard. 1995. "A Theory of Homicidal Behaviour Among Women." *Criminology* Vol 33. No. 2. pp. 173-191.

Pearson, P. 1997. *When She Was Bad. How and Why Women Get Away With Murder.* Toronto: Vintage Canada.

Philipson, I. J. and K.V. Hansen. 1990. "Women, Class and the Feminist Imagination: An Introduction." In K.V. Hansen and I.J. Philipson (Eds.), *Women, Class and the Feminist Imagination: A Socialist Feminist Reader*: pp. 1-39. Philadelphia: Temple University Press.

Pollak, O. 1961. *The Criminality of Women.* New York: A. S. Barnes.

Priest, L. 1992. *Women who Killed.* Toronto: McClelland & Stewart.

Robertson, E, R. Bankier and L. Schwartz. 1987. "The Female Offender: A Canadian Study." *Canadian Journal of Psychiatry* Vol. 32. (December).

Rosenblatt, E. and C. Greenland. 1974. "Female Crimes of Violence." *Canadian Journal of Criminology and Corrections* 16: 173-80.

Segal, L. 1987. *Is the Future Female?: Troubled Thoughts on Contemporary Feminism.* London: Virago Press.

Schur, E. 1983. *Labelling Women Deviant. Gender, Stigma and Social Control.* United States: Random House.

Schwartz, M. and W. DeKeseredy. 1993. "The Return of the 'Battered Husband Syndrome': Through the Typification of Women as Violent." *Crime, Law and Social Change* Vol. 20 pp. 249-265.

Shaw, M. 1989. *Survey of Federally Sentenced Women.* Ottawa: Minister of the Solicitor General of Canada.

Shaw, M. 1991. *The Federal Female Offender. Report on a Preliminary Study.* Ottawa: Correctional Services of Canada.

Shaw, M. 1995a. *Understanding Violent Women.* Ottawa: Correctional Services of Canada.

Shaw, M. 1995b. "Conceptualizing Violence by Women." In R. Emerson, R. Dobash, R. Dobash and L. Noaks (Eds.), *Gender and Crime*: pp. 115-131.

Shaw, M., K. Rodgers, J. Blanchette, T. Hattem, L. Thomas and L. Tamarack. 1992. *Paying the Price. Federally Sentenced Women in Context.* Ottawa: Correctional Services of Canada.

Silverman, R. and L. Kennedy. 1993. "Special Offenders: Women, Children and the Elderly." In R. Silverman and L. Kennedy (Eds.). *Deadly Deeds: Murder in Canada*. Scarborough: Nelson Canada. Pp. 141-177.

Silverman, R. and J. Teveen. 1980. *Crime in Canadian Society*. Toronto: Butterworth and Company (Canada) Ltd..

Simon, R. 1975. *The Contemporary Woman and Crime*. Washington, D.C.: National Institute of Mental Health.

Simpson, S. 1991. "Caste, Class and Violent Crime: Explaining Differences in Female Offending." *Criminology* Vol. 29. No. 1. pp. 115-135.

Singer, M., J. Bussey, L. Song and L. Lunghofer. 1995. "The Psychological Issues of Women Serving Time in Jail." *Journal of the National Association of Social Workers* Vol. 40. No. 2. pp. 103-113.

Smart, C. 1976. *Women, Crime and Criminology: A Feminist Critique*. London: Routledge & Kegan Paul.

Sommers, E.K. 1995. *Voices from Within: Women Who have Broken the Law*. Toronto: University of Toronto Press.

Sommers, I. and D. Baskin. 1994. "Factors Related to Female Adolescent Initiation into Violent Street Crime." *Youth & Society* Vol. 25. No. 4 (June) pp. 468—474.

Steffensmeier, D. and E. Allan. 1996. "Gender and Crime: Toward a Gendered Theory of Female Offending." *Annual Review of Sociology*, 1996. No. 22, pp. 459-487.

Steinmetz, S. 1977/78. "The Battered Husband Syndrome." *Victimology*, (3/4) pp. 499-509.

Straus, M.A., R.J. Gelles and S.K. Steinmetz. 1980. *Behind Closed Doors*. New York: Anchor Books.

Thomas, C. 1994. "Women Who Kill." *The National Association Review* Vol. 279. No. 3. (May—June), pp. 4-6.

Thomas, W.I. 1923. *The Unadjusted Girl*. New York: Harper & Row.

Tong, R. 1989. *Feminist Thought. A Comprehensive Introduction*. Boulder: Westview Press.

Ussher, J. 1992. *Women's Madness: Misogyny or Mental Illness?* Massachusetts: University of Massachusetts.

Walford, B. 1987. *Lifers. The Stories of Eleven Women Serving Life Sentences for Murder*. Montreal: Eden Press.

Walklate, S. 1995. *Gender and Crime*. London: Prentice Hall/Harvester Wheatsheaf.

Ward, D., M. Jackson and R. Ward. 1979. "Crimes of Violence by Women." In F. Adler and R. Simon (Eds.). *The Criminology of Deviant Women*. MA: Houghton Mifflin Company. Pp. 114-138.

The Winnipeg Sun. Friday, November 22, 1996. Vol. 16. No. 327. "Freedom Possible for 6 Female Killers" by Nadia Moharib. Winnipeg, Manitoba.

Wolf, N. 199). *The Beauty Myth*. Toronto: Vintage Books.

Wolfgang, M. E. 195). *Pattern in Criminal Homicide.* Pennsylvania: University of Pennsylvania Press.

York, G. 1992. *The Dispossessed. Life and Death in Native Canada.* Toronto: Little, Brown and Company (Canada) Limited.

Young, I. 1980. "Socialist Feminism and the Limits of Dual Systems Theory." *Socialist Review* Vol. 10. Nos. 2-3 (March—June). pp. 174-183.

The Crime of Authenticity: Regulating Boundaries of Identity around Jewish Community through the Image of Russian Jewish Criminality

Kelly Amanda Train
York University

Introduction

The image of the Jew as a criminal is nothing new. This image has prevailed throughout history and been illustrated in various forms; most notably in Shakespeare's character Shylock who embodied the stereotype of the Jew as miserly and money-grubbing.[1] This criminalization of the Jew has operated as a way in which Jews have historically been racialized as other. Criminalization, then, refers to one process by which racialized Jewish difference has been imagined. In this sense, the process of criminalization metaphorically signifies and exemplifies the Jew as other through the image of the Jew as a criminal. This image of criminality signifies and renders identifiable Jewish racialized difference and otherness through such imagery.[2]

What is interesting is that the image of Jewish criminality has recently been appropriated by hegemonic forces within the Jewish community and used to marginalize Jews who are not seen to fit the authentic identity of who or what is a Jew. The image of criminality has been taken up within the Jewish community to reinforce, even police and regulate, what constitutes an authentic Jewish identity. The irony is that forms of othering (i.e., through the processes of criminalization) used within the Jewish community to marginalize Jews who do not fit the notion of the authentic Jew mirror those same forms of othering used to marginalize Jews in general within the broader context of society. The criminalization of Russian Jews within the Jewish community operates to marginalize these Jews within the Jewish community and, even more so, articulates their identity as a false (not authentic) Jewish identity. In this sense, the metaphor of criminality replaces how Russian nationality, culture and immigrant status exclude and deny claims of authenticity to Jewish identity and ultimately deny true or full membership within Jewish community.

This article focuses on destabilizing the imagery of the Russian Jewish immigrant as a criminal. I am arguing that the image of criminality is being used as a metaphor in place of the notions of nationality, culture and immigration that situate Russian Jews outside of an authentic Jewish identity.[3] The use of the notion of the Russian Jew as a criminal is based in these barriers and contains these notions of difference (via nationality, cultural difference and immigrant status) within its meaning and imagery. To talk about the Russian Jew as a criminal necessarily infers Russian Jewish otherness within the Jewish community through nationality, culture and immigrant status. Based on this imagery, I am taking up Russian Jewish criminalization as a means by which Russian Jewish exclusion and marginalization from the Jewish community has been legitimated and has replaced the metaphors of exclusion of nationality, cultural difference and immigrant status. I am looking specifically at the Israeli context of Russian Jewish immigration to Israel and how these immigrants are situated outside of an authentic Jewish identity. I am also concerned with how this marginalization and exclusion is articulated through immigration and absorption processes that politically regulate a specific Jewish identity and force this identity upon Russian Jewish immigrants. In this sense, Israeli immigration policies operate to police and regulate an authentic Jewish identity. Within this framework, the Russian Jew as a criminal is exemplified through immigration processes.

Immigration and the Construction of an Authentic Identity

The existence of the state of Israel is based on the notion of Israel as a Jewish state.[4] The struggle for the creation of the state of Israel, as well as the basis behind all of its governing laws, is the idea of Israel as a place of safety, security and refuge for all Jews from persecution and anti-Semitism. On this basis, all Israeli rights and laws are based on the identity of its citizens as Jews[5] (Barsky 1996). This is reflected in Israeli nation-building whereby Israeli immigration policy legally grants unconditional citizenship to any and all Jews. Under the Law of Return, the legal definition of who is a Jew is understood to be anyone who can claim Jewish heritage or descent as far back as three generations (Barsky 1996).

There has recently been a huge influx of immigrants to Israel from the former Soviet Union (known collectively as Russian Jews) and Ethiopia. The mass immigration of Russian and Ethiopian Jews to Israel is due to the intense institutionalized and individual anti-Semitism in their home countries. In the case of Russian Jews, while they see themselves as Jews because of their experiences of anti-Semitism in the Russian context, many do not fit within the Israeli cultural meanings of who is a Jew. In this sense, many of these Russian Jews are not Jewish *per se*. Many have either recently converted to Christianity as a result of present-day pressure to become Russian Orthodox within the former Soviet Union or have no Judaic religious basis or beliefs as a result of surviving and being raised within a communist regime. These Russian Jews, in many cases, have at least one Jewish grandparent, yet they themselves were not brought up as Jews within a religious or cultural context. On the basis of Jewish ancestry, however, they have been racialized as Jews within the Russian context. As a result, they have suffered from severe persecution as Jews in Russia (Barsky 1996). The opening up of the former Soviet Union has made emigration from Russia much easier. This, in combination with strict and limited immigration quotas to the US and Canada, and the large-scale establishment of Israeli Jewish agencies across Russia to promote *aliyah*[6] (and ultimately to bring these Jews back to the homeland) have brought large numbers of Russians who have been racialized within the Russian context as Jews to Israel (Moskovich 1990). This racialization is also recognized within the Israeli context whereby, under the Law of Return, legally these Russian Jews are deemed as Jews. Yet, there is a disjuncture between the legal definition of Jewish identity under the Law of Return and the recognition of who is a Jew within rabbinic law (this being a religious identity based in Judaism) (Barsky 1996). Who is recognized as a Jew in Israel in the everyday sense largely hinges on being positioned within both definitions. Thus, Jewish identity in Israel is based in both a religious and racialized identity.

Russian Jews who enter Israel on the basis of Jewish heritage or ancestry are legally seen as Jews. This Jewish identity is legally inscribed or marked on Israeli identity cards that indicate their nationality as Israeli (Barsky 1996). Jews, whether immigrant or Israeli born, are legally identified under the nationality category as Israeli, while non-Jews are defined as Russian or Arab. What is important to note is that all Jews who have gone to Israel to claim citizenship are denoted as having Israeli nationality. In contrast, non-Jews with citizenship in Israel (i.e., Palestinians and the non-Jewish Russian spouses of Russian Jewish immigrants) are legally defined in the nationality section of their Israeli identity cards by the country of their origins (as in the case of non-Jewish Russian or Ukrainian spouses) or their racialized identity (i.e., the marking of Arab). The purpose of indicating nationality is not about actually identifying one's nationality, but rather to illuminate those who are non-Jews from those who are legally recognized as Jews. The indication of one's Jewish status via the demarcation of their nationality as Israeli (whether recent immigrant or Israeli born) is to make legal sense of who individuals are, how to categorize and organize people and ultimately how to deal with or treat people in a legal and everyday sense (Barsky 1996). Although there is a hierarchy in the way that Jews are treated in relation to other Jews (specifically the treatment of Sephardi[7] and Mizrachi[8] Jews as subordinate and second-class Jews in relation to Ashkenazi[9] Jews (see Shohat 1988)), Jews in general are treated differently and given privileges that are unavailable to non-Jews, particularly non-Jewish Arabs and Palestinians, in Israel.

What needs to be stressed here is that Jewishness is conceptualized differently among Jews. The meanings of Jewishness are contingent on a specific socio-historical and cultural context. Within the Russian context, Jewishness is exemplified first and foremost as a racialized identity of otherness, although it may have other socio-cultural meanings attached to it. While Jewish identity has been legally defined through Russian state processes as a nationality, the marking of nationality as Jewish on Russian passports is used primarily as a means of organizing its citizens into racialized categories and racialized subjects. This legal organization of Russian citizens with Jewish ancestry is articulated through the stamping of Russian passports demarcating Jewish identity for nationality. This demarcation of nationality as Jewish does not change with religious conversion to Christianity (Barsky 1996). Rather, who is a Jew within the Russian context has to do with Jewish ancestry and ultimately Jewish racialized identity, and not a religious or national identity. The demarcation of Russian passports with Jewish identity for nationality can be seen to produce Jewish subjects as racialized others outside of an authentic Russian identity. Ultimately, this authentic Russian identity is produced reflexively through the production of racialized others. In this case, an authentic Russian is, of course, not Jewish. Russian Jews understand their Jewishness through their racialized identity as other, which is attached to a history and present-day experience of anti-Semitism and Jewish persecution within the former Soviet Union.

We might also see here how the historical articulation of race is directly tied to nationality. In this sense, the articulation of Jewish identity as a nationality in the Russian context and the articulation of Israeli nationality as a metaphor for Jewish identity in the Israeli context operate through legal processes to socially organize people into categories of normative and other. In both cases specifically, these processes legally mark who is a Jew. Yet, in both cases the consequences and effects of such markings prove very different results. In the Russian context, this legal process organizes Jews into a visible legal category of other or outsider. In the Israeli context, such processes legally define everyone who, under the Law of Return, is considered Jewish as part of a normative, inclusive nationality and racialized identity through an Israeli/Jewish identity. Built within these metaphors of nationality and racialized identity is the legal organization of who belongs and who does not, and separates people into categories of us and them.

While Russian Jews are legally recognized as Jews under the Law of Return, they experience discrimination, many have even called it persecution[10] (see Barsky 1996), in Israel because they are not recognized as Jews within the Israeli context of the social, cultural and religious meanings of who or what is a Jew. As a result, Russian Jews, while legally defined within the boundaries of inclusion, are simultaneously positioned outside of an authentic Jewish identity. As part of the immigration process and in return for the governmental financial and housing subsidies provided to new immigrants, new immigrants are forced to go through absorption processes as a means of tailoring their identity to fit within the construction of the authentic Jew. This means taking Hebrew and Jewish history and philosophy classes, converting to Judaism and moulding their way of life to fit within the Israeli cultural context of what it means to be a Jew. Specifically, this means adopting Judaism and incorporating its religious laws to some extent in the everyday way of life. The basis behind this kind of absorption is to make Russian Jews into good Israelis or good Jews. As Barsky (1996) argues, Russian immigrants are subject to intense pressure to adopt Judaism as a religious identity and cultural way of life. The refusal to do so leads to the loss of housing and employment, as well as outright hostility from other Israeli Jews (Barsky 1996).

The Criminalization of Russian Jews

While Russian Jews are legally defined as Israeli through the processes of *aliyah*, the reality is that they are continuously situated and marked as other within their everyday lives through the metaphor of the immigrant. The use of the term immigrant in the Israeli context is used to express those Jews who have recently claimed *aliyah* but do not fit within the construct of the authentic Jew. In this sense, immigrant tends to be reserved for Ethiopians and Russians.[11] In the Ethiopian case, their skin colour and cultural way of being Jewish denotes their racialized difference from being true or authentic Israelis. In the Russian case, their language, their Russian look (see Barsky 1996) and, most importantly, their Jewish identity, which is detached from any Judaic religious identity and is often even situated within their atheist or even Christian religious beliefs and values, place them outside of a true or authentic Israeli identity. In both cases, their construction as immigrant in Israel reinforces their inability to fully fit or belong within a true or authentic Israeli identity, which essentially translates to the inability to fit within a true or authentic Jewish identity (as Israeli and Jewish in the Israeli context are interchangeable).

The construction of both Ethiopians and Russians as immigrants brings with it specific imagery that operates to legitimate, reify and signify their exclusion. Recently, the exclusion of Ethiopian Jews has been legitimated through their stigmatization as HIV/AIDS carriers in light of the recent blood donation crisis in Israel.[12] In the Russian case, the imagery that has recently plagued their arrival has been that of the criminal. For example,

> We've lived in the same apartment in Neve Ya'akov for the
> past ten years. It's a pretty crummy place. All the criminals
> from the U.S.S.R. got dumped in my backyard. You'd think
> I was happy that a thousand blond girls moved into my
> development. But there are two thousand fathers and
> brothers watching them like hawks. Besides, I don't speak
> their language. The only language they want to hear is money.
> (Rafi in Mozeson and Stavsky 1994)

Such imagery exemplifies Russian Jewish criminality as similar
imagery to that of Shylock, that Russian Jews are money-grubbing
and miserly. Such imagery is entrenched in Western images of
communist criminality, communist corruption and the Russian mafia.
This imagery is necessarily juxtaposed to the Israeli socio-economic
system, which is imagined as providing equal opportunity to all Jews.[13]
The production of the Russian Jew as a criminal through such imagery
operates strictly as a means of imagining difference and articulating
exclusion from the notion of the authentic Jew. This imagery, then, is
not about criminality *per se*, but rather about community membership.
To elaborate further, the point is not whether such crime exists or
not, but rather that such imagery persists as a means of reifying and
legitimating a proper and recognizable Jewish identity that polices
not only who can belong but who embodies a proper and recognizable
Jewish identity and who finds themselves marginalized within the
community. We might say, then, that the imagery of Russian Jewish
criminality renders Russian Jewish otherness intelligible.

The imagery of Russian Jewish criminality as a metaphor for the
immigrant other within Jewish community is not isolated to the present-
day Israeli case. Such imagery has been borrowed from the early-
twentieth-century North American context and transformed to fit the
Israeli scenario. In the North American context, Russian Jewish
criminality was used as a metaphor to illustrate oppositional positions
within the Jewish community of immigrant and assimilated. Joselit
writes:

> [Frank] Moss depicted "Old Israel"—the German-Jewish
> community—as respectable citizens, in contrast to "New
> Israel"—the Eastern European Jewish community—whose
> people lived lives of unbridled license ... the Lower East
> Side, the civic reformer concluded, "is a distinct centre of

> crime ... and the criminal instincts that are so often found
> naturally in Russian and Polish Jews came to the surface
> here in such ways as to warrant the opinion that these
> people are the *worst element in the entire make-up of New
> York life.* [original emphasis] (Joselit 1983:6)

Such imagery illustrates how an authentic Jewish identity is produced through metaphors of Old and New World, which exemplify images of exclusion and inclusion. In the above quote, Old Israel designates an established, assimilated Jewish community that immigrated at a much earlier time period. New Israel, in contrast, articulates a Jewish community of recent immigrants. Through this imagery, the assimilated, established Western Jew is situated in opposition to the Eastern European Jewish immigrant. Inherent within such images are the notions of Eastern European corruption in contrast to a civilized, hence assimilated, Western Jewish way of being. The power of the established community enables them to define the boundaries around membership within the community. These boundaries are constituted around the identity of those who hold power within the community. On this basis, these boundaries are legitimated through such imagery of criminality.

This earlier North American example of images of Russian Jewish immigrant criminality is directly applicable to the present-day Israeli case. For example:

> I swear, people just don't like the Russians. They have their
> own little gangs. And they smell bad. They take all the
> money and all the jobs. You can believe me because I'm
> Russian, too. At least my parents were born there. They
> came here [Israel] twenty-three years ago, so I don't feel
> close to these smelly newcomers. (Limor in Mozeson and
> Stavsky 1994:83)

This illustrates the binary relation established between the pure or authentic Jewish community and those situated on the periphery. In the above case, authenticity is entrenched in an assimilated Israeli identity. Those who fall outside of this authenticity are deemed immigrants, and in the case of Russian Jewish immigrants, this marking is accompanied by images of criminality that are associated with Old World/Russian corruption, such as gangs. Such images of criminality are entrenched in the articulation of cultural differences that are expressed as images which are used to exemplify criminality itself, such as in this case the signification of Russian Jews as "dirty" or "smelly."

Importantly, the construction of the category of Russian Jews as criminals reflexively establishes a binary category of the authentic Jew as an innocent bystander. Jewish community and Jewish identity are conceptualized as absolute whereby the community reifies its conception of itself through such imagery of what it is not. The imagery of Russian Jewish criminality operates to reify those outside of the construction of the *authentic* Jew, and therefore reinforce an us versus them community identity. Belonging within the "them," in this case being imagined within the imagery of Russian Jewish criminality, necessarily denies membership in the "us" or the pure community as such imagery establishes strict oppositional barriers of innocence/ purity and criminality. As a result, Russian Jewish immigrants are denied the authenticity of belonging and placed outside of this realm of community identity. In other words, they are deemed as not being real Jews.

Conclusion

The criminalization of Russian Jews within Israel and the Jewish community operates to signify Russian Jewish otherness within the Jewish community. This signification reflexively produces an authentic Jewish identity. The criminalization of Russian Jews, then, is not about actual criminality; rather, the crime is perhaps the claim of Jewish identity which does not fit within the hegemonic community construct of who is a Jew. Thus, the imagery of Russian Jewish criminality operates to police and regulate the hegemonic construction of the authentic Jew. What becomes apparent through the process of criminalization is that the boundaries around Jewish community are rigid, not fluid, and depend upon a singular common identity as the basis from which community membership can be rendered intelligible. This authentic or common identity does not allow for diversity within the meanings and lived realities of Jewishness. We might then argue that Israeli nation-building is about the construction of an authentic Jewish identity. As a result, Jewish community membership is based on the premise of exclusion rather than inclusion. Perhaps in

deconstructing notions of internal community otherness we might begin
to rethink essentialized notions of community identity, thereby making
community an inclusive, rather than exclusive, place.

Endnotes

[1] For further discussion on images of Jewish criminality, and more specifically
on the racialization of Jewish criminality, see Sander Gilman (1991) and
(1986).

[2] Historically and in the present, Jews have been denoted as a separate
racialized construct, different from normative constructs of whiteness and
from other racialized others such as blacks, Asians, South Asians and
Arabs. By normative racialized identities, I am referring to racialized identity
which is seen as invisible because it is normative. In contrast, othered
racialized identities are rendered visible through social meanings attached
to skin colour, cultural traditions, rituals, customs and ways of being, as
well as such imagery as criminality, which is discursively imposed upon
racialized others. Today we recognize racialized identity as derived from
the social meanings attached to skin colour and culture. Yet, historically
racialized identity has been attached to nationality (Miles, 1993). This
identity is tied to birthright, as national identity was not simply denoted as
one's own national identity but as part of a historical bloodline of national
identity; i.e., the national identity of one's parents, grandparents, etc.
Historically, then, racial identity was seen in terms of national identity,
such as the German race, the British race, etc. and was only deemed
authentic if one could trace one's roots adequately to substantiate one's
claims to that national racialized identity. Claims to this authentic national
identity meant that one could not be situated within other racialized
identities, such as Jewishness, Blackness, etc. Thus, it is necessary to
recognize that the construction of race is not static, but rather has
transformed over time and place.

[3] It is important to note that in using the term, Russian Jew, I am referring
to new immigrants from Russia (and the former Soviet Union) as outside
the construct of the authentic Jew. This is an important point as the
construct of the authentic Jew is based in the image of the Ashkenazic
Jew (Eastern European Jews), primarily those with Russian, Polish and
German ancestry.

[4] The Zionist dream of a Jewish state has fundamental roots in the history
of Jewish persecution. The basis of a Jewish state was meant to provide
a place of safety, security and refuge in the form of a Jewish homeland.
The location and place of this homeland is symbolic of the historical

homeland of the Jews from which they were expelled 2000 years ago. Thus, Jewish immigration to Israel is seen as not simply a place of safety and security from Jewish persecution but also a spiritual and religious homecoming. This spiritual return through immigration is known in Hebrew as *aliyah*, which means more than simply the immigration to Israel, but rather the spiritual and religious, as well as material, return to the Jewish homeland. Under Israeli immigration policy, this is known as the Law of Return or, in Hebrew, *aliyah*.

5   This is exemplified through Israeli treatment of non-Jewish Arab Israelis and Palestinians. Both are legally dealt with and treated as second-class citizens (see Shohat 1988; Mayer 1994; Young 1992).

6   See footnote 4.

7   Sephardi Jews are the descendants of the Jews of Spain. These Jews left Spain during the Spanish Inquisition to escape persecution and settled in North Africa (i.e., Tunisia and Morocco), the Middle East (i.e., Iran, Iraq, Egypt, Libya, Syria, Yemen and other Arab countries), Turkey and Greece.

8   Mizrachi Jews (in English known as Oriental Jews) is the term used in Israel to refer to Jews who are not Ashkenazi—descendants of Eastern European Jews. Mizrachi is used in Israel as an umbrella term to denote all non-Ashkenazic Jews much in the same way as we in North America use the umbrella term people of colour to incorporate South Asians, blacks, Asians and Latinos. Incorporated within this category are Sephardi Jews, Indian Jews, Ethiopian Jews and Middle Eastern Jews (some Middle Eastern Jews do not call themselves Sephardi and instead identify as being Jews from a specific Middle Eastern country, i.e., Yemenite Jews).

9   Ashkenazi Jews are Jews who are the descendants of Eastern European Jews. These Jews tend to have their roots in Russia, Poland, Lithuania, Romania, the Ukraine, the Czech Republic and other parts of the former Soviet Union, as well as Germany, England and France, etc.

10   Some Russian Jews have tried to immigrate to Canada from Israel under humanitarian refugee claims by articulating the discrimination and persecution they have suffered in Israel because they are not authentic Jews (see Barsky 1996; Glickman 1996), and even more so, not seen as Jews at all outside of their legal status.

11   North American Jews who make aliyah are not seen as immigrants because they are recognized as having the right or authentic Jewish identity.

12   I have elaborated on this imagery in detail elsewhere. See Train 1996.

13   For further elaboration see Shohat 1988, Gottlieb 1993 and Gayle-Deutsch 1994.

Bibliography

Barsky, Robert F. 1996. "Refugees from Israel: A Threat to Canadian Jewish Identity?" In Howard Adelman and John H. Simpson (Eds.), *Multiculturalism, Jews and Identities in Canada*: pp. 219-262. Jerusalem: The Magnes Press, The Hebrew University.

Gayle-Deutsch, Alisa. 1994. "Challenging Fragmentation: White Privilege, Jewish Oppression and Lesbian Identity." In Mona Oikawa, Dionne Falconer and Ann Decter (Eds.), *Resist: Essays Against a Homophobic Culture*: pp. 96-114. Toronto: Women's Press.

Gilman, Sander L. 1986. *Jewish Self-Hatred: Anti-Semitism and the Hidden Language of the Jews*. Baltimore: The Johns Hopkins University Press.

Gilman, Sander L. 1991. *The Jew's Body*. New York: Routledge.

Glickman, Yaacov. 1996. "Russian Jews in Canada: Threat to Identity or Promise of Renewal?" In Howard Adelman and John H. Simpson (Eds.), *Multiculturalism, Jews and Identities in Canada*: pp. 192-218. Jerusalem: The Magnes Press, The Hebrew University.

Gottlieb, Amy. 1993. "Not In My Name: A Jewish Feminist Challenges Loyalty to Israel." In Linda Carty (Ed.), *And Still We Rise: Feminist Political Mobilizing in Contemporary Canada*: pp. 53-72. Toronto: Women's Press.

Joselit, Jenna Weissman. 1983. *Our Gang: Jewish Crime and the New York Jewish Community 1900-1940*. Bloomington: Indiana University Press.

Mayer, Tamar. 1994. "Heightened Palestinian Nationalism: Military Occupation, Repression, Difference and Gender." In Tamar Mayer (Ed.), *Women and the Israeli Occupation: The Politics of Change*: pp. 62-87. London: Routledge.

Miles, Robert. 1993. *Racism After 'Race Relations'*. London: Routledge.

Moskovich, Wolf. 1990. *Rising to the Challenge: Israel and the Absorption of Soviet Jews*. London: Institute of Jewish Affairs.

Mozeson, I.E. and Lois Stavsky. 1994. *Jerusalem Mosaic: Young Voices from the Holy City*. New York: Four Winds Press.

Shohat, Ella. 1988. "Sephardim in Israel: Zionism from the Standpoint of its Jewish Victims," *Social Text* 19/20:1-35.

Train, Kelly Amanda. 1996. "AIDS, Race, and the Construction of Jewish Community: Ethiopian Jews in Israel." *Response: A Contemporary Jewish Review*, 66(Summer/Fall):51-55.

Young, Elise G. 1992. *Keepers of the History: Women and the Israeli-Palestinian Conflict*. New York: Teachers College Press, Teachers College, Columbia University.

Negotiating Deviance and Normativity: Performance Art, Boundary Transgressions, and Social Change

Britta B. Wheeler
New York University

Introduction

Contemporary art explores identity and challenges taken-for-granted assumptions about self and society. These practices come from the tradition of the avant garde and promote social justice through art, which often uses provocative and direct modes of representation to enact difficult subject matter and to call attention to social problems. The history and practice of avant garde art, specifically performance art, relies on the use of disjunctive and contradictory images, boundary transgressing methods and shock tactics to subvert status quo ideals and institutions. Thus contemporary avant garde artists and their work are often known, constructed, labelled, and stigmatized as deviant by those who do not understand or disagree with these art world norms. Deviance is, however, contextual—in the eye of the beholder—determined not by inherent qualities in the act but by the power to label and the power to enforce the label (Becker 1963; Erikson 1966). But a paradox exists in the realm of art: rule-breaking behaviour is thought to be preserved against sanctions imposed on common sociality because of its context inside the art frame, and it is conversely labelled and sanctioned as deviant by those outside of the art context who find it a real threat to more conventional notions of social and artistic decorum. Cutting edge contemporary art is intentionally deviant; pushing the limits of accepted boundaries, on one hand, and the victim of being labelled and sanctioned as such, on the other. Thus, because of the work of contemporary performance artists, the contradictions embedded in the notion of what is normal and good (for whom, where, and when) become increasingly visible as the stakes over the struggle to define normality heighten when artists challenge norms of acceptable representation and a conventional status quo ideal of art and public expression. In this chapter, I discuss the ways performance artists produce social change by experimenting with and confronting social and personal boundaries, the limitations imposed by these and their constructions. First I describe the works of more radical performance artists and their uses of artistic content and form to invoke social change. Then I talk about the resistances to artists' work by a conservative backlash in a controversy over US government funding for the arts. In this public crisis, divergent groups competed over authority to define core societal values and the symbolic representation of these. Finally I show how artists use pedagogical strategies to accomplish smaller social and political changes after the outcry against radical art. I use data from field work, interviews and public records of performance events and controversies.

Performance Art[1]

Performance art provides a creative locale where art making and socio-political concerns merge because of the open-ended nature of the art form, its historical basis in radical intention, its anti-aesthetics, and low-tech requirements. Performance artists are interested in broadening traditional moral boundaries and oppressive assumptions about marginal members of society and hold the possibility of creating a society based on an overall acceptance of difference rather than an either/or, good/bad set of definitional assumptions. They create ritual art and performance art that cross the boundaries between art and life and resist traditionally confining definitions of identity, providing space where alternative realities are examined and presented. By doing this they contest definitions of marginal identities, including that of the artist as irrelevant to the regular mechanisms of society.

Performance art intentionally plays with the lines between art and audience, content and form. Artists may confront audiences with work that does not fit conventional definitions of beauty. The artist may bring the audience into the art work by directly confronting them or making the work on the street or in other non-traditional artistic venues. This work poses more of a threat to social norms than art that provides more of a distance between art and real life or art and audience because it refuses audiences role as passive observer (see Wheeler 1997 for a discussion of aesthetic distance and contemporary art). Thus, the use of formal techniques, perhaps those that assert the opposite of traditional aesthetics, works also to subvert art world hierarchies. Avant garde performance art rejects of the separation of art from society and challenges the institution of art that promotes this division between the aesthetic and social realms (Benjamin 1968; Ridless 1984). Nehring (Nehring 1993) suggests that avant garde art include such cultural production as punk rock music and attitudes because they bring art into the everyday, making it relevant to social discourse. This definition of avant garde art differs from a more conventional one focused primarily on avant garde art as primarily an art world innovator located in museums and for the purposes of maintaining art world distinctions of high and low culture. But crossing boundaries, even between generalized concepts like art and life, is not always easy and is often taken as rule-breaking. Performance artists in the late 1980s pushed limits of acceptable representation in their attempts to create social change and awareness. In doing so, definitions of deviance and the moral order of society were called into question.

Theories of Deviance

Sociological theories of deviance rest on a common assumption that definitions of what is known as deviant change over time and place. Deviance is contingent on processes of symbolic and actual labelling, prevailing definitions of the normative moral order and the power to deny legitimacy to those labelled deviant (Goode and Ben-Yehuda 1994; Pfohl 1994; Sumner 1994) Therefore, labelling is concurrent with social norms, but these norms change over time and place.

Definitions of deviance are constructed through conflicted social processes and organized efforts to change collective meanings of social behaviour. Sellin (Sellin 1938; Kelly 1993) marked the way that conflicts between divergent cultures arise when norms and symbols conflict in the borders between them. This occurs "when the law of one cultural group is extended to cover the territory of another" or when members of migrate across groups (Sellin 1938: 74). These boundary crossings produce tensions and struggles and often result in members of one group taking action to define the situation according to their own goals. They promote causes in order to shape social norms to coincide with their vision of the issues at hand. These "moral entrepreneurs" (Becker 1963: 128) use organized means to gain publicity for personal interests and make or enforce social rules through individual promotion and campaigns for their causes.

Performance artists are moral entrepreneurs in that they promote social change in their art work. Their goals are loosely constructed around an artistic practice of identity politics interested in gaining a public voice and to increase visibility for individuals and groups with traditionally marginal, silent and invisible identities (Hirsch 1972; Marsh and Kent 1984; Phelan 1993). Artists do this by talking openly and assertively about race, sex and gender. When performance artists cross boundaries of standard social decorum, they meet resistance from others offended by their openness and disregard for normative social rules. Thus a conflict occurs over definitions, representations and modes of representation. A "moral panic" arises when such contestations become collective disputes and "a condition, an episode, person or group of persons emerges to become defined as a threat to societal values and interests ... " (Cohen 1972: 9). In the controversy over US arts funding in the late 1980s and 1990s, competing groups of moral entrepreneurs—artists on one hand, conservative congressmen, on the other—attempted to define art and the social good in different ways to gain support for their respective reform strategies. Thus a cultural clash ensued over the definition of art, publicly acceptable modes of expression, the government funding of art and the use of symbols as markers of social norms in each of these.

Turner's theory (Turner 1969) of "social dramas," similar to the idea of moral panics,[2] frames such collective crises as moments of possibility that show social processes as a set of events, like a narrative, occuring in sequence and leading to a range of possible social functions and outcomes. Social dramas can reveal ongoing reproduction of social relations that are otherwise obscured by routine daily practices. A social drama can become the focal point and functional remedy for a society in crisis and artists who intended their work to promote such a moment of possibility. Crisis moments reflected in a social drama may allow for an increased level of reflection to occur and may provide potentially "liminal" moments (i.e., a moment of activity that is difficult to define; one that causes uncertainty), which allow for social transformation (Turner 1969; Wagner-Pacifici 1986). Artists attempted to create social drama through their individual performative practices in order to call attention to their concerns on a larger stage.

A social drama allows change because public themes are called into question as a result of the conflict being played out in the social drama. Subsequently a re-evaluation of the conflicting themes takes place, creating some form of social change or renewal of social values. Performance art strategies that conflate life with art allow liminality to happen because taken-for-granted boundaries are crossed, thus highlighting a boundary that was previously invisible. In the words of performance artist, Ray Langenbach

> [in a performance that crosses boundaries] people are able to become more aware of that which already is. [This social behaviour] becomes a dynamic thing: the figure to look at rather than just the ground. The perceptual field around it changes. It is not always clear if things get better or if things get worse, it becomes a moment of crisis. Then hopefully some resolution of that crisis, you know, comes out of it, but that is something that generally either in politics, religion, or in performance art, the performer, in the larger sense of that word, has very little control over. It becomes a social dynamic, and the performer is basically just scratching the edge and then the thing happens out of that.... It is very problematic in some ways, but there is that element in social life and a group will deal with it when they have to. When something appears in a different frame than usual, then suddenly it has to be dealt with. It is usually just buried and people go on with their lives, but I guess that there is hope that there is some resonance that keeps on going with people and then forever that thing is no longer just the cliché that it was before. (Personal telephone interview, 1998)

Artists "create a crisis" in order to instigate liminality in the hope of creating new awareness and social change. Performance artists assert their marginal identity statuses to create crises as points of empowerment[3] and, during the late 1980s and throughout the 1990s, artists gained the most attention when confronted those identities most directly embedded in the conflicts over sex, sexual identity, sexual politics and AIDS. As a response to the AIDS crisis, the ongoing degradation of women, and the denial and repression of alternative sexual identities, artists openly discussed and displayed sexual acts in the public realm in order to increase objective understanding of sexual experience. Performance artists David Wojnarowitz, Holly Hughes, Tim Miller and John Fleck vocalized the experience of being gay and refused the negative social stigma attributed to it by enacting the ACT-UP[4] tenet that "silence = death." They addressed the public denial and the unequal positions of being gay in society by using their art speak directly to powerful public figures and to redefine normativity based on their experiences.

David Wojnarowicz wrote an essay for an exhibition catalogue in which he attacked public figures who stood against funding AIDS research and publicly opposed homosexuality. Wojnarowicz described Cardinal John O'Connor as a "fat cannibal from that house of walking swastikas up on Fifth Avenue" and with increased outrage in his angry tirade, he imagined how he could "douse [Jesse] Helms with a bucket of gasoline and set his putrid ass on fire" and "throw Rep. William Dannemeyer off the Empire State Building" (Wojnarowicz 1989). He also made complexly layered collages that combined political imagery with homoerotic subject matter and performed his angry monologues as critiques of "cultural excesses and politics of exclusion".

Holly Hughes created unequivocally lesbian plays that refused any adherence to white male heteronormativity by simply ignoring it. (Heteronormativity is a term that suggests the social construction of social sexual relationships that are taken for granted in most contemporary cultures. In other words, this term refers to the notion that heterosexual unions and the societal institutions that support these are not necessarily natural, but require an ongoing enforcement in order to maintain them.) "There is no subterranean appeal to dominant culture for understanding" (Davy 1993: 55). Taking the standpoint of a lesbian subjectivity subverted traditional normative rules about being silent and submissive as a person with an outsider status.

Tim Miller's work took place in performance spaces and with ACT-UP/LA. Integrating his staged work with other life works, Miller's performance art took the form of organizing the gay community, asserting the social and political needs there and making the connections between the gay community and other socially marginal groups (Harper 1998: 31-40).

Other performance artists, like Annie Sprinkle and Karen Finley,[5] took representations of women into their own hands by distorting and remaking stereotypical images. Annie Sprinkle started doing performance art after a career as a porn star in order to call attention to double messages about female sexuality. Sprinkle "demystified" the female body by showing her cervix to audience members and demonstrating orgasm on stage (Schneider 1997).

Karen Finley raged about the way women were patronized and ridiculed. She smeared chocolate on her body in order to represent how women were treated like dirt. This performance was said to defy any notion of the female body as sexual and therefore Finley "renders pornography impotent" (Carr 1993). The general tenor of her work takes the form of an angry tirade against the abuse of power in both political and personal realms. Finley responded in a letter to the editor of the *Washington Post* (May 19,1990). "Actually, my work speaks out against sexual violence, degradation of women, incest and homophobia. When I smear chocolate on my body, it is a symbol of women being treated like dirt," Finley stated (1990).

Appropriation of the Social Drama

The frank nature of the material and the combination of public and private realms provoked rapid moral outrage from right-wing members of the US Congress who used the excuse of government funding to create a national panic over government funds for "pornography." These artists hit the core social issues of representation, meaning and the authority to define, and through their work called direct attention to the social, political and representational injustices against marginalized groups occuring at that time. The social drama crisis created by artists was quickly appropriated by more institutionalized and powerful members of society.[6]

Social dramas unfold as a series of four steps: naming the threat, building a consensus for this definition, continued labelling and implementing institutional power (Alexander 1988). Individuals and groups with institutional power come to take control of a social drama by defining another group as deviant and enlisting others in a consensus to label this deviant behaviour as a concerted threat to the core values of society.[7] For resolution of the threat to occur, institutional and legitimate means of social control must be drawn upon to stop these potentially "polluting forces" in order to resolve the conflict posed by them. Counter-centres emerge when these social control efforts rely on multiple contingencies to enforce centralized norms as the generally agreed upon outcome of the conflict. And lastly, in this process of crisis and renewal, symbolic processes derived from an alliance of those interested in containing social transgression continue to label and differentiate normative social values from those that pose a significant threat to these values. The social drama as a struggle over values and these attempts to define the sacred centre of society against transgressive actions reveals the broader mechanisms of the social construction of deviance in effect in this crisis.

Artists attempted to label oppressive social systems deviant by calling them out, enacting them, refusing and ignoring them. However, artists' power lies in shock and confrontation and in redefining the social landscape through artistic action. The moment at which artists cease to perform for audiences already committed to their causes is the simultaneous moment of most and least power. It is these moments of provocation and their accomplishments that show the relative power of the marginal and the institutional.

Right-wing congressmen and the family values coalition redefined this crisis as one about good and evil and used this religious platform to attack funding of the arts. The NEA-funded (i.e., the National Endowment for the Arts) exhibitions by photographers Robert Mapplethorpe and Andres Serrano led to this controversy over artistic representation of social values because of their use of directly sexual and religious imagery. Mapplethorpe and Serrano used similar techniques as those of performance artists to cross over the distinctions between what is real and what is staged. Therefore, as photographs, even staged works take on the tone of reality.

An initial letter from April 5, 1989, written by the executive director of the American Family Association, called attention to Serrano's photograph "Piss Christ." The primary focus of this initial letter was the "bias and bigotry" against Christians by both popular cultural productions as well as ones supported by government funds. It was Jesse Helms's May 18, 1989 letter to the NEA chairman, Hugh Southern, protesting the use of government funds for the art of Andres Serrano that brought attention to "government supported infractions against Christians."

Mr. President, several weeks ago, I began to receive a number of letters, phone calls, and postcards from constituents throughout the State concerning art work by Andres Serrano. They express a feeling of shock, of outrage, and anger.

They said, "How dare you spend our taxpayers' money on this trash." They all objected to taxpayers' money being used for a piece of so-called art work which, to be quite candid, I am somewhat reluctant to utter its title. This so-called piece of art is a deplorable, despicable display of vulgarity. The art work in question is a photograph of the crucifix submerged in the artist's urine.

This artist received $15,000 for his work from the National Endowment for the Arts, through the Southeastern Center for Contemporary Art.

Well if this is what contemporary art has sunk to, this level, this outrage, this indignity—some may want to sanction that, and that is fine. But not with the use of taxpayers' money. This is not a question of free speech. This is a question of abuse of taxpayers' money. If we allow this group of so-called art experts to get away with this, to defame us and to use our money, well then we do not deserve to be in office.

That is why, Mr. President, I am proud of the Members, who in literally a matter of minutes—over 20, about 25—joined me in signing a strong letter of protest to the Endowment. Here is a picture, and the title is "Piss Christ." Incredible.

... The purpose for which the Endowment was established, and I quote, "to support the survival of the best of all forms that reflect the American heritage in its full range of cultural and ethnic diversity and to provide national leadership on behalf of the arts."

Mr. President, I submit this is a distortion of those purposes. It does not reflect on the full range of cultural and ethnic diversity; rather, it is a perversion of those principles. If people want to be perverse, in terms of what they recognize as art or culture, so be it, but not with my money, not with the taxpayers' dollars, and certainly not under the mantle of this great Nation. This is a disgrace. (Bolton 1992: 28-9)

Helms uses the authority of traditional religious morality to assert his definition of deviance and to implicate the government use of arts funds in this matter as an assault against the normal moral good. His statement makes blanket assumptions about the unification of religious communities and the values of the American people, and simultaneously creates Serrano as the criminal against these general moral concerns. It is also interesting to note how Helms distances himself from the "government" while aligning with the concerns of "vast majority of the American people."

Building Consensus

Along with the religious organizations and individuals who found art that dealt with sexual and religious identity offensive, the old guard art world became confused and concerned about the recent turn towards broad inclusion of a range of aesthetic principles and multicultural themes imbued with political messages. Consensus, then, was built over loosely structured generational alliances rather than traditional political or religious affiliations. Painter Helen Frankenthaler provides an example of how this occurred as she expressed her concerns in the *New York Times* in July of 1989.

> When I was appointed to the advisory council of the National Endowment for the Arts, I understood that the council received its charter from the Federal government. It functions as an autonomous body devoted to the pursuit and support of quality in the art and culture of America—past, present, and future.
>
> ... I, for one, would not want to support the two artists mentioned, but once supported, we must allow them to be shown. With all the fuss, I think a number of crucial points have to be made.
>
> Granted, we are "fed" by Government permit and budgets, but censorship and Government interference in the directions and standards of art are dangerous and not part of the democratic process.... If that healthy atmosphere is censored or dictated, the life of every citizen is at stake....
>
> But there are other issues in these particular cases. It is heartbreaking both as an artist *and* as a taxpayer(!), for me to make these remarks, and as a painter on the council I find myself in a bind: Congress in a censoring uproar on

one hand and, alas, a mediocre art enterprise on the other! Sad, indeed.

By "mediocre art enterprise" I mean: Has the council run its course in terms of doing a necessary quality job? Should it change its course from within? Is it possible? I myself find the council—the recommendations of the panels and the grants given—of dubious quality. Is the council, once a helping hand, now beginning to spawn an art monster? Do we lose art along the way, in the guise of endorsing experimentation? ...

Despite the deserved grants, I see more and more non-deserving recipients. I feel there was a time when I experienced loftier minds, relatively unloaded with politics, fashion and chic. They encouraged the endurance of a great tradition and protected important development in the arts. I recall spirited, productive discussions and arguments.

Naturally, it is assumed that many of us often feel aghast at some of the awards, but I feel that way more and more, and I am not alone. Have we "had it"—like many, now defunct, once productive, agencies? (Frankenthaler 1989)

The elite consensus was built not along the lines of those for or against arts funding but from the viewpoint that American art and culture had become one of increasingly questionable quality. One can only assume this disintegration of culture is a result of the increasingly blurred distinctions between popular culture and high art and the continued inclusion of multicultural content, which often deals specifically with identity issues and challenges the viewer to look at culturally constructed assumptions about these.

Consensus around the misuse of government funds occured through a general misunderstanding of contemporary art. The complexities of artistic specializations and the paradigms they express cannot be understood and critiqued by immediate judgments. The value is not always self-evident, though the reasons for dismissal may appear to be. Simplistic interpretations leave the viewer bereft, but the skills needed to make a more complete reading are embedded in obscure language and thought processes. Current art theory assumes, to quote an official of the Hirshhorn Museum in Washington, D.C., that art "often deals with extremities of the Human condition. It is not to be expected that ... everyone is going to be pleased or happy with it." The criterion of art thus becomes its ability to outrage, to (in the Hirshhorn official's words) "really touch raw nerves" (Lipman 1989, in Bolton 1992: 41).

Thus, social conservatives tapped into a ripe place for public outrage.[9] Significant social consensus between the elite groups privy to this argument centred on the disdain for public funding of such art and found that the funding of this art and the art itself were outright affronts on taxpayers' expectations. Artists, politicians, religious leaders, and the media were all surprised at the power of art to cause upheaval in moral and social sensibilities.

Continued Labelling

The performance artists discussed above served as targets of the Right for the continued process of labelling needed to further take control of the social drama and solidify the institutional mechanisms to contain it. After the initial attack on Mapplethorpe and Serrano, social conservatives closely scrutinized other uses of NEA funds calling attention to Karen Finley, Tim Miller, Holly Hughes and John Fleck. The NEA recalled grants given to these four performance artists and they became the object of continued controversy over free speech, the definition of obscenity and the use of government funds for art.

Institutional Implementations

Social conservatives were successful in creating a public controversy and a climate of fear for artists and arts presenters as well as imposing restrictions on the arts in the US, but they did not easily define and control what kinds of values were regarded as central and important to the majority of Americans. A poll taken in 1990 revealed that most United States citizens believed that even if they were offended by particular images, others had the right to view them, and supported the National Endowment for the Arts against funding cuts and other restrictions (Poll by Forecast, Incorporated, July 13,1990, see Bolton 1992: 249), hence revealing a disjuncture between the power and interests of the rule-makers and the overall beliefs of the population.

Despite the voice of the populous siding in favour of artists and government funding of the arts, real economic sanctions did take place. During July of 1989, a symbolic cut of $45,000 was implemented to the NEA budget as punishment for equivalent funding to Serrano and the Mapplethorpe retrospective. Individual artist grants were eliminated in 1994, and the NEA budget was cut in half between 1990 and 1998 to a level of $98 million. Each year a battle ensues in Congress when the negotiation for the NEA budget is on the floor.

The argument over arts funding and the crisis over the renewal of values was not resolved in any easy or clean way for either group. Senator Jesse Helms's 1989 obscenity clause[10] suggested restrictions against arts funding and denied support for artwork deemed objectionable. A year later an independent commission investigating the grantmaking procedures at the NEA recommended that the Helms amendment be disregarded as the "NEA is an inappropriate tribunal for the legal determination of obscenity" (Bolton 1992: 360). Further reforms for the NEA were recommended by the commission at that time to ensure more clear criteria for arts funding.

The 1998 Supreme Court decision *Finley v. NEA* finalized this social drama by determining the fate of the governmental role in funding the arts. The Supreme Court sided in favour of the NEA in withdrawing grants from four performance artists and upheld Helms's obscenity clause, leaving the definition of obscenity to be settled by the NEA at any given time.[11] But this decision did not conclude the outcome of how individuals with alternative definitions of normativity attempted to renew society in other cultural arenas. The right-wing "harbingers of morality" were successful in controlling the public controversy and creating a climate of fear for artists and arts presenters as well as imposing restrictions on the arts in the US. But, they did not easily define and control what kinds of values were regarded as central and important to the majority of Americans. Nor did they curtail the attempts made by artists to effect social change towards increased pluralism and social awareness of alternative modes of thinking and marginal social identities.

Artists Try Other Techniques

Here I discuss the performance practices of three artists who are interested in social change, but do so in a less radical way than the artists I mentioned previously.[12] These artists negotiate boundaries by using interactive pedagogical strategies—listening, then pushing, then pulling back and knowing the context in which change is possible. They understand the power of art making as a tool for both individual and social change, and they walk the line between making art consisting of more overt confrontations and using their skills to subtly disrupt social boundaries.

Ray Langenbach, an American-born artist living and teaching in Singapore, uses the moment of chaos/crisis liminality for potential change, but he does not expect to be able to speak to a broad audience with his work. "I see my performance as somehow being able to have an impact in a limited range.... We become stronger by critiquing ourselves" (personal interview). Langenbach uses the performance platform to challenge like-minded and like-educated individuals.

In a performance at the 1996 Penn State Symposium for Culture, Performance Art and Pedagogy, Langenbach challenged the mostly white, middle-class, highly educated audience by creating a situation of uncertainty among the conference presenters. Sending letters from a Singaporean artist, which contained condemnations about the hegemonic nature of the US art world and veiled threats, to each of the conference presenters, he created a stir among those in the inside circles of the conference. A buzz over these threats occured through gossip networks. Langenbach's formal presentation took place on the last evening of the conference in the manner of a highly theoretical monologue delivered in a militaristically fascist fashion. The meaning of the words was hard to comprehend because the delivery was intensely focused and engaged in a high level of theory. Many of the audience members felt alienated and angry as a result. Most did not realize the connection between the earlier letter and the staged performance.

The meaning of the entire performance became clear in an informal dialogue at the post-performance reception when Langenbach and a group of other performance artists in attendance put all their interpretations together. After much heated dialogue, Langenbach revealed his intentions to scathingly critique US cultural authority in the world and the seemingly unified assumptions of the art world. He presented his critique as someone with the same cultural skills as most of the artists in attendance but shattered these assumptions of a unified art world discourse and intention when his performance justified fascism. Thus, he called attention to the way performance artists reproduce a hegemonic discourse even when they disrupt such dominant representations. Delivering this presentation to a less sophisticated audience would have led to even further misunderstanding and outrage. To Langenbach, the art becomes ineffective when it is presented to inappropriate audiences and taken out of a certain range. He speaks to the audiences with whom he is most connected in order to effect change there; when there is less of a social distance between artist and audience, there is less resistance to the message being given. By working within one identity location—here that of the art world—rather than speaking to audiences across different perspectival locations, Langenbach finds the technique of boundary crossing most effective when there is a limited range of differences between artist and audience. This performance had a limited influence on a like-minded audience, but it was eye-opening to the artists in attendance because it took them off guard, provided a new perspective from which to view the relationship between the artist and the world of cultural production and allowed artists to critique their own relationship to global production of art. Langenbach limits boundary crossing to settings where individuals will be more receptive to engaging in the themes of the performance and be enlightened by it through the labour of understanding it.

Wendy Morris, a Minneapolis performance artist/choreographer, teaches art and consults in various organizations. She uses her skills as an artist to help corporations with various issues at hand.

> W.M.: I tend to find roles within institutions where I get to have my own creative influence.
> B.W: Isn't that threatening to them, sometimes?
> W.M.: That has not been my experience .... [I have learned a [great deal] from the work of] Liz Lehrman [from Washington, D.C.] ... She's got one company called 'Dancers of the Third Age' which is made of all seniors. Liz does a lot of teaching and I remember her saying once that if she goes in and she's working with a group of people and she's coming up with resistance, it's because she missed a step somewhere along the line. She skipped something. She didn't break things down. I think that if I come up with resistance it's

because I missed something. It's like I've gone too—
farther than they were ready to go.

Morris uses her knowledge derived from different groups of
people.

So part of it is working with organizations depending on
where the organization is at .... I did a session with these—
I mean these are insurance brokers who are owning the
country.... One time during a break, I noticed they started
to get tight in their abdomens.... We were just gossiping
about office stuff, and I noticed a man's foot tapping. And
while we were talking, carrying on this conversation ...
without anyone noticing it, I just had a little ball in my
pocket and I slid it on the floor to him. I dropped it on the
floor and I kicked it to him. Meanwhile they're carrying on
this conversation and he kicked it back to me. I kicked it to
him again. He kicked it to somebody else. And then another
one. Five minutes later, without anyone knowing how it
happened, there's fifteen people in the room running
everywhere, twenty balls on the floor, kicking them back
and forth and somebody said, "how did this happen?" This
is, you know, this was their bathroom break ... and so it's all
about looking for where the point of opening is. You know,
that's all the skills of improvisation. The body gestures are
clues.

Morris uses her skills as a dancer to pay attention to elements
outside the normal range of vision. She is able to negotiate between
knowing how much to push and in what direction and stepping back.

Taking a more distanced, relaxed approach, like Morris does,
may not get things done with as much drama or vigour, or create a
national crisis, but this approach starts from the place where the
participants and audiences are able to begin the process of building
new awareness and understanding. These openings differ from place
to place in a multicultural society. Working in corporations may only
allow individuals to simply feel more creative and may enable them
to continue to work from the same basic assumptions about entitlement
and individualism that the more radical and deviantized artists
condemn. But, this technique of using the context of the situation at

hand to determine the amount of distance an artist can go in pushing an agenda is useful in understanding the relationship between boundaries and resistance. It may help those interested in moving towards greater social change to undermine resistances and stalemates.

To other performance artists, the teaching process is integral to what making art is all about. Charles Garoian, a professor at Penn State, thinks of his site of art production as the classroom. Performance to him is

> done within the context of academia [rather than the art world or alone in one's studio] in order to basically question and critique the structures of learning that tend to inscribe themselves on the bodies of the students. [When I first started teaching] the only thing that came out of my mouth was, "Look, you guys. I know a little bit about art and that's what I've been studying for several years now. You guys know a lot about your lives and your cultures, and so what we're going to do is learn from each other." And, therein lies the basis for my teaching, in that I began to realize that the best way to get my kids to get creative was to make room for their own cultural identities, their own memories and histories and other things that they were studying, their experiences as a whole. That was going to be the only way to get them to think critically and creatively, to create works of art that were meaningful.

Garoian uses performance art as a way to get students to understand their own stories and to show them what it means to be collaborative. In a society so fully invested in competitive strategies, collaboration can be a stepping stone for social and political cognizance. Garoian developed his performance pedagogy while teaching high school art:

> Performance became a way of contesting the assumptions of history. [One example of doing this was] the ice piece .... There were five tons of ice delivered to the school on the particular morning. The administration called me on the carpet ... because I was disrupting classes, and I said, "Well, the sculpture students and I .. have been working in plaster,

we've been working in wood and metal and now we're beginning to talk about the ephemeral conditions of art.... You knew questioning whether or not objects ought to be made to last for centuries or whether something that was ephemeral could function as an art work. Okay?" So I always presented my administrators the rationale as it was an opportunity to educate them. In much the same way that Suzanne Lacy has worked with the public policy-makers.... Here is an opportunity for me not only to educate students and myself but also to educate the administrators to think about larger ramifications of art within the culture at large, but more importantly, within the context of the curriculum of the school.

And, they got it. And you know, five tons of ice showed up that morning and the students had to decide, based on the way ... because we asked for the water to be frozen in any shape or form, and people put it in plastic bags, they put it in milk cartons, they put it in plastic buckets, so we had all these different shapes and the students had to come up with some sort of an architectonic form in order to assemble all these parts. Well, at first it was one big pile, then they realized that they weren't really taking advantage of the shapes, so they in a sense created a wall, a wall that was transparent and a wall that was melting away.

Rather than looking at art as merely this kind of discipline-based enterprise within the school, one that was most often marginalized within the context of the curriculum, that it had to go underground and work in ways that one would not expect. You know, no one would have guessed that we were doing anything but monkey business or playing around like a bunch of kids until finally the rationale of ephemerality was presented. That rationale was too strong. But that became an underground means in order to question the very stability of what curriculum is all about. In other words, just as a bronze sculpture will last thirty thousand years, so does a curriculum last for; you know, it comes across in a very structured manner to the point where it's not even permeated by any kind of human life.

Using the art making process to create metaphors for social life allows students to start to question basic assumptions about what is given to them, as well as to question the role of authority in providing the normative definitions of reality. Garoian's art making and teaching strategies bring new understanding to the students, the school administration, and the community who brought the ice. By giving the rationale of the project and framing it pedagogically, the school administration did not find it threatening, but found their own opening into it.

Performance art methods shape the dynamics of power in society by pulling the raw materials into areas not usually touched by art. Artists use performance art methods differently across the various contexts in which they exist. Performance art as a technique to implement social change is manifested both within normal boundaries, paying careful attention to the context and the moment where appropriate action can take place, and refusing the very notion of normality. When art is taken out of its immediate context and the audience for which it was created, the stakes for its reception and understanding increase. Using performance art/life techniques redefines what is known as sacred by opening up the taboos surrounding it. Work in this realm can be relatively smooth, with the use of appropriate boundaries and expectations about relative influence, understanding the context and the limits embedded there, and the use of a clear rationale. Or, it can be confrontational and jarring, with the intentions of using shock value to provoke changes in social groups who resist these changes. Changing society depends on working at different paces in many different arenas.

Conclusion

Through these examples we see the way artists use boundary crossing techniques to both create crises and invoke more subtle changes in personal and community belief systems. Several kinds of questions occur as a result of this discussion. Does art cause social change? Does social change depend on deviance? Is boundary crossing an integral part of the way artists attempt social change?

The more radical artists discussed here did cause social change in the form of provoking a social drama, calling attention to themselves and the meaning and definition of art. But the changes that occurred were not necessarily the ones they had intended. Arts funding was the target. However, artists were successful in pushing their agenda and pushing the acceptable limits of public discussion of sexuality and representations of alternative sexualities in the mass media and the wider culture generally. For instance, gay and lesbian lifestyles were depicted on prime-time television when women were shown kissing.

In terms of arts funding, the historical avant garde held a goal of bringing art back into life and ending its separate status as a patronized part of an elite art world institution. In terms of this goal, artists were successful at making new links between popular culture and the art world and at attacking the institution and elite definition of art. The result of this is mixed. On one hand, funding of art is now held to a stricter standard, there is less money available, and the status of art has diminished. On the other hand, more diversity is acceptable in popular representations. When postmodern identity-based individuals, socialized in a mediatized, fluid and momentary culture, come into contact with modernist hierarchies, a conflict over central social values occurs. Radical artists accomplished a goal of killing the institution of art by getting defunded, bringing the work into the realm of the social, political and the personal. What was once defined as deviant across society is now only defined as such by a small group who happen to inhabit powerful social positions. Because of this, definitions of democracy should also come under scrutiny.

When artists continue to create works that challenge taken-for-granted assumptions about the wider social life or in smaller occupational settings, the work of social change continues. Even the most minute increase in awareness may be part of a larger effort to gain further equality, if all awareness leads to increased social justice. But this remains a question for discussion and future research.

Endnotes

[1] Though the field of performance art is very diverse and has become more so since the 1989-90 debates over arts funding, my definition of performance art here rests on the particular form of performance art that became most visible at that time. Since that time performance an has burgeoned and has, as is the case when any avant garde art becomes widely accepted and practised, become less radical and shocking. I will discuss some of these adaptations at the end of this paper. Firstly, however, I focus on the definition of performance art during the late 1980s and

early 1990s, which denoted intentional norm reversal practices. Performance art has become a term which denotes a broad range of art, theatre, dance activities, most of that are not interested in shocking and reviling audiences.

[2] Moral panics, like social dramas, "serve as a mechanism for simultaneously strengthening and redrawing society's moral boundaries—that line between morality and immorality, just where one leaves the territory of good and enters that of evil" (Goode 1994: 52). The difference between the two concepts lies primarily in the use of deviance. For Goode and Ben-Yehuda, moral panics are negotiations of deviance. Turner, on the other hand, sees the crises in social dramas as mechanisms for defining normativity. I use them as two sides of the same coin.

[3] The actions of performance artists are similar to subcultural resistance to domination as described by Hall and his colleagues in their work on British youth culture. Hall et al. discuss subcultures and resistance to hegemonic social controls as a result of class locations, but artists hold a very paradoxical class location in contemporary society which cannot be solely described as working class. Bourdieu (1993) best explains the particular class location of artists as being the "dominated among the dominant," caught in the double bind of an "economic system reversed." Traditionally, when an avant garde artist makes a large sum of money, the artistic value of her work diminishes as she "sells out" to the "profane" values of the mundane economic world. Though artists in contemporary US society have mostly overturned this notion, the role of artists, especially performance artists, is still caught between class locations, and either held up as genius or dismissed as madness. This dichotomous position of artists in society is still a tension despite recent changes in both economic conditions and technological advances. Performance artists are often opposed to the commodification of art, which in turn places them in this elitist notion that art is beyond or above utility and practicality. Performance artists generally create their work without much pay and are rarely able to make a living from it. In fact, performance artists often advocate a regular day job as central to their commitment of keeping art outside of the commodity culture. The actions of radical artists rely on a resistance to the dominant culture. Thus the class location of performance artists, though different in some crucial ways from working class youth culture, still can be understood in Hall's terms.

[4] The AIDS Coalition to Unleash Power is a gay activist group that uses public performances as part of its strategy for subverting AIDS discrimination (see Kistenberg 1995)

[5] Some, but not all, of this work received monetary support from the National Endowment for the Arts. Karen Finley, Holly Hughes, Tim Miller and

John Fleck had their NEA grants rescinded because of their use of explicit sexual materials. They became known as the "NEA Four" because of their suit against the NEA and their challenge to Jesse Helms's 1989 amendment to the NEA guidelines which included an "obscenity clause" which prohibits the funding of "obscenities" as art.

6   The relative power between various social groups is important to highlight here. Though some say marginal groups hold a powerful social position in this case, it lies primarily in the power of threat through words and symbols and is not backed up by institutional power.

7   From a functionalist perspective a normative order of society exists around a set of core values. I argue along with Foucault (Foucault 1979) that these normative values are continually being contested, revised, asserted and appropriated. And, while it may appear that dominant values remain pervasive, they are not static and unified nor are they resistant to subversion.

8   The 1990s conflicts about art and government support of the arts are not new. The National Endowment for the Arts has been controversial since its inception because the Puritan history of the United States makes support of the arts suspect. When the implementation of arts funding became manifest, it was a response to the fear of falling behind in the Cold War competition (Ayers 1992) and an attempt to use the symbolic as a force for political power. Consensus for the idea of national support for cultural production occured when conservatives could see the utilitarian value in using cultural prominence to assert authority over the Russians. The National Endowment for the Arts was established in 1965 and grew to a budget of 171.22 million in 1990 (Bolton 1992).

9   It could be argued that the photographers and performance artists in question here were also tapping into this public sentiment, trying to create spectacle to call attention to themselves and to tap into public outrage about inequality. Several crucial points show the distinction between these two arenas. 1) Art is made within an "art frame." Things that are called art are traditionally kept sacred and separate from the regular workings of rational society. 2) Art is viewed and understood from a different set of assumptions than is public policy. Contemporary art works form the notion that, even though it looks and feels to the viewer like it is "real life" it is not, even though it is playing with this distinction and prefers to remain ambiguous in its contemporary forms. More than likely it is asking the viewer to look beyond what appears to be happening in the specific art piece and to question the underlying content and assumptions involved both in the art and the reaction to it. 3) Senators are expected to be rational, thoughtful, non-erratic individuals who call upon logic of democracy to support their arguments. Religious fervour is to be kept separate from policy analysis.

10   It stated, "None of the funds authorized to be appropriated pursuant to

this Act may be used to promote, disseminate, or produce 1) obscene or indecent materials, including but not limited to depictions of sadomasochism, homoeroticism, the exploitation of children, or individuals engaged in sex acts; or 2) material which denigrates the objects or beliefs of the adherents of a particular religion or non-religion; or 3) material which denigrates, debases, or reviles a person, group, or class of citizens on the basis of race, creed, sex, handicap, age, or national origin" (Bolton 1992: 347).

[11] According to Nina Totenberg on National Public Radio (March 31,1998) this was a "lose-lose situation" for the NEA because even if the Supreme Court sided in favour of the continued role of government in funding free speech, inevitably Congress and its right-wing pundits would continue to hack away at the NEA. Even though the NEA had the right to decide its own definition of obscenity, as a government agency it would be subject to continued public disputes shaped by a conservative common denominator.

[12] The data are taken from a snowball sample of thirty artists interviewed between 1994 and 1997 and ethnographic observations conducted during that same time in a variety of locations where performance art was being presented and discussed. All the artists gave permission to be known by name.

Bibliography

Alexander, J. 1988. "Culture and Political Crisis: 'Watergate' and Durkheimian Sociology." *Durkheimian Sociology: Cultural Studies*, J. Alexander (ed.). Cambridge: Cambridge University Press: 187-224.

Ayers, S. M. 1992. *The Selection Process of the National Endowment for the Arts Theater Program: An Historical/Critical Study*. New York: Peter Lang.

Becker, H. 1963. *Outsiders: Studies in the Sociology of Deviance*. New York: The Free Press.

Benjamin, W. 1968. *Illuminations*. New York: Schocken.

Blinderman, B. (Ed.). 1990. *David Wojnarowicz: Tongues of Flame*. Normal, Illinois: University Galleries Illinois State University.

Bolton, R. (Ed.) 1992. *Culture Wars: Documents from the Recent Controversies in the Arts*. New York: New Press.

Bourdieu, P. 1993. *The Field of Cultural Production: Essays on Art and Literature*. New York: Columbia University Press.

Carr, C. 1993. "Unspeakable Practices, Unnatural Acts: The Taboo Art of Karen Finley." *Acting Out: Feminist Performances*. L. Hart and P. Phelan. Ann Arbor: University of Michigan Press: 141-152.

Cohen, S. 1972. *Folk Devils and Moral Panics: The Creation of Mods and Rockers*. London: MacGibbon and Kee.

Davy, K. 1993. "From Lady Dick to Ladylike: The Work of Holly Hughes." *Acting Out: Feminist Performances*. P. P. Lynda Hart. Ann Arbor: University of Michigan Press: 55-84.

Erikson, K. 1966. *Wayward Puritans: A Study in the Sociology of Deviance*. New York: John Wiley and Sons.

Finley, K. 1990. Letter to the Editor. *Washington Post*. Washington, D.C. May 19, 1990.

Foucault, M. 1979. *Discipline and Punish: The Birth of the Prison*. New York: Vintage Books.

Frankenthaler, H. 1989. "Did We Spawn an Arts Monster?" *New York Times*. New York. July 17, 1989.

Goode, E. and N. Ben-Yehuda. 1994. *Moral Panics: The Social Construction of Deviance*. Cambridge, Mass: Blackwell Press.

Hall, S. and T. Jefferson, (Eds.) (1976). *Resistance through Ritual: Youth Subcultures in Post-war Britain*. London: Harper Collins.

Harper, G. (Ed.) 1998. *Interventions and Provocations: Conversations on Art Culture and Resistance*. Albany, NY: State University of New York Press.

Hirsch, P. 1972. "Processing Fads and Fashions: An Organization-set Analysis of Cultural Industry Systems." *American Journal of Sociology* 77: 639-659.

Kelly, D. H. (Ed.) 1993. *Deviant Behavior: A Text-Reader in the Sociology of Deviance*. New York: St. Martin's Press.

Kistenberg, C. 1995. *AIDS, Social Change and Theater*. New York: Garland Publishing Inc.

Lipman, S. 1989. Say No to Trash. *New York Times*. New York. June 23, 1989.

Marsh, A. and J. Kent, (Eds.) 1984. *Live Art: Australia and America*. Adelaide: Anne Marsh and Jane Kent.

Nehring, N. 1993. *Flowers in the Dustbin: Culture, Anarchy, and Postwar England*. Ann Arbor: University of Michigan Press.

Pfohl, S. 1994. *Images of Deviance and Social Control: A Sociological History*. New York: McGraw-Hill.

Phelan, P. 1993. *Unmarked: The Politics of Performance*. London: Routledge.

Ridless, R. 1984. *Ideology and Art: Theories of Mass Culture from Walter Benjamin to Umberto Eco*. New York: Peter Lang.

Schneider, R. 1997. *The Explicit Body in Performance*. London: Routledge.

Sellin, T. 1938. *The Conflict of Conduct Norms. A Report of the Subcommittee on Delinquency of the Committee on Personality and Culture*. New York: Social Science Research Council Bulletin.

Sumner, C. 1994. *The Sociology of Deviance: An Obituary.* New York: Continuum.

Turner, V. 1969. *The Ritual Process: Structure and Anti-Structure.* Chicago: Aldine.

Wagner-Pacifici. 1986. *The Moro Morality Play: Terrorism and Social Drama.* Chicago: University of Chicago Press.

Wheeler, B. B. 1997. "The Performance of Distance and the Art of Catharsis: Performance Art, Artists and Audience Response." *The Journal of Arts Management, Law, and Society* Vol. 27 (No. 1): 37-49.

Wojnarowicz, D. 1989. "Postcards from America: X-rays from Hell." *Witnesses Exhibition Catalogue.* New York: Artists' Space.

Sickdopers: A Reconceptualization of Becker's Marijuana Theory as Applied to Chemotherapy Patients

Timothy P. Rouse
Middle Tennessee State University

You're Sick and You're Beautiful
Artificial Joy Club

This work explores Howard Becker's classic 1953 article "Becoming a Marijuana User" and applies the theoretical propositions to a phenomenon I term *sickdopers*. Becker's (1953; 1967) research rendered the importance of social dynamics in understanding how marijuana was smoked. Essentially, Becker (1953: 236-239) posited that marijuana use involved, foremost, actors learning the proper ingestion technique, next, learning to become conscious of what it means to be "high as a result of the drug," and finally, to view the efficacy of ingestion as pleasurable. Adler and Adler (1978) extended Becker's thesis by noting there are key developmental issues for very young children (i.e., *tinydopers*, eight years and younger) that precludes Becker's notions of how perceptual efficacy is conceptualized.

Adler and Adler (1978) delineate a sequential model of social change that addresses the diffusion and legitimation of marijuana (Adler and Adler cited in Kelly 1996:238). This model begins with stigmatized outgroups, followed by two subterranean groups, then a middle-class acceptance of marijuana and its use, and finally what they refer to aptly as sacred groups (i.e., children). I would add to that model the category of *sickdopers*, which refers to "sick groups" circa 1984, near the time of Nancy Reagan's war on drugs and increasing media attention to AIDS. About this time there were increased media reports on sick populations and the efficacious effects of cannabis used by AIDS, cancer, MS and glaucoma patients.

In 1992, the Bush administration, following DEA advice, axed federal support of marijuana as a therapeutic substance. Drug Czar William Bennett tried to revive the "reefer madness" moral panic of pot as a gateway drug and was appearing on CNN's *Larry King Live* noting that if US policy included shooting marijuana users there would be fewer problems with the substance. Currently, the Cannabis Buyer's Club in San Francisco has received much media attention because of its open defiance of marijuana laws in their efforts to sell marijuana to sickdopers. The US Comprehensive Drug Abuse Prevention and Control Act categorizes marijuana as a Schedule I substance. Moreover, marijuana's medical status has been amended in twenty-five states (i.e., has been approved for medical use). Given the federal government's refusal to reclassify marijuana as a Schedule II drug, authorities do not want to appear soft on drugs or of sending a message of drug advocacy; the twenty-five states that recognize medicinal qualities of the drug (with the exceptions of California and Arizona) have slowly caved to the pressures (Goode 1993).

Historically, drugs have been used as a scapegoat to deal with marginalized populations by political and economic elites (Musto 1987; Rumbarger 1989; Rouse 1991; Goode 1993). This paper deals with cancer patients who are chemotherapy patients and cannabis users. The configuration of these terms implies sundry groups that have been marginalized in various ways. According to Szasz, the root of the Greek term *pharmakos* had little to do with pharmacology or medicine, instead it implied "scapegoat" (Szasz 1985:19). Typically, scapegoats had the troubles of the community put on their backs to be either sacrificed or sent into the wilderness. Cancer patients to some degree suffer the apprehension of sacrifice or the experience of moving toward a wilderness. The use of marijuana by those who have chosen this route also procures the troubles of the community in legal terms.

Methods

Like Becker's (1953:235) original work, the purpose of this paper is to "describe the sequences of changes in attitude and experience which lead to" (departing from Becker's) the use of marijuana as medicine. The primary pattern of behaviour is medicinal. The phrase "use as a medicine" implies the use of marijuana in self-regulated dosages when needed to ameliorate the pernicious effects of chemotherapy.

This current piece is based on earlier research of sickdopers and the techniques of neutralization they innovated to excuse or justify their participation in illicit drug use. Elsewhere, I have detailed the sampling and data collection procedures by these sickdopers. This paper is intended to be illustrative and conceptual. My aim is not to test Becker's theory but rather to describe how it applies, with some modification, to sickdopers.

My sample involved twenty-six cancer patients who reported the use of marijuana to ameliorate the negative effects of chemotherapy (i.e., nausea, apositia, mild depression, lethargy and fatigue). Sixteen of the research subjects were women; there were more elderly women using marijuana than there were elderly men. In addition to the semi-structured, open-ended interviewing of subjects with cancer, supportive data were drawn from interviews with five physicians, eleven nurses, and three medical technicians. All interviews were conducted face-to-face except for two, one on the Internet and another by telephone. The time-frame was two years and the setting was in the mid-southern United States. All of the subjects can be described as either blue-collar (proletarians) or middle class. Two oncology clinics and cancer support groups served as sites for making contacts and using a snowball sampling technique. While observing behaviour in painful places might present difficulties in entry, my rapport (as well as interest in the subject) was spawned by my own diagnosis of cancer. The genesis of my role of participant observer can be described as follows.

> In early June of 1995 I received a phone call on a biopsy of the umbilicus performed by a surgical oncologist: "Dr. Rouse, I have the report on your biopsy and I'm sorry to tell you that my worst nightmare has come true, you have adenocarcinoma."
>
> My nightmare began since I didn't know what adenocarcinoma was! I learned all I could about it and what I learned was cold and serious. I focused on survival techniques

and one of those went back to graduate school where my mentors always reminded me that as a sociologist I was "always on duty." By the time I got through the first surgery and began my first year of chemotherapy I realized I was sitting in a research site.

Thus, I did not assume the role of an "invisible flâneur" (Wilson 1995); I have participated in many of the practices and behaviours of the research subjects. This does not preclude me from gleaning interpretive insights from the work of Becker and then applying them to the data. The data here are the narratives provided by the sickdopers.

The problem that this research addresses is theoretical. It is a problem of ontological security and extential anxiety that Giddens has described:

The notion of ontological security ties closely to the tacit character of practical consciousness—or in phenomenological terms, to the "bracketings" presumed by the "natural attitude" in everyday life. On the other side of what might appear to be quite trivial aspects of day-to-day action and discourse, chaos lurks. And this chaos is not just the disorganization, but the loss of a sense of the very reality of things and of other persons. (Giddens 1991:36)

Mostly, this research is exploratory and suggestive. Much has already been studied about the effects of marijuana, positive and negative, on varied populations. Likewise, the technical aspects of the chemical composition of the drug and its interactive effects in the human organism has been discussed (Ray and Ksir 1996). And it is not my intention here to be redundant. Further, a good deal of legal debate exists (Inciardi 1991). My intention is to apply Becker where appropriate and describe the variance as it is sociologically applied to sickdopers.

Initiation

Step One

For Becker, learning the proper technique in marijuana smoking is nascent. Becoming sick is the first step in the sequence of sickdoping. Freidson (1970) posited that illness can better be understood if grasped "as a social concept rather than a medical fact" (Brissett and Edgley 1975:314). It was Parsons (1951:428-447) who first delineated the social meaning of the sick role. Freidson developed a processural model that showed little difference in the stages of becoming ill or criminal. His comparative analysis was based on a social psychology that addressed illness as a class-based form of social deviance. Much of his analysis rested on the premise of labelling theory that posits legitimacy is confirred upon actors via audience reaction. Like serious criminals, the serious ill face sundry forms of social death and stigma (see Nessim and Ellis 1991:150-181 for discussion of stigma myths in cancer; also Goffman [1963] and Patterson [1985] regarding the death of the social). Thus, the social reality of illness is that the seriously ill will confront a myriad of actors (caregivers) who will remove some of the privileges and freedoms normatively granted the non-sick (e.g., what to eat, where to travel for help, what machines and procedures to be subjected to routinely). Consequently, like becoming criminal, becoming sick means losing some personal control while having the role of the helpless imputed to the actor.

Stigmatized populations are often controlled populations *qua* specific agencies of social control (i.e., law and medicine). Following Goffman (1963), stigma means to spoil one's identity. Goffman spoke of three types of stigma: blemishes of the body; blemishes of character; and blemishes of the tribe. Indeed, the seriously ill may encounter all three. According to one patient:

> The chemo turned the veins in my arm and I had some splotches on face and back. Nobody could see my back, but I couldn't forget about my spots.
>
> I lost all of my hair and covered it with a wig. I wasn't certain if others could tell if I was wearing a wig or not. My husband reassured me others couldn't. My shirt covered the scar where my left breast used to be. I couldn't hide that no matter how I tried.
>
> I had been tattooed. I had little blue x's on my jaw and the back of my neck from where they were aiming the radiation gun. Sometimes I'd see other people looking at me. I hated to go out anywhere.

Blemishes of character are invisible, there are no outward badges to differentiate the actor. Still subjects stated how they felt they were full of blame and doubt:

I didn't know what to do. What did I do to cause this cancer?
Did I not exercise enough, eat the right foods, pray hard
enough, drink too much? Why me? was my recital. I felt like
a bad person. A defective person with defective genes.

And, blemishes of the tribe:

I belonged to a club I didn't want to join. I can't go to the
survivor groups. I'm not the sort to talk about private matters.
I don't want people's sympathy. I don't want people seeing
me as less than a whole person.... I don't want to be seen
as weak.

To be sick then is to be tagged with a label that finds the patient
typed by the self or others. Current therapy for cancer patients relies
on what is often referred to as either "slash, burn or poison" (i.e.,
surgery, radiation or chemotherapy). Once an actor becomes
enmeshed in the medical system, the potential for a "dramatization
of evil" (Tannenbaum 1938) has been framed.

Step Two

The next step in the sequence of becoming a sickdoper is to
learn of the existence of marijuana as a therapeutic substance and to
deconstruct previous meanings of cannabis, *mutatis mutandis*. This
means that the use of cannabis as medicine is constituted first in the
language actors encounter. These are response cries for relief. The
phrase "use of cannabis as medicine" is meant to emphasize the
ameliorative effects of the drug and the state of personal control an
actor has in choosing to use cannabis. Patients hear others' accounts
and reflexively ponder the self as a potential candidate for the
treatment:

I heard a guy in my survivorship group talk about marijuana.
He didn't talk about it in the group, it was after when we
were having coffee and cookies. I had read something about
it in *Time* and I saw some stories on TV ... but this guy was
the last person in the world I thought would smoke marijuana,
I mean he seemed very conservative and we never talked
about it until about two months after I met him. He said it
helped him and I started wondering if it could help me. I
eventually talked with him about it.

Cancer patients are not looking to get "high" in the recreational frame Becker discussed (Becker 1953:235-236). Rather, if they are looking, they are seeking relief; relief from many stresses but confined here to being sick, especially nausea. Sometimes this relief is sought so that other normal functions may be maintained, such as eating:

> I've been on and off chemo for over three years. I'd usually throw up three or four times before and during dinner. Then I'd wait about twenty minutes and start eating again. That's usually what it was like at least three or four times a week. When I first started using pot, I'd wait until I started feeling queasy, like I was gonna lose it. So I'd smoke some dope and I'd be OK. Now I just smoke some weed about a half an hour before dinner, no need to cut it so close.

In spite of the fact that there are many more middle-class users of marijuana (Goode 1969, 1970, 1993; Adler and Adler 1978; Hathaway 1997), a class that is typically more politically active (Eitzen and Zinn 1997) and have organized to offer not only social support for drug users but also to eradicate draconian drug laws (Jenks 1995), there persists a view of marijuana use as deviant because it is criminal. For forty years this tautological thinking was perhaps just the reverse (i.e., it should be criminal because deviants use it). While it is true that not all deviant behaviour is criminal, and vice-versa, this thinking may persist since two major institutions of social control have created a specific image, via medicine and law. If medicine were to wholeheartedly endorse marijuana as medicine it could affect middle-class views of the drug in the polity. Albeit, marijuana arrests for small amounts carry a less serious fine than forty years ago, and there is what Stebbins (1996) refers to as criminal tolerable deviance—acts that are criminal according to the law yet tolerated and often challenged. Most of the sickdopers do indeed fear the added stress of criminal charges. Such thinking regarding the social status of marijuana was common to the majority of subjects in this research, yet the benefits of cannabis use outweighed the risk for most:

> Of course I am a law-abiding citizen. I don't like breaking any laws. But the ends here justify the means. I guess I don't like the terrible bouts with vomitting more than I fear getting popped for the weed.... I've heard the drug czar—Barry

> McCaffrey—saying that marijuana is a dangerous substance
> and doesn't have any medical benefit. All I can say is, let's
> see what kind of a he-man he'll be if he gets cancer. He isn't
> a doctor, is he?

Most of the sickdopers had concerns about the law and the social
acceptance of marijuana (i.e., especially getting busted and having
their name in the press), and while all of them felt the laws on
marijuana as medicine ought to be repealed, the overwhelming
majority of them also believed that marijuana for recreational purposes
should be legalized.[1]

This angst of living within the confines of two major institutions of
social control, law and medicine, was a common narrative especially
among those who had never used an illicit substance. In the following
narrative, the subject is aware that she is capable of being labelled a
"criminal" by a justice system that is only an abstract concept, but she
has reconstituted her status as "patient" in the form of a master
status subsequently minimizing or rendering obsolete her concerns
with criminality:

> I'm an old woman … I've been blessed with a good life.
> There is obviously some reason I have this cancer and the
> trials that I've had. Still, I don't believe the Lord intends for
> me to suffer needlessly. The marijuana for me is a medicine.
> I don't want people to know I'm using it, many of my friends
> would look at me as crazy. You know, I shouldn't care what
> they think, but I still do…. I have been used to taking lots of
> medicines that make me feel bad and sometimes "strange"….
> The marijuana was strange at first. I was told the first few
> times that it would take some getting used to. After the first
> time I was really affected by it. I though I was losing my
> mind. I didn't think I would use it, but the fact that my
> nausea left me was a blessing. I can't imagine why I am
> breaking any laws.

The need for companionship or the function of conviviality is
sometimes enhanced by the euphoria of the drug:

> I found that while I was taking the marijuana I could visit
> with others. Not only could I visit but I looked forward to
> visiting and talking with others. Otherwise, I was preoccupied

with my sickness (especially bowel movements, gas and stomach cramps) and didn't care to have company. The drug seemed to make me more sociable and less concerned about my physical problems.

However, the sociability is not one that calls forth cancer survivors to share marijuana together in a group. Once the route of administration is learned, most of the pot smoking is done alone. Occasionally, non-sickdopers join the afflicted:

My grandfather had lung cancer—he smoked cigarettes all his life. Near the end he had to quit. My brother suggested he smoke pot to counteract the effects of the chemo and radiation sickness (my brother and I smoked pot for years). Grandpa had no problem saying yes. We think he liked smoking joints because it reminded him of cigarettes. He smoked two or three joints throughout the day! After starting the pot, he was always a lot more chipper when he had guests and he was always eating. He did well right up till the day he died.... Prior to the pot smoking he was often listless and almost always grumpy.... Me and my brother smoked dope with him and he liked our company. We'd play music. He started listening to some of "our" music and he actually liked it! We listened to some old music from his day and we all had a good time. The last couple of months he was alive were the closest we ever were.

Thus, there exists a sense of comraderie that one finds in certain survivorship social worlds (e.g., Alcoholics Anonymous, POWs):[2]

I know there are quite a few of us smoking marijuana. I don't know many others personally, maybe two or three people, but I know there are many. We've paid our dues ... I don't want cops or politicians deciding what's medicine for me. I've got enough goddamned scars on my body to show I paid my dues. Are they really worried we're "hurtin' somebody" ... if you really want to know how I feel, they can go fuck themselves and quit arresting the sick because they want to feel better; assholes, I tell 'ya, assholes. I guess they need some bodies to fill up the jails.

Often, marijuana as medicine is encouraged for the elderly by the young:

> My granddaughter is the one who told me, "Granny, I want you to seriously think of smoking some marijuana so you can eat and not have to feel so bad, I can get you some."

The reconceptualization of marijuana from that of a "street drug" to one which has therapeutic benefits is objectified in the constant preoccupation with being a survivor. Lyotard (1995:144-146) has discussed a survivor in terms of that which should not exist, should be finished, dead, yet exists.[3] This survivorship state is a personal reflection of time gone by and yet to come. Sickdopers may be inclined to try out new behaviours that under normal past circumstances would not be an option. The more serious cancer stage sickdopers often feel the problematic of time as a "stay of death." Given a reprieve, one may live in a taciturn manner or one may gaze at and in turn indulge in experimenting in new and uncommon behaviours. Either way, this sense of survivorship is internalized by the path that cancer has carved for the actors involved.[4]

This phenomenon of survivability is comprised in what Bourdieu (1977) terms *Habitus*, that is, a way of life structured here by the experience of structured suffering and structured relief from suffering, to wit, the marijuana experience; or, an expression of the collective subjectivities of such a population. *Habitus* tends to describe this phenomenon better than lifestyle or subculture in that it covers a particular *Weltanschauung* of the sickdoper regardless of the actors' backgrounds.

Contact

Step Three

Having become sick and learning of cannabis as a reasonable source of relief, *mutatis mutandis*, the next step is to conceptualize the technique of cannabis use as a medical procedure. Typically, the sickdoper is one which has not used marijuana before. Only five of the subjects had previous experience with marijuana and all of them had quit using it as a recreational drug years earlier. One such respondent put it this way:

I smoked dope in the sixties and quit by the mid-seventies. I
just quit. I was tired of it. I had a family, a job and just didn't
care about it much. I was also thinking about just getting
healthier. I quit smoking cigarettes and cut down on alcohol,
too. Strange, one of the reasons I quit smoking pot is because
it used to make my heart palpatate, you know, beat faster. I
also go on these strange paranoia death trips when I was
high. That was only near the end of my "smoking pot for
fun" days—about the last year. I'd get loaded and start thinking
about everyone or everything I loved—even the dog—dying.
I couldn't stand it. That's a big reason I quit. Now, twenty
years later, I've started smoking pot again. I only smoke on
the days I get my chemo, because of the nausea and this
metallic taste I get in my mouth and maybe a couple of
times during the week to help me with my appetite. I don't
smoke a lot, maybe a total of three bowls a week. The pot
is a lot stronger now than in the sixties, and it's expensive,
I only smoke it when I need it; a bag lasts me a long time.
I'm not crazy about getting "high," since I do have a good
deal of work to do at home in my office, but I do enjoy the
high, no magnified "death trips." That's weird, since I've
been closer to death this past two years.

Consequently, while some sickdopers had previous experience with
the drug and had to reidentify with the effects, others did not and had
to learn the technique.

In Becker's second sequence, users had to learn to recognize the
effects of what it meant to be "high." Becker elaborated the
importance of the other's role in teaching the novice first how to
properly smoke marijuana, that is to hold it in the lungs longer than
tobacco, and to identify the subjective effects as normal outcomes of
the drug and not the result of psychosis. Similarly, sickdopers have to
conceptually define how cannabis precludes sickness. Becker
underscored "the important role of interaction with other users in
acquiring the concepts that make this awareness possible" (Becker
1953:238). Consequently, contact with other users was an integral
part of the process for the novice:

I was about to start a new type of chemo that had some
serious nausea associated with it. I met a man in my support
group who told me that I should try some pot to deal with

the side-effects. He said he'd show me how to smoke it, how to hold it in my lungs, and how much I'd need. I told my husband about it first and he was encouraging me to do whatever would help me. He used to smoke some pot a few years ago and quit. Well this guy came over and all three of us smoked. I was surprised my husband jumped in ... we had a good time and it has helped me with the nausea and eating, I can really eat and I enjoy it!

Often, the cancer support group serves the latent function as a place of contact:

One night I heard this guy in the group talk about smoking pot and how it helped him. A couple other members didn't think it was a good idea because it was illegal. I had some drugs the doctor prescribed for nausea, some of them gave me diarrhea. I already had enough of that from the chemo I was getting—twelve to fifteen bowel movements a day—all my nutrients went down the toilet, besides that I didn't have much desire for food. I talked to the guy and tried some pot. I went to his house and he showed me how to smoke it and what to expect. It helped. I didn't like the "woozy" feeling at first, but I got used to it and it was actually OK, my wife thought I was pretty damned silly, but I'm also hungry and don't have to throw up as much—I'll put up with the silliness. It's been better than the stuff my doc gave me.

Additionally, what both groups did have in common was the dilemma of "where" to find the drug and "how" to use it. Sickdopers learned of marijuana as a useful substance by talking with others who have had cancer. This was often accomplished by talking to relatives, neighbours or friends who knew someone with cancer that used the substance to mollify the nausea. Sometimes this awareness was gleaned by talking with people at the chemo clinic or in weekly cancer support groups. Often, nurses knew of someone using pot. In fact, in one clinic in the Rocky Mountain region, some nurses would arrange meetings between patients expressing a desire to learn more about pot and current patients who were sickdopers. Two nurses reported:

We both worked in the west and I don't want to say that the atmosphere at the clinic was more "liberal" but it was certainly more tolerant, even encouraging of marijuana as a remedy.

Working in the east and the south, I've encountered more of a conservative attitude. Here, if doctors know a patient is using pot they ignore it or don't discuss it. Back west I actually worked for one doctor that would tell patients that they could buy pot. That would never happen here.

Sickdopers subsequently learn that encouragement from cannabis as medicine will either come from other sickdopers, family members or nurses. It may not always come from the primary caregiver. One patient described his experience informing his oncologist of his marijuana use:

Patient: I'm smoking some marijuana to help with the bad effects of the chemo.
Physician: Isn't that risky?
Patient: How so?
Physician: I mean, don't you have to buy it on the street? You don't know what you're getting and you have to get it from people you don't know.
Patient: I get it from a colleague at work whose brother-in-law grows it.
Physician: Oh.

In this instance the oncologist didn't ask, "does it help?" or "how does it help?" Rather, the concern was with legality and purity of the substance. Indeed, this may reflect the physician's scepticism of marijuana as a therapeutic substance and the physician's fear of illicitly prescribing non-legal drugs. The patient's subjective or anecdotal experience is minimized or ignored.

Maintenance

Step Four

In the final phase, when an afflicted individual uses marijuana as medicine, the effects are conceptualized as integral to the well-being of the patient. Much has already been said in this present work about medicinal issues; a related topic is dosage. Learning to control dosage is also an integral part of becoming accustomed to cannabis as medicine:

> I sometimes realized I was working too much. I suppose I was smoking tiny pipeful every time I felt nausea. A friend of mine who got me the marijuana told me to slow down a little, he also instructed me that there were different strengths to marijuana. So sometimes I could get some that was quicker acting and at other times not as intense. I felt that the stronger marijuana made me more light-headed and drunk-like, but it got to the nausea faster. Anyway, about two or three weeks of use I realized how much I needed to smoke. Two or three full pipes can last me a week.

Central to this experimentation is the realization that patients can have some exercise of control in their medical treatments. This means, too, that patients will frequently discontinue cannabis use when they have finished their chemotherapy regime.

> I wanted to have total control of my mind, my work required it. When I finished chemo I also quit using grass. Yes, it was enjoyable, but I was never crazy about my mind wandering so fast or being laid back to the degree that I was. Overall, I like being straight. The grass served its function [relief from the deleterious side-effects]. Besides, when I quit smoking grass, about a month after the chemo was finished, I felt like I was truly on the road to total recovery. I didn't want to jeopardize that by putting more smoke in my lungs.

Clearly, these sickdopers are committed to using cannabis as a therapeutic substance, but they are also committed to discontinuing such use when they feel they are getting well. The terminally ill who believe they are doomed do not discontinue their cannabis use since they feel it adds to the quality of the time they have left:

> I don't like to think about how much time I have left, just what I can do in that time in the least amount of pain. The marijuana I smoke allows me to eat, not vomit as often, and the high is pleasurable. I'm not worried about lung diseases. I take a good deal of morphine, what's a little pot? The stuff's in my bones, I'd rather not think about it.

Such drug use is subsumed in existential issues of suffering and pain.

Perhaps it is the physician who manages the most salient impression on the patient. Yet, physicians may often not prescribe marijuana because it has not achieved widespread acceptance as an ethical drug. As one physician related:

> I was one of the first in this state to prescribe marijuana for my patients. Several of my patients were using it and I instructed them how to use it and what to expect. I guess I now believe we have many other drugs to counteract the nausea. Still, there is a lot of controversy surrounding the drug ... I prescribe a regiment of several different drugs.... I suppose one could make an argument that the marijuana did serve several functions.

While it is true that physicians who prescribe the drug lend credibility to it, the patients on their own efforts have negotiated a social reality that ascribes credibility to the drug.

Discussion

This research explores a unique social group that regularly participates in illicit drug use, namely, sickdopers. While there are parallels to Becker's landmark contribution, this work underscores the differences of the types of groups.

To be certain, learning the proper technique in sickdoping follows a similar pattern to what Becker outlined (1953:237). That is,

> If the person is to become a user ... he must learn to use the proper smoking technique in order that his use of the drug will produce some effects in terms of which his conception of it can change. (1953:237)

Such a change is, as might be expected, a result of the individual's participation in groups in which marijuana is used. However, the types of groups are crucial in this instance. The groups that the user attaches himself or herself to are not subterranean groups like jazz musicians, hippies or bohemians. These are sick groups. Sick groups are seeking remedies. And, certainly, there's little difference in what recreational groups are seeking for pleasure and sick groups are seeking for relief—to feel better. The differences are that recreational users enhance the moment that is free of physical pain or discomfort; the sickdopers experience a level of discomfort and are not using the substance to enhance the taste of food, but merely to keep the food down.

While learning the technique is important; for sickdopers, controlling the dosage is more important. Some sickdopers had used the prescribed synthetic cannabis drug Marinol and complained of either not getting enough or too little effect (in addition, Marinol is quite expensive compared to one-quarter of an ounce of marijuana). Smoking marijuana in a pipe or joint allows the user to anticipate what is necessary. This anticipation either comes from experimentation with the substance or listening to others claim how much they need it. Some were merely frustrated with what they had been taking:

> My doctor gave me some Zofron for nausea, it worked a little. I was also using Raglan, Levsin and Atropine. Some of these had nausea as a side-effect. Others had diarrhea. Hell, I had enough diarrhea! Smoking the pot made it simpler, I didn't have any side-effects and I felt good, I tried to tell my doctor about it, but he didn't have much to say—I told him I feel better. His only response was, "That's good."

Others resonate what the doctor who prescribed cannabis stated:

> Look, the marijuana allows me to eat and not puke, or at least not constantly feel like I'm going to puke. It also takes me out of myself so I'm not so damned blue. It settles my stomach and mellows me out for sleep. Now, I can take at least four or five different pills for what I just take a little pot for.

Sickdopers continued to use cannabis because for them it works. Working means that their subjective state is temporarily aligned with relief.

In a later work Becker argued:

> Before engaging in the activity on a more or less regular basis, the person has no notion of the pleasures to be derived from it; he learns these in the course of interaction with more experienced deviance. (1963:30)

While the intersubjective nature of this statement is true for this study, some modification is in order. First, actors may have prior notions of the medicinal qualities to be derived, they may not have the subjective experience but they have in fact garnered some form of talk—truth claims—that communicates that relief is to be found in cannabis. Next, actors do indeed learn in the course of interaction— not necessarily with social deviance but more so in the realm of how Freidson (1970) discussed the sick as deviant. To wit, actors learn with more experienced sickdopers.

As Freidson illustrated, these are actors that have either been granted conditional legitimacy due to their temporary condition that exempts them from normal obligations while granting them some extra privileges on the grounds that they seek help, or they may be ascribed unconditional legitimacy, which is to say that they are permanently exempted from normal obligations and additional privileges that they may obtain are often unquestioned (cited in Brissett and Edgley 1975:324).

Returning to Becker and the reconceptualization of sickdoper motives, Becker stated of the novice:

> He learns to be aware of new kinds of experiences and to think of them as pleasurable. What may well have been a random impulse to try something new becomes a settled taste for something already known. (1963:30)

Certainly sickdopers have to acclimate to the effects of marijuana described by Becker, but the sickdoper has justified or excused his or her behaviour by finding a medical motive. Thus, techniques of neutralization are utilized that appeal to biology. The new experiences of relief from nausea, mild depression and loss of appetite in exchange for a pleasant euphoria that instigates hunger, mental activity and no nausea are immediately welcomed. Further, this has not been a random impulse; it is a concerted desire to try something new. Seeing that the substance has brought mitigation elevates the theoretical desire to a level of praxis.

Conclusion

Like gravy and gasoline (Artificial Joy Club), two profound directions of twentieth-century thought, Marxism and existentialism, converge to cover the question of personal control. For Marxism, being human embraces the product of human labour. Capitalism separates workers from their productions. Marx termed the social phenomenon alienation. Cancer patients are often alienated from their treatment regime. They experience a social reality of being told what to do, where and when. The goal here is for some expanded role of persona and some anxiety reduction in controlling the direction of one's existence in approaching a state of anomie.

Sartre and Heidegger contravened that being in the world was lost; for Sartre, freedom was found in the individual's ability to say no; for Heidegger, freedom and authenticity were accomplished by embracing human finitude (Kurtz 1979:168-169). To be sure, humans are both in the world and of the world. To be in the world is to attempt to write one story, to be of the world means the outcome most likely will be unplanned:

> To investigate such matters on the level of abstract philosophical discussion is, of course, quite different from actually 'living' them. The chaos that threatens on the other side of ordinariness of everyday conventions can be seen psychologically as dread in Kierkegaard's sense: the prospect of being overwhelmed by anxieties that reach to the very roots of our coherent sense of 'being in the world.' (Giddens 1991:37)

The decision to use cannabis as therapy is part of an ongoing capacity of the self that maintains a particular narrative—a contiguous story of self (Giddens 1991:54); perhaps only an attempt to support "normal appearances." Normal appearances, with the routine aid of cannabis, allow the self to appear regularized and in control of one's body; an identity found "in the capacity to *keep a particular narrative going*" (original emphasis) (Giddens 1991:54).

Cancer victims (like other seriously ill populations) experience fragmented and terrorized selves. The possibility of a wretched death is compounded by the fear of a criminalizing justice system when one decides to partake in relief from cannabis. As Giddens (1991:188) asserts, modernity fragments, but it also unites. For the sickdoper, unity is manufactured in the social world of other users. Whether the social world occurs in concert with others or is constituted as a *Habitus*, it has a unifying effect.

This research was reflexively conducted in the *umwelt* (i.e., face-to-face, "we" relations) of the sickdoper's life-world. It can only be read as a text in the social world of the *mitwelt* (the larger abstract "they"). The natural attitude (i.e., the taken-for-granted everyday beliefs) for all of these sickdopers was corrupted by the discovery of their cancers. By becoming sickdopers, their natural attitude has been bracketed in a new vocabulary of motives that not only allow relief from some of the stresses associated with their illnesses but reconceptualizes their story of self. Giddens describes the *umwelt* as "a 'moving' world of normalcy which the individual takes around from situation to situation, although this feat depends also on others who confirm, or take part in, reproducing that world" (1991:128).

This research is similar to Becker's in that it focuses on social process and uses the subject's voice in telling the story. Like Becker's, it is an interpretative study of contemporary society. It attempts to sanitize the deviantized sick. It involves the micro politics of emancipation for the sick to have control of their medical treatment regimes. It is different than Becker's in that the groups are different since they are driven by different motives. Becker's research took place in modernity; this research occurred in postmodernity. Postmodernity prescribes a plethora of contradictions.

Marcus and Fischer (1986:8) have argued that postmodernism constitutes a "crisis of representation." On the one hand, illicit drugs are prescribed and acceptable since they might fight diseases. On the other hand, proscribed drugs ingested by the group's own accord that make them feel good are unacceptable because they are illicit. Thus, in one form or another, suffering continues.

Suffering is endemic to existence. Kleinman and Kleinman (1996) assert that suffering can be coterminously conceptualized in two ways:

> 1) Collective models of experience shape individual perceptions and expressions. Those modes are visible patterns of how to undergo troubles, and they are taught and learned, sometimes openly, often indirectly. 2) Social interactions enter into an illness experience ... both aspects of social experience—its collective mode and intersubjective processes—can be shown to be reshaped by the distinctive cultural meanings of time and place. (1996:2)

Substantively, Becker's early marijuana work was valuable because it revealed and meticulously described the importance of the social in learning not only what but "how" it meant to be "high." This work has attempted to describe the life-world of the sickdoper and highlight the differences in the context of time and place. My work focused primarily on proletarian and middle-class sickdopers. Further research might investigate how this works for the poor.

Endnotes

[1]   Elsewhere, Becker (1955) has described the assimilation process of becoming a marijuana user when normative societal controls are broken down. Recently, Hathaway (1997) has revised Becker's work and applied it to contemporary norms.

[2]   To some degree, all of the following have discussed this phenomenon in ideolographic terms, see Wilson 1939; Rudy 1986; Denzin 1987; and Rouse 1996.

[3]   See Lyotard (1995) for an elaboration; also see Kurtz (1979) for a detailed discussion of existentialist issues centring around alcoholics and meaning in survivorship; Denzin (1987) and Rouse (1996) discussed similar issues in phenomenonological terms.

[4]   The integrity of this survivalship in cancer and AIDS has been compared to prisoners of war and those who have suffered from Post-Traumatic Stress Disorder. Most notably, the social connection, and that which leads to increasing the social, leads to longer survivability rates. See Hirshberg and Barasch (1995:179-240), *op cit.*

References

Adler, Patricia A. and Peter Adler. 1978. "Tinydopers: A Case Study of Deviant Socialization." *Symbolic Interaction*, 1:90-105.

Becker, Howard S. 1953. "Becoming a Marihuana User." *The American Journal of Sociology*. 59:235-242.

———. 1955. "Marihuana Use and Social Control." *Social Problems* 3:35-44.

———. 1963. *Outsiders: Studies in the Sociology of Deviance*. NY: Free Press.

———. 1967. "History, Culture and Subjective Experience." *Journal of Health and Social Behavior* 8:163-176.

Bourdieu, Pierre. 1977. *Outline of a Theory of Practice*. Cambridge: Cambridge University Press.

Brissett, Dennis and Charles Edgley. 1975. *Life As Theater: A Dramaturgical Sourcebook*. Chicago: Aldine.

Denzin, Norman K. 1987. *The Alcoholic Self*. Beverley Hills: Sage.

Eitzen, D. Stanley and Maxine Baca Zinn. 1997. *Social Problems*. Boston: Allyn and Bacon.

Freidson, Elliot. 1970. *Profession of Medicine*. New York: Dodd, Mead and Co.

Giddens, Anthony. 1991. *Modernity and Self Identity: Self and Society in the Late Modern Age*. Stanford: Stanford University Press.

Goffman, Erving. 1963. *Stigma: Notes on the Management of Spoiled Identity*. Englewood Cliffs: Spectrum Books.

Goode, Erich. 1969. *Marijuana*. New York: Atherton Press.

———. 1970. *The Marijuana Smokers*. New York: Basic Books.

———. 1993. *Drugs in American Society*. New York: McGraw-Hill.

Hathaway, Andrew. 1997. "Marijuana and Tolerance: Revisiting Becker's Sources of Control," *Deviant Behavior* 18:103-124.

Hirshberg, Caryle and Marc Ian Barasch. 1995. *Remarkable Recovery: What Extraordinary Healings Tell Us About Getting Well and Staying Well*. New York: Riverhead Books.

Inciardi, James A. 1991. *The Drug Legalization Debate*. Newbury Park: Sage.

Jenks, Shepherd M., Jr. 1995. "An Analysis of Risk Reduction Among Organized Groups That Promote Marijuana and Psychedlic Drugs." *Journal of Drug Issues* 25:629-647.

Kelly, Delos. 1996. *Deviant Behavior*. New York: St. Martin's Press.

Kleinman, Arthur and Joan Kleinman. 1996. "The Appeal of Experience; The Dismay of Images: Cultural Appropriations of Suffering in Our Times." *Daedalus* (Winter): 1-23.

Kurtz, Ernest. 1979. *Not God—A History of Alcoholics Anonymous*. Center City: Hazelden.

Lyotard, Jean-Francois. 1995. *Toward the Post-Modern*. Atlantic Highlands: Humanities Press.

Marcus, George E. and Michael M.J. Fischer. 1986. *Anthropology as Cultural Critique: An Experimental Moment in the Human Sciences*. Chicago: University of Chicago Press.

Musto, David F. 1987. *The American Disease: Origins of Narcotic Control*. New Haven: Yale University Press.

Nessim, Susan and Judith Ellis. 1991. *Cancervive*. New York: Houghton Mifflin Co.

Parsons, Talcott. 1951. *The Social System*. New York: Free Press.

Patterson, Orlando. 1985. *Slavery and Social Death*. Boston: Harvard University Press.

Ray, Oakley and Charles Ksir. 1996. *Drugs, Society, and Human Behavior*. St. Louis: Mosby.

Rouse, Timothy P. 1991. "Sociologists and American Prohibition: A Study of Early Works in The American Journal of Sociology 1895-1935." *The American Sociologist* (Fall/Winter):232-243.

———. 1996. "Conditions of a Successful Status Elevation Ceremony." *Deviant Behavior* 17:21-42.

Rudy, David. 1986. *Becoming Alcoholic: Alcoholics Anonymous and the Reality of Alcoholism*. Carbondale: Southern Illinois University Press.

Rumbarger, John. 1989. *Profits, Power and Prohibition: Alcohol Reform and the Industrializing of America 1800-1930*. Albany: State University of New York Press.

Stebbins, R.A. 1996. *Tolerable Differences: Living with Deviance*. Whitby: McGraw-Hill Ryerson.

Szasz, Thomas. 1985. *Ceremonial Chemistry: The Ritual Persecution of Drugs, Addicts and Pushers*. Holmes Beach: Learning Publications, Inc.

Tannenbaum, Frank. 1938. *Crime and the Community*. Boston: Ginn and Co.

Wilson, Elizabeth. 1995. "The Invisible Flâneur." In Sophie Watson and Katherine Gibson (Eds.), *Postmodern Cities and Spaces*. Cambridge: Blackwell. Pp. 59-79.

Wilson, William. 1939. *Alcoholics Anonymous*. New York: Alcoholics Anonymous World Services, Inc.

Do the Current Social and Psychological Theories Really Explain the Initial Causes of Drug Use?

Peter J. Venturelli
Valparaiso University

The data comprising this research consists of approximately sixty in-depth life history interviews and twenty-four open-ended interviews as follow-up research conducted at a midwestern university community between 1994 and 1998. The interviews consist of males and females ranging from eighteen through fifty-four years of age who are avid licit and mostly illicit drug users with approximately twenty who have abstained from their drug usage (in a separate paper the twenty that have recently abstained from chronic drug use will be analyzed separately).

The research is divided into three parts. The first part summarizes the findings of the reccurring motives and reasons for drug use and abuse from life history drug users. Both recreational and chronic, mostly illicit drug users comprise the interviewees. Throughout this section, only the more repetitive patterns for drug use are reported.

The second part of the research discusses the most salient primary theories that explain the reasons for drug use. The third section

This is a completely revised research paper originally prepared for presentation at the 1998 meetings of the Society for the Study of Social Problems, Drinking and Drugs Division, presented at Hotel Nikko, Pink Pearl room, San Francisco, CA, Saturday, August 22, 1998. Session: #80, Roundtable 3: Other Drug Issues, Problems and Findings: Users vs. Non Drug Users, Domestic Violence, Pregnancy and Drug Use, and Sexual Risk Behavior.

discusses the adequacy of the current theoretical explanations for illicit drug use. The application of more plausible theories to the findings is questioned concerning its ability to ultimately explain the initial use and persistence of drug use.

Life History as a Method

The life history method is unique for comprehending drug use. Through the life history, the individual "comes alive" through his or her detailed descriptions and accounts involving drug use. Life histories detail the surrounding specific events that affect and effect the motivations behind and the reasons for drug use (also referred to as justifications and rationalizations). In summary, life histories provide much of the qualitative information for comprehending people's motives and their drug use behaviour.

Who are the Drug Users?

As far back as history is recorded, people have used drugs. No culture has avoided this problem. There have always been people who have searched for and found substances that alter their moods, feelings or thoughts. Is this so unnatural? Do people often look for ways to feel different or strange in search of a stimulating or exciting experience? Kids often twirl around and get dizzy. People pay $35 or $40 per day to go to large amusement parks where roller coasters and other devices will hang them upside done, throw them back and forth and take them to the edge of sickness—all in search of a thrill.

Historically, several naturally occurring substances have been used and abused as methods to become drunk or to feel different, to escape from reality. As science matured, some learned to concentrate these naturally occurring substances into drug derivatives, which are sometimes one hundred or more times stronger than the original substances.

Before the development of modern transportation, people did not distribute these substances to other countries; they just used them at home. But as modern transportation improved and as people started moving about the earth more easily, they sometimes took their drugs to other cultures or countries for personal use, to use as seeds for planting and cropping, or to sell. Drugs were on the move. Wars have been fought over drugs: the opium wars between the

British, who had occupied what is known as India today, and China, which had tried to disallow the importation of opium into its society. The subject of drugs has always inspired passion often because of the large amount of money associated with their use and trade.

Today, possibly every drug that has ever been discovered in the history of the world is available for use in the US. No drug of abuse has ever been eliminated completely. Trends in drug use change, but the drugs themselves tend to weather all storms. Drugs continue to be used to alleviate anxiety and pain, produce relaxation, provide relief from boredom, increase strength or work tolerance or provide a temporary distortion of reality.

If we consider the use of coffee and tea, vitamins and mineral supplements, nearly every one is a drug user. As mentioned above, studies carried out by the Social Research Group of George Washington University, the Institute for Research in Social Behavior in Berkeley, California and others provide detailed, in-depth data showing that drug use is universal (Hanson and Venturelli 1998: 13). Mainly, this research focuses on interviewees that either are using or have used and abused what are referred to as licit and illicit drugs, such as alcohol, tobacco, marijuana, cocaine, hallucinogens, heroin, etc.; mainly, psychoactive-type drugs that pharmacologically interfere with either or both the functions of the body or mind in an adverse manner.

As mentioned above, this study comprises sixty life histories that were conducted between 1994 and 1998. From these life histories, the following main reasons are given regarding why drug use began:

Family Influences
1. Father drank extensively and usually had many mood shifts.
2. Mom and dad were always drunk. They were very happy people when they drank together.
3. I did drugs because I wanted to try them; besides, my uncle first got me drunk at age eight.
4. Mom was the first one to give me a bowl at age sixteen.
5. Mom gave me alcohol at fourteen or fifteen; it was usually some beer.
6. Dad gave me sips; mom did not like it because her father was an alcoholic all his life. My dad would just laugh when I felt "tipsy" from the alcohol. I also drank to get revenge from mom who was always grounding me.

7. Older brother would buy my friends and me alcohol when I was sixteen.
8. I always remember how my dad would hug me when he smelled of beer.
9. My older brother was abusive.
10. My mother would always criticize me for everything.
11. I came from an abusive family; my dad would hit my mom and my mom used to hit me.
12. We have a long history of depression in our family.
13. Since as long as I can remember, my parents use to deal drugs. Parents, uncles and aunts drank and smoked weed.
14. My girlfriend or boyfriend was a heavy drug user.
15. After my dad died unexpectedly from heart complications at thirty-two, I was just fifteen and all I wanted to do was "get fucked up."
16. I hated my stepmother so I would like to get drunk often.
17. Parents appeared straight, but I remember finding weed in their bedroom one day.

Personal and/or Peer Influences:
1. Pot made me feel good about myself and allowed me to forget all the other things that were happening to me.
2. I was just kind of hanging out and all my older friends drank and smoked cigarettes and dope.
3. I feel like it's a special bond when I smoke dope with my friends. A bond that keeps renewing itself the more times we get high together.
4. Everyone I knew back then used drugs extensively.
5. I was very shy, that is where drugs helped my shyness. I often became the centre of the crowd when I was flying really high.
6. I really do not know who I am without drugs. Pot is part of my personality. I cannot imagine a life without alcohol, cigarettes and pot. If I had to I could give up cigarettes, but never the other two.
7. Drugs minimize boundaries while maximizing emotions.
8. The world is clearer and more fun when I am high.
9. Drugs allowed me to forget my parents.
10. I was very fat in high school, so I would get high to forget my body shape.
11. Had a homosexual affair with a kid my age, before that it

was my uncle. Drugs use to make me forget that different part of myself. Often, when I am high I like to have sex with either a male or female. I really don't care who it is. I like both sexes for sex. Drugs help me to appreciate my real self — feel good about myself. This is why I want to live in a bisexual area when I leave this dead and homophobic town.

12. Just plain peer pressure, I really wasn't pressured, I was the one who pressured others to try it.

13. First started to use dope in Vietnam. I used it to quiet my nerves in those jungles. Thirty years later, I still use it to quiet my nerves — especially when the wife is bitching. Sometimes, I can get my wife to smoke dope with me, then we make love after quarrelling. If she is having PMS, then nothing works, not even the pot.

14. We just have better sex when we get high. Everything is slower while fucking.

15. When high, I don't have to worry what society thinks. You just don't care what anyone thinks when you are doing drugs with your real friends.

Above are some of the more salient responses. Many similar responses where repeated by other interviewees in one form or another.

Research Findings and Plausible Theoretical Explanations

Psychological theories that deal with internal mental and/or emotional states are theories that analyze the learning process. Applicable theories such as the process of habituation; Bejerot's "addiction to pleasure" theory (Bejerot 1965, 1972, 1975); and social psychological learning theories, namely differential reinforcement theories (Akers 1992), were examined considering the research data.

Further, more sociologically based theories such as social learning theory/role of significant others (Edwin Sutherland (1947: 5-9)—better known as differential association theory, labelling (Akers 1968, 1992; Plummer 1979; Heitzeg 1996; Cheron 1992; Becker 1963; and Hewitt 1994); subculture theory (Cohen 1955); and control theory (Hirschi 1971; Reckless 1961) were also examined. Thus, after reviewing these theories and comparing the findings from the life histories, the following theories appear to best explain plausible explanations regarding factors most responsible for drug use in the life histories.

One of the psychological theories that offer a better explanation for the findings than other theories has to include Bejerot's "addiction to pleasure theory." The basic process by which learning mechanisms can lead a person into drug use is described in this theory. The theory assumes that it is biologically normal to continue a pleasure stimulus when once begun. Even recent research supports this theory, showing that "a strong, biologically based need for stimulation appears to make sensation-seeking young adults more vulnerable to drug abuse" (Mathias 1995: 1). Sensation-seeking individuals are defined as a category of people who characteristically seek new or novel thrills in their experiences. They maintain a constant preoccupation with getting high or are known to have a relentless desire to pursue physical stimulation or dangerous behaviour. The pleasure derived from stimulation may become habitual when new and shorter nerve course comes into function and higher centres are disconnected. For example, the pleasure associated with getting high may become a learned conditioned response if opiate users discover that the drug and sexual stimulation are mutually reinforcing. Opiate use becomes addictive when the two stimuli become mutually reinforcing. At this point, for example, drug use and sexual stimulation are mutually reinforced thorough paired associate learning.

Another example when drug use is associated with receiving affection or approval is in a social setting, such as within a peer group relationship. Initially, the actual use of certain drugs may not be very important or pleasurable to the individual. However, the affection experienced during intimate interaction when drugs are used becomes paired with ingesting, inhaling or injecting the drug. The pleasure derived from peer approval—especially the intimacy often associated with such "secret" interaction from conventional society most often associated with such interaction coupled with the drug use—can become paired and associated. In this example, drug use and intimacy may become perceived as very worthwhile.[1]

Specific support for this theory from direct quotes of life history interviewees includes:

1. Interviewer: What do you think about sex and being high on pot, alcohol, and some coke? Female interviewee age twenty-

four: It's just a lot to say . . . it makes things more sensual, like slower. It's more like both of you will take your time more, enjoy the moments, celebrate the pleasures together, I am very concerned with totally pleasing her and she is equally sensitive to fully stimulating me. Your sense of touch is so much more; it makes you more relaxed. It definitely heightens sensual pleasure; it's totally erotic. This is true whether I am with a woman having sex or with a man! Though here in this example I am referring to when I am having sex with my boyfriend.

2. Interviewer: What is so different about smoking weed with good friends? Interviewee, male, age twenty-six: I feel like it's a special bond when I smoke dope with my friends — I mean really good friends. A bond that keeps renewing itself each time we all smoke together. Even when I smoke with someone that I think I would like as a friend, when we smoke, a special, new relationship begins to develop.

3. Interviewer: What is so special or different when using drugs as opposed to sipping a non-alcoholic drink with friends? Interviewee, male, age nineteen: When I am drunk I get more crazy, I love to dance and just have fun, it's the bomb dude! On the other hand, when I am high on weed, I am a lot more mellow and just love to sit there and have great conversation. I become very humourous and my friends usually love me more. When you are drinking pop, it's OK but never the same intensity.

4. Interviewer: John (pseudonym), what do you do with yourself when you both (girlfriend and boyfriend) do drugs together? Interviewee, male, age twenty-one: My girl and I love to have sex when we are high. First we enjoy chatting and joking with friends; then, as the night wears on she and I get horny based on past sex we had while high. Sex and drugs, wow! What a combination. Why I think we are addicted to each other's bodies when high. Sometimes, I feel like my soul is inside her body and I am part female! One night we were so high on acid, that I was imagining being a baby inside her womb. Then, we also love to have other types of sex together — of course. I won't go into that unless you want me to, I'd rather leave it up to your imagination.

Such expressions regarding the linkage between erotic pleasure and the use of drugs are adequately explained by Bejerot's "addiction to pleasure theory."

Regarding the sociological explanations, social learning theory possessed the most amount of explanatory power, followed by Reckless's containment theory. Sutherland's differential association theory explains drug use as a form of learned behaviour where conventional learning occurs through imitation, trial and error, improvisation, rewarding appropriate behaviour and when cognitive mental processes are at work. Social learning theory focuses directly on how drug use and abuse are acquired through interaction with others who use and abuse drugs. This theory emphasizes the pervasive influence of primary groups, or groups that share a high amount of intimacy and spontaneity where members are emotionally bonded. Families and residents of tightly knit urban neighbourhoods are examples of primary groups. In contrast, secondary groups are groups that share segmented social roles where interaction is based on prescribed role patterns. As known, social learning theory addresses a type of interaction that is highly specific. This type of interaction involves learning specific motives, techniques and appropriate meanings that are commonly attached to a particular type of drug. Some more illustrative examples from the life history research include:

1. We were always happy together smoking dope. I grew up with these three guys. We went to the same grade school, junior high and high school. I really cannot remember who taught me how to smoke dope. We just watched each other at first. Even my older brother was with us the first time. I remember he showed us at age thirteen how to hold in the smoke. My brother was seventeen at the time. Three years later he died in a car accident. I can still say that my brother taught me everything, even dope smoking.

2. When I was about six years old, I use to watch my mom smoke dope with her girlfriends. I always thought that everyone does this at the time. I remember how happy they used to be, laughing and talking constantly while high in that memorable living room. I also remember that I wished to be with them and wanted to be older so that I could join in.

From literally dozens of life histories that offer similar examples, these are just two examples where social learning theory directly applies.

Finally, containment theory also possesses adequate explanatory power for understanding the motivation to use illicit drugs. According to this theory, the socialization process results in the creation of strong or weak internal and external control systems. The degree of self-control, high or low frustration tolerance, positive or negative self-perception, successful or unsuccessful goal achievement and resistance or adherence to deviant behaviour determines internal control. Environmental pressures, such as social conditions, may limit the accomplishment of goal-striving behaviour, such conditions include poverty, minority group status, inferior education and lack of employment. The external control system consists of effective or ineffective supervision and discipline, consistent or inconsistent moral training, positive or negative acceptance, identity and self-worth. Examples are latchkey children who become delinquent and alcoholic parents who are inconsistent with disciplining their offspring. They provide another example of the breakdown in social control.[2] A small sampling of direct quotes from oral histories that support this theory includes:

1. Every time I plan to quit doing drugs, along come my friends with lines like: "Come on, Why quit now? You can quit later when you are older, married and living the boring life."
2. I am often tempted to graduate to other drugs like pot, cocaine and acid. But, so far I am happy with my beer. I like to watch my friends get high, but I only drink alcohol.
3. I would do drugs in a heartbeat, but my wife would kill me. That was one thing I promised her when I wanted to marry her. Her father died of a cocaine overdose. He had a heart condition and didn't know it. Since her father's death, Cindy [a pseudonym], my wife, is scared to death of drugs. A little alcohol is ok but I really can't drink much in front of her. And, I don't drink behind her back because I love her too much. Since I stay away from bars and certain friends, I am OK … drug-free. But gosh, I miss it once in a while.
4. I never even thought much about drugs when I was studying to be a priest in the seminary. But then, I had to have sex on a more regular basis and just quit the seminary. Now, I am

with a bunch of dudes who drink and smoke dope all the time. So, guess what, I do the same.

Discussion

While the psychological and sociological theories mentioned in this research add more insight than other theories, the evidence for explaining why people initially begin using and/or abusing drugs is not really adequately answered. While the theories appear to explain the use of drugs in this research, a lingering question remains. Why do peers initially influence drug users when many others are not influenced by peers and commonly avoid habitual, drug-using peers? Why does only a proportion of drug users finds the linkage in using drugs coupled with sex, while another proportion does not? Examples include making a linkage with other types of pleasures, such as meditation, stimulating conversation, bungee jumping, movies and theatre, simply enjoying an unaltered state of consciousness etc. One would think that theories should explain more of the variation. Why are the current theories so fragmented? Again, why do some people couple sex with drugs while countless others do not? Is there something in the personality structure of drug users that leads them to use or abuse drugs, while countless others will either not use or only use licit-type drugs with moderation throughout their lifetime?

Can answers regarding why a certain percentage are attracted to drugs be more adequately explained by personality characteristics such as levels of self-esteem, depressive disorders, etc?

How about bio-physiological and genetic theories? Social scientists need to construct theories that integrate the fragmented social and psychological theories that on their own are limited in their explanations. There simply are too many theories that on their own explain too little. As we approach the turn of the century, we need to take stock of our fragmented theories and possess the spirit of Talcott Parsons and, of course, devoid ourselves of any attachments to functionalism per se. Why should differential reinforcement, differential association, labelling, subculture, control, social learning and containment theories not allow some genetic aspects of social behaviour? All of us have genes, we now know that at least some aspect of our behaviour emanates from genetic makeup. Why not include this in our theorizing?

Could there be something in our lives that can more likely cause or hasten an initial attraction to illicit-type drugs? What about economic causes? Perhaps Marx's theory of alienation in capitalistic societies should be revised to alienation *via* chemical usage. Is the use of illicit-type drugs similar to *soma* in the book *1984* ? Is illicit drug use or abuse explained better by looking at the current structural arrangements found in postmodern capitalistic societies? Further, are the causes for initial drug use the same across cultures? Does the man in India who uses marijuana use this drug for the same reason as the man using drugs in the United States? In effect, are there pan-universal explanations for why people extensively abuse drugs destructively?

More social scientists should begin looking at the multiple reasons for drug use. Why not look more intensively at how structural arrangements and political ideology affect drug use behaviour? Are the current answers for explaining illicit drug use based on overly reductionistic analyses of peer group, socialization and community influences? While standard explanations such as the role of peer influence are widely accepted, how many of us do things that are contrary to our opinion solely because of peer influence? How many people who are from severely dysfunctional families have never really been handicapped by poor socialization? How many respected leaders have been spawned forth from societies who came from so-called dysfunctional families. How, for example, do the socialization theories explain such occurrences? They do not; socialization theorists avoid either such cases or term such cases as exceptional. If, for example, my brother experiences a life of crime and I experience a life of success and hard work, how can theories based on socialization explain the variance? They do not, therein lies the flaw.

Are the current drug laws against illicit drug use beneficial or harmful—especially when increasingly larger percentages of the incarcerated are imprisoned solely for drug law violations (many for simple possession)? Are legislators viewing drug use or abuse based on fallacious, stereotyped images of drug users that are inappropriate, inaccurate and outdated? This may be especially true since criminal justice systems in countries with a parliamentary-type system of government using a more punitive approach to the use of illicit drugs have never been able to curb drug use effectively. Moreover, this is true even though many of these countries spend literally billions of dollars on law enforcement, prosecution and incarceration with very poor results in curbing total illicit drug use.

Is the use of drugs adequately explained by single theories within the confinement of specific disciplines? If so, why does the application of one theory often explain certain types of drug users while the same theory does not apply to other drug users? Now is the time to begin constructing theories that are interdisciplinary and can explain more of the variations in the types of users and their reason(s) for drug use. Let us begin to remove our disciplinary blinders

Conclusion

The sixty life histories and the twenty-four follow-up in-depth interviews reveal both family and personal and/or peer influences regarding the motivation for drug use. While only the recurring responses are reported, such consistencies do not vary much from oral history to oral history. The second part of the research examined the most applicable theories that best explain the interviewees' reasons for drug use and/or abuse. The discussion in the final part questions whether the current single discipline-driven theories really explain why people use illicit-type drugs, to the extent where drug users are willing to jeopardize their health, social relationships and community standing.

This author is asking for a more critical re-examination of widely accepted explanations such as peer influence and the adequacy of socialization for drug usage. Perhaps, more marcroscopic and multi-disciplinary theories need to be developed in place of naively believing that the current single discipline-driven microscopic explanations adequately explain drug use and/or abuse.

Endnotes

[1]   More elaboration on this point will be made in a forthcoming research paper.

[2]   Further elaboration will be made in a forthcoming research paper.

Selected Bibliography

Akers, Ronald L. 1992. *Drugs, Alcohol, and Society: Social Structure, Process, and Policy.* Belmont, CA: Wadsworth Inc.

————. 1968. "Problems in the Sociology of Deviance: Social Definition and Behavior." *Social Forces* 6 (June): 455-465.

Becker, H. S. 1963. *Outsiders: Studies in the Sociology of Deviance.* New York: Free Press.

Bejerot, N. 1975. "The Biological and Social Character of Drug Dependence." Edited by Kisker, K. P., Meyer, J.E., Muller, C. and Stromogrew, E., *Psychiatrie der Gegenwait, Forshung und Praxis*, Vol. III, 2nd ed. Berlin: Springer Verlag, pp. 488-518.

————. 1972. *Addiction: An Artificially Induced Drive.* Springfield, Ill.: Charles C. Thomas.

————. 1965. "Current Problems of Drug Addicted." (Swed.) *Lakartidingen*, 62 (50): 4231-4238.

Cheron, J. M. 1992. *Symbolic Interactionism: An Introduction, an Interpretation, an Integration*, 4th Ed. Englewood Cliffs, NJ: Prentice-Hall.

Cohen, A. K. 1955. *Delinquent Boys: The Culture of the Gang.* Glencoe, IL: Free Press.

Hanson, G. and P. Venturelli. 1988. *Drugs and Society*, fifth Edition. Sudbury, MA: Jones and Bartlett Publishers.

Heitzeg, N. A. 1966. *Deviance: Rulemakers and Rulebreakers.* Minneapolis: West Publishing.

Hewitt, J. P. 1994. *Self and Society: A Symbolic Interactionist Social Psychology*, sixth ed. Boston: Allyn and Bacon.

Hirschi, T. 1971. *Causes of Delinquency*, 2nd ed. Los Angeles: University of California Press.

Mathias, R. 1995. "Novelty Seekers and Drug Abusers Tap Same Brain Reward System, Animal Studies Show." *NIDA Notes* 10, 4 (July/August). Pp. 1-2.

Plummer, Kenneth. 1979. "Misunderstanding Labeling Perspectives." In David Downes and Paul Rock, (Eds.), *Deviant Interpretations.* London: Martin Robertson, pp. 85-121.

Reckless, W. C. 1961. "A New Theory of Delinquency." *Federal Probation* 25: 42-46.

Sutherland. E. 1947. *Principles of Criminology*, 4th ed. Philadelphia: Lippincott.

Gender Differences in the Impact of Incarceration on the Children and Families of Drug Offenders

Susan F. Sharp, Susan T. Marcus-Mendoza, Robert G. Bentley,
Debra B. Simpson and Sharon R. Love
University of Oklahoma

As state and federal prison systems across the country incarcerate increasing numbers of prisoners, researchers have begun to explore the social implications of incarceration (Fulbright 1996). Many question the wisdom of massive incarceration programs, suggesting that the costs for individuals, families and communities may far outweigh the benefits (Watts and Nightingale 1996). These concerns are of particular interest in Oklahoma where the incarceration rate has increased by more than 30% between 1992 and 1996. Almost 75% of the offenders incarcerated in 1996 committed nonviolent crimes, which further invites examination of whether the benefits of such mass incarceration compensate for the toll it is taking on Oklahoma's families (Oklahoma Department of Corrections 1996) The largest segment of nonviolent offenders incarcerated in Oklahoma are incarcerated for drug-related offences. This study is an initial analysis of the effects of incarceration on the children and families of drug offenders from the inmate's perspective. We pay particular attention to gender differences and similarities in

This project was supported by a grant from the Oklahoma Department of Corrections. The opinions expressed in this paper are our own and do not necessarily reflect policies or procedures of the Oklahoma Department of Corrections.

these effects. We will give a brief overview of the effects of incarceration on communities, families, and children, and then explore the findings of our study.

The Negative Effects of Incarceration on Communities

Recent research has suggested that there are many far-reaching, negative consequences to the increasing use of incarceration in the United States. In an overview of the literature, Moore (1996) found that high rates of incarceration weaken communities. Removing individuals from the infrastructure of the community creates economic hardships on the remaining residents and leads to stress, stigmatization and displacement of children. Prison strengthens gang ties, which are then carried back into the community, further disrupting the community structure. Individuals released from prison are likely to be homeless, jobless and have difficulty forming and maintaining relationships. These individuals place an economic and emotional burden on the community. They are also poor role models for children who live in areas with high incarceration rates. Such children learn to view prison as a common, and potentially unavoidable, aspect of their future. Obviously, the outlook for communities with high incarceration rates is grim.

Furthermore, incarceration does not appear to be the cure-all to our burgeoning crime problem. Large-scale incarceration may actually increase crime in our communities, thereby counteracting any positive effects of prison. According to Clear (1996), incarceration increases crime in three ways. First, the removal of large numbers of offenders from a community creates a need for new recruits who can fill the void left by those we have imprisoned. And as criminal enterprises look for replacements, more young people are being drawn into criminal careers. Second, as prison becomes a common and familiar experience, it is less likely to be a deterrent to crime. "It is not the actual brutality of prison life that deters, it is imagining the prison experience ... the widespread use of prison will continue to create growing numbers of informed consumers who know people who have survived and count them among friends and family" (p. 13). Lastly, research has linked high rates of incarceration to many of the social problems that lead to criminality such as social disorder, disruption of families and economic inequality. Therefore, Clear suggests that the increasing rate of incarceration has "backfired" by proliferating rather than reducing our crime problem.

The Negative Effects of Incarceration on Children and Families of Offenders

Research has also documented the negative effects of massive incarceration in the United States on the emotional and financial well-being of families and children of inmates as well as communities. Some of these impacts on the family and children may differ for the families of male and female inmates.

Incarceration of men can lead to mild tension in the family, legal separation or even divorce (Hairston 1991; Weisheit and Klofas 1989). Wives of incarcerated men often experience difficulty in meeting the family's basic needs for food, clothing and housing. They feel isolated, experiencing demeaning treatment by the prison system, and report feeling imprisoned by the responsibilities and pressure placed upon them by their husbands (Fishman 1995). Additionally, these women report significant problems with children due to the absence of the fathers, particularly in terms of getting the children to obey (Daniel and Barret 1981; Girshick 1996).

Incarceration of mothers may cause different problems for families. A majority of incarcerated mothers have had primary or sole responsibility for the care of their offspring, raising the possibility that their children may have to move to settings with non-parental caretakers (Harris 1993). A 1994 report by the Bureau of Justice Statistics revealed that nearly 90% of male inmates with children under the age of eighteen reported that their minor children were living with their mothers (Bureau of Justice Statistics 1994). In contrast, the majority of incarcerated mothers reported that their children were living with grandparents. Only one-quarter reported that the children were in the care of their fathers.

Children of both male and female inmates suffer greatly when a parent is incarcerated. Studies have linked incarceration of a parent to poor school performance, aggressive behaviour and emotional problems in children (Hairston 1991; Johnston 1995a; Kampfer 1995). Children of incarcerated parents even appear to suffer a post-traumatic stress syndrome similar to children whose parents have died (Kampfer 1995). Theorists have also suggested that economic deprivation, reduced parental supervision and lack of relationships with parents may lead to deviant behaviours among the children (Hagan 1996; Merton 1938; Messner and Rosenfield 1993).

Whereas children of both male and female inmates are subject to the problems mentioned above, the children of female inmates are less likely to have the other parent in the home and are, therefore, more likely to be placed in alternative living arrangements. This poses obvious problems for children including unfamiliar people and surroundings (Sobel 1982). First, the family is the primary institution of socialization and nurturance in American society (Lindsey 1997). Thus, changes in the family structure will affect socialization. Second, alternative caretakers may not be optimal substitutes for parents. According to a study published by the National Council on Crime and Delinquency (Bloom and Steinhart 1993), "the ability of caregivers to cope with their new parenting roles vary with the caregiver's age, job and income status and other personal characteristics" (p. 34). Some older caregivers may not have the stamina, patience or financial resources needed to raise young children, and younger caregivers often have their own children to care for in addition to their new charges. Children may be separated from their siblings and have to learn to adapt to new rules and forge new relationships (Johnston 1995b). They are often confused about the relationship between themselves and their caregiver. Girshick (1997) argues that we should consider community-based alternatives to incarceration for female offenders, in part due to their roles as primary caretakers of children.

The effects of incarceration, however, are not always negative. In some cases, there may be beneficial effects on families when an offender is incarcerated (Gabel and Johnston 1995). In cases where parents' behaviour is endangering the child, the children's safety must be the primary consideration. However, many researchers argue that the trauma involved in incarceration of a parent is outweighed by the benefits (Bloom and Steinhart 1993; Clear 1996; Gabel and Johnston 1995).

There is a need for the collection of detailed information concerning the families of both male and female inmates. This should include whether the offender was married or cohabiting at the time of incarceration, as well as detailed information on the number of children, their ages, whether they lived with the inmate prior to his or her incarceration, the current living arrangements of spouses and children and the planned living arrangements after the release of the offender. This information could prove valuable in developing more comprehensive studies of the effects of incarceration on families of inmates.

This study is an initial analysis of the gender differences in the impact of incarceration on the family members of incarcerated individuals from the offenders' perspective. Since drug offenders constitute the single largest category of offenders in Oklahoma (Oklahoma Department of Corrections 1996), we focused on the families of individuals incarcerated for drug offences, from the perspective of the offenders.

We hypothesized that the data would indicate that incarceration is associated with a number of negative effects on the families of offenders. Furthermore, we predicted that the effects would differ according to the gender of the parent. We anticipated the following specific differences:

1. Families of male inmates would experience more economic disruption as a result of incarceration.
2. Children of female inmates would be more likely than those of male inmates to be placed in a non-parental household.

Method

Participants

We obtained from the Oklahoma Department of Corrections lists of inmates at five institutions who were incarcerated for drug offences. Those lists were ordered numerically based on chronological entry into the Oklahoma Department of Corrections system. Random samples were drawn by computer to reflect the range of inmates from those in the system for long periods to those newly brought under the department's supervision. Due to department transfers and inmate work assignments, at several institutions all available inmates meeting the selection criteria participated in the project to ensure adequate sample size. Almost all inmates selected for the study completed the survey.

The research team administered the survey to a total of 268 male and female inmates at five facilities: Dr. Eddie Warrior Correctional Center (EWCC—female inmates, minimum security prison), Jackie Brannon Correctional Center (JBCC—male inmates, minimum security prison), Clara Waters Community Correctional Center (CWCCC—male inmates, community custody), Oklahoma City Correctional Center (OKCCC—male inmates, community custody), and Kate Barnard Correctional Center (KBCCC—female inmates, community custody). Female inmates represent approximately 10% of the total inmate population in the US (US Department of Justice 1996). However, to facilitate comparisons between male and female inmates, we oversampled female participants to obtain similar number of males (N = 124) and females (N = 144) participants.

Survey Instrument

The survey instrument contained questions about families, including economic changes, placement of children, problems with children, domestic violence and the effects of incarceration on the family, as well as questions about demographics, criminal record and drug usage. The instrument included questions from existing measures as well questions constructed by the research team. Some questions were drawn from the National Youth Survey, Wave VI (Elliot 1993), Men's Relationship Study (Umberson 1995), Inmate Population Survey (Marcus-Mendoza and Brody 1996) and the AIDS Initial Assessment (National Institute on Drug Abuse 1993). We added questions about changes in family income and problems that children may have faced, as well as open-ended questions concerning their perceptions of the positive and negative effects of their incarceration on their families.

Inmates completed the survey in group settings under the supervision of the research team, taking approximately forty-five minutes on average. Members of the research team assisted inmates who needed help reading the questionnaire. We assured the inmates of the anonymity of their responses and instructed them not to write their name or other identifying information on the survey form. Participation was voluntary, and we obtained informed consent from all participants.

Results

Demographic Data and Inmate Backgrounds

Participants were asked to self-identify race. Almost half the inmates were white, one-third were African-American and about 14% were Native American. The vast majority were Protestant. The modal educational category was high school graduation or GED. However, males were more likely than females to report some post-high school education (31.4% versus 20.6%). It is worth noting that the women at Kate Barnard Community Correction Center were far less likely to report post-secondary education than any other group (10.9%). The majority of both male inmates (65.9%) and female inmates (55.6%) reported prior felony convictions, although a higher percentage of male inmates reported prior incarcerations. Almost half the men and more than one-third of the women reported full-time employment prior to this incarceration.

Nearly half of both the male and female inmates reported prior participation in an alcohol or drug treatment program. Additionally, almost half were the first in their family to go to prison, although a larger percentage of the females reported that another family member had been incarcerated in the past. Females were also significantly more likely to report having a spouse or common-law partner who has been incarcerated ($\chi2= 38.5999$, $p < 0.001$). A higher percentage of females than males reported a spouse being an accomplice in their current offence, but this was not significantly different.

Females were significantly more likely than males to report a history of physical abuse ($\chi^2 = 13.108$, $p < 0.001$), as well as a history of sexual abuse ($\chi^2 = 28.650$, $p < 0.001$). A large percentage of both male and female inmates had experienced domestic violence as adults, although females were more likely to report being victims ($\chi= 67.594$, $p < 0.001$) and males were more likely to describe themselves as perpetrators of domestic violence ($\chi^2= 10.533$, $p < 0.005$).

Table 1 contains alcohol and drug history. We reported the mean age of taking the first drink, daily drinking, first usage of drugs other than alcohol and first injection of drugs (where applicable). Males reported earlier use for all four measures.

Living Arrangements, Family Composition and the Financial Effects of Incarceration

A relatively small number of inmates reported divorce subsequent to incarceration. However, only thirty-four women and thirty-two men reported being legally married at the time of incarceration. Of these, fifteen women and sixteen men reported that they had at least discussed divorce with their spouse and, in most cases, someone had already filed for divorce. Nine males indicated their spouse had filed, an additional three said their spouse had discussed divorce and four

Table 1: Mean age at initiation of alcohol and drug use

	Females	Males
Mean age at first drink (in yrs.)	15.6	13.2
Mean age began daily drinking (in yrs.)	19.0	18.4
Mean age first used drugs (in yrs.)	18.3	16.2
Mean age first injected drugs (in yrs.)	18.6	17.8

reported they had filed for divorce themselves. In contrast, only three females reported their spouse had filed, an additional two reported their spouse had discussed divorce, but ten females inmates reported filing for divorce themselves.

In addition to marital status, we also examined where and with whom inmates reported living prior to incarceration. Inmates were asked whether they had lived with certain individuals prior to their incarceration, and a series of dummy variables were created to reflect their responses, with affirmative responses coded one, negative coded zero. The findings are presented in Table 2. The majority of both male and female inmates indicated they lived in their own homes. Slightly more than half the males and slightly less than half the females reported living with a spouse or common-law partner prior to incarceration. However, 36% of the females indicated that they lived with one or more of their children immediately prior to incarceration, compared to less than 21% of the males (t_{258} = -3.0794, p = .002). This suggests more disruption in family composition for children of female inmates. We will return to a more in-depth discussion of the perceived effects on children in the following section.

One of the potentially negative effects of incarceration is disruption not only of the family composition but also of the family environment. We examined several possible changes families may have to face. Table 3 presents inmate responses to questions about family moves since the inmate's incarceration. Surprisingly few inmates reported that their families had moved to a cheaper home. However, a fairly large number of inmates (n = 92) reported that their families had moved in with others. There was not a significant difference between

Table 2: Living arrangements prior to incarceration

Variable	Females	Males
Lived with my child	36.0%	20.7%
Lived with my spouse	20.3%	20.7%
Lived with my common-law spouse	26.8%	30.6%
Lived in my own home	60.6%	67.5%
Plan to return to same home	28.1%	29.2%

T-tests were conducted for differences by sex for each variable. The only significant difference was for the variable "lived with my child," $t_{258} = -3.0794$, p = .002.

male and female inmates on this question. Males and females differed significantly in terms of knowing whether their families' living arrangements had changed, with males far more likely to report not knowing.

We asked inmates what their greatest concerns were about the effect of incarceration on their families. Several inmates appeared concerned about changes in living arrangements of their families:

> They are all cramped up with their aunts and really confused about why (male).

> My youngest daughter has bounced from place to place because her mother is having a real hard time (male).

> The adjustment my children had to make when they moved to Texas—changing schools, friends (male).

We also explored the effects of incarceration on family income. However, it is important to note that many of the income questions contained high numbers of missing responses, so we are only able to report on a limited number of cases. We do not know whether inmates who did not respond chose to omit the information or whether they simply did not know the answer. Female inmates reported a mean family income of $29,402 prior to incarceration, with only 50% (n = 72) women responding to this question. Fifty-two percent of the

Table 3: Changes in family living arrangements since incarceration

	Females	Males	Total
Has your family moved to a cheaper home?	9 (n = 117)	15 (n = 92)	24 (N = 209)
Has your family moved in with others?	57 (n = 118)	35 (n = 93)	92 (N = 211)
Has your family moved to a better home?	7 (n = 118)	9 (n = 93)	16 (N = 211)
Don't know where they are living	6 (n = 119)	20 (n = 93)	26 (N = 212)

males (n = 65) indicated a mean prior income of $34,485. Estimates of current family income were $10,693 for females (n = 41, 28.5%) and $6634 for males (n = 43, 34.7%). We do not know if these estimates include illegally earned income.

Table 4 displays responses to a series of questions about family sources of support prior to incarceration. Females were significantly more likely than males to report both Aid to Families with Dependent Children (AFDC) (χ^2 = 20.577, p = .001) and child support (χ^2 = 8.891, p = .005) as a prior source of support. A significant number of both males and females indicated that their own work and their spouse's work helped support the family. Although not included in Table 4, it is worth noting that sixteen males and nineteen females indicated illegal income as a source of support for their families. We then explored how the sources of support have changed. In Table 5 we examined inmates' responses concerning support of families since incarceration. There were significant differences between the responses of females and males for two questions. Males were significantly more likely to state that their spouse was supporting their family (χ^2= 8.952, p = .005), while females

Table 4: Method of supporting family prior to incarceration, by gender

Variables	Females	Males	Total	χ^2	p
Respondent worked	62	75	137	18.750	ns
Spouse worked	33	20	53	0.923	ns
Received AFDC	32	3	35	20.577	.001
Received child support	11	0	11	8.891	.005
Family helped	19	10	29	1.0897	ns

Table 5: Current support of family, by gender

Variables	Females	Males	Total	χ^2	p
Spouse works	25	37	62	8.952	.005
	(n = 129)	(n = 101)	(N= 230)		
AFDC	17	14	31	.035	ns
	(n = 129)	(n = 101)	(N = 230)		
Family help	42	21	63	3.891	.05
	(n = 129)	(n = 101)	(N = 230)		

were more likely to report family help as a source of support (χ^2 = 3.891, p = .05). It is worth noting that about 25% fewer females reported a spouse's work as a current source of income compared to a prior source of income. However, for males the number reporting a spouse's job as the current source of support was nearly double those reporting a spouse's job as a source of support prior to incarceration. We also explored inmate perceptions of the effect of their incarceration on the family's income. Sixty-three percent of the female inmates answering this question indicated that the family's income was less than it was prior to their incarceration, as compared to 78% of the males who responded. This difference is statistically significant, (χ^2= 22.142, p = .001).

In response to the open-ended question about their greatest concern, a number of male inmates indicated that the economic impact on their families was a primary concern:

My sister is paying my house payment wish (*sic*) takes away from her family (male).

Standard of living (male).

Bills piling up, mortgage behind, Kids hasn't (*sic*) had clothes bought for them (male).

No child support (male).

Lower income, lower standard of living, less parental supervision/attention, less family oriented activity, less money/gifts/responsibilities—you name it (male).

Overall, inmates thought that incarceration had diminished their families' income. Only seven females and one male reported that the family's income was the same, while a majority of both males and females reported that income was "somewhat less" or "much less" since their incarceration, with males being slightly more likely to indicate the latter.

The Effects of Incarceration on Children

Table 6 presents the mean number of children inmates reported. On average, male inmates had slightly fewer than two children under age eighteen, and female inmates had slightly more than two children. However, the mean number of children living with female inmates prior to incarceration was almost double that for male inmates; this difference was statistically significant ($t = -4.73$, $p = .001$). There were also significant differences in the number of minor children not living with the inmate at the time of his or her incarceration. In this instance, the mean for males was almost double that for females; this difference was also significant ($t = 2.8505$, $p = .005$.)

It is quickly apparent that incarceration of a parent affects a large number of children. To explore the effects, we examined the current living arrangements of these minor children. In Table 7 we

Table 6: Mean number of children under age 18

Variable	Females	Males
Number of children under age 18	2.01	1.69
Number of children living with me at time of arrest*	1.39	0.74
Number of minor children living elsewhere at time of arrest*	0.69	1.24

* T-tests revealed significant differences between males and females for the variable "Number of children living with me," t_{252} = -4.73, p = .001, and for the variable "Number of minor children living elsewhere," t_{157} = 2.8505, p = 0.005.

Table 7: Current living arrangements of children living with inmate prior to this incarceration, by gender

Variable	Female	Male	Total
Child now with other parent	29	37	66
Child with inmate's mother	47	7	54
Child with inmate's father	12	4	16
Child with inmate's grandparent	1	3	4
Child with inmate's sibling	15	2	17
Child with partner's mother	5	3	8
Child with partner's father	0	2	2
Child with partner's grandparent	1	0	1
Child with partner's sibling	1	0	1
Child in foster home	4	0	4
Child with agency	3	0	3
Don't know where child is	2	3	5
Total	120	61	181

* χ^2 tests conducted on first six variables (remaining six had too small of cell frequencies.) χ^2 was significant for "Child now with other parent" (22.988, p = .001), "Child now with inmate's mother" (16.566, p = .001), and "Child with inmate's sibling" (4.311, p = .038.)

present information for those children living with the inmate at the time of his or her incarceration. Males were significantly more likely to report that the child is now living with the other parent, while women were significantly more likely to report that the child is now living with the inmate's mother or sibling. A small number of women but no men reported children were living in foster homes or had been placed with agencies.

In Table 8 the current living arrangements of those children who did not live with the inmate at the time of incarceration are presented. Again, males were significantly more likely to report that the child was with the other parent, while siblings of the inmates or parents of the inmate or inmate's partner were providing homes for the children of females.

An open-ended question invited inmates to share their feelings about their children's current living situations. Responses fell into four broad categories: positive feelings about the situation, mixed feelings, negative feelings and lack of knowledge about the children's situation.

A large number of inmates indicated that they felt good about the situation. Generally, these responses focused on family members providing good care. Some inmates reported that their children were with the other parent, who was providing good care:

They are better off with their mother (male).

I feel They (*sic*) are in good hand's (*sic*) with my wife (male).

They are in good hand (*sic*) they mother (*sic*) love them (male).

In some cases, other family members were providing care. The most common other caretakers reported were the inmates' mothers or siblings. Inmates tended to report positive feelings about their children's situation in these cases, often expressing relief that the children were safe and were receiving good care:

I feel good about it—totally secure that my mother takes excellent care of her (male).

I feel good about it. She with my mother (female).

Table 8: Current living arrangements of inmate's children not living with inmate prior to this incarceration, by gender

Variables	Females	Males	Total
Child now with other parent	15	49	64
Child with inmate's mother	7	5	12
Child with inmate's father	1	1	2
Child with inmate's grandparent	2	2	4
Child with inmate's sibling	7	2	9
Child with partner's mother	8	2	10
Child with partner's father	2	0	2
Child with partner's grandparent	0	1	1
Child with partner's sibling	0	0	0
Child in foster home	1	1	2
Child with agency	2	0	2
Don't know where child is	0	4	4
Total	45	67	112

$^*\chi^2$ significant only for variable "Child now with other parent" (29.800, p = .001).

I feel my sister is doing the best she can do with my current situation (female).

I'm very lucky that my mother and stepbrother take very good care of my son (female).

In a few cases, children were not with family members. One inmate eloquently described the care his children are receiving from friends, expressing gratitude that the children's safety as well as their educational needs were being provided:

I am grateful to friends who have come forward to meet my children's needs. They are in school and their grades have be (sic) commendable. I know that they are safe (male).

Another inmate expressed trust in the agency caring for her infant:

> ... my two mo (*sic*) old is living with a Christian Organized Housing Program and though I trust them with her I wish it didn't have to be (female).

Some female inmates reported mixed feelings. Although they acknowledged that their caretakers largely met their children's physical and safety needs, these inmates also expressed concern about the children's emotional needs. Female inmates tended to focus on the mother-child bond, expressing concern that their children were unhappy due to their absence:

> I need to be home with her. She will be a year old this month. I haven't gotten to bond. My mother takes good care of her and so does the organization A Touch of Love (female).

> I feel sad. The people are great. But she and I were best friends. Now she has her whole world tore upside down, I feel the same way (female).

> I know they are safe and well cared for. But they're not happy. We are very close. My baby doesn't understand why mom can't come home. They need me, I need them (female).

> They are with my familia. The person they are with is a very good mother. But I'm ready to take care of my own children (female).

> They love their grandparents, but it is hurting them terribly bad, we have never been away from each other till now. They want me home (female).

Male inmates, however, expressed different concerns. Several expressed concern that their children lacked adequate guidance without the inmate present. Others were concerned about the financial impact of their incarceration on their children:

> It needs to become better, because I don't want them to only have one person to depend on. A child needs two

parents to become a complete, responsibly (sic) adult. Even though some excel with one. They still have a void in their life and it does affect them (male).

I don't like it! I want to be with them to guide them through life (male).

They need a father figure around. Sober and filled with the Holy Spirit. They are having a difficult time accepting the separation and dealing with the changes (male).

A substantial number of inmates mentioned lack of safety and supervision of their children. Several men expressed concern that the mother of the children was unfit to care for them:

I took full custody of my children after proving my wife unfit to care for them. At that time, she of course brought up all pertinent information regarding my drug usage and the judge still found me competent. Now my kids are forced to live in the same squalor and abuse that I spent time and money to rescue them from (male).

I think it has been hard on them, and my ex-wife is not a very stable person and she is a bad influence on them (male).

I don't like them living with their mother. She's a junkie (male).

don't like current situation. Mother works all day so daughter runs wild. No discipline when my daughters (sic) mother is at home (male).

It is interesting to note that no female inmates expressed concern about the father being unfit. This may be because the father was less likely to have the children of an incarcerated female. Females were also significantly more likely to have had a spouse or partner who was incarcerated, which may have contributed to the small numbers reporting the father had current custody. It is interesting that the only female indicating that she did not know where her child lived currently was a woman whose child was adopted at birth. In contrast, a number of male inmates did not know about their children's current living situation.

A few inmates provided information about effects on children other than their biological children. One inmate reports he was helping his sister raise her children:

> I do not have any children of my own, however, I was assisting my sister in the upbringing of her newly born. Since I am no longer helping her raise my nephew, my sister has had to go on welfare and been forced to move in with our parents. My nephew's home, as he once knew it, has changed (male).

> I don't like it, that my stepchildren got taken away and put in foster homes because of my stupidity (male).

Some inmates expressed concern about how their incarceration would affect their own position in the family. For these inmates, there was concern about whether their family would be able to trust them and if their children would remember them:

> Hopefully, they have not gave up on me. I am a better person than I have ever been since I became addicted (male).

> Will my daughter know that I am her father upon my release (male).

> That my children will not trust me or want to live with me when I get out (female).

> Out of sight, out of mind (female).

Whereas both female and male inmates expressed concern about their relationships with family members, female inmates were more likely than male inmates to express concern about emotional damage to their children and other family members. These inmates focused on the harm that their incarceration caused their family members:

> My children are missing out on everything a healthy home environment offers. I'm afraid they have deep abandonment fears (female).

I don't want my son to be lonely missing me and worrying about me which take away from his happiness and his ability to concentrate on his school work (female).

How are they physically, mentally, emotionally. I was daddy. They never expected me being here or using drugs (male).

The survey included a question about inmates' perceptions of the supervision their children received since their incarceration. The results are presented in Table 9.

Here there was a significant gender difference ($\chi2=16.849$, p = .002). Higher percentages of female inmates reported that their children were getting the same or more supervision, while higher percentages of males state their children were getting much less supervision. Inmates also reported concerns about children getting into trouble as a result of their incarceration:

Table 9: Perceived supervision of children since incarceration

Variables	Females	Males
Much less	12.3%	26.3%
	(16)	(30)
Somewhat less	12.3%	10.5%
	(16)	(12)
Same	16.9%	6.1%
	(22)	(7)
Somewhat more	10.8%	4.4%
	(14)	(5)
Much more	7.7%	3.5%
	(10)	(4)
Don't know	11.5%	12.3%
	(15)	(14)

(35 of the 130 females responding to this question said it was not applicable to them, as did 42 of the 114 males who responded to this question.)
* χ^2 conducted for difference by sex was significant (16.849, p = .002).

My oldest daughter just running crazy out there (female).

Kids getting involved with things their piers (*sic*) pressure them into (male).

Seems that my incarceration is a status symbol for my daughter. Instead of being a deterrent, she think its "cool." No discipline or quality time is being spent with her since my incarceration (male).

My daughter (16) has left home, my sons have become angry (male).

To gain more knowledge about specific problems experienced by children, we included a question dealing with inmates' perceptions of problems that their children may have experienced. A number of potential problems were presented, and answer choices include "no," "yes, but it was a problem before I was incarcerated," "yes, and has only been a problem since I was incarcerated," "was a problem before I was incarcerated but is not now" and "don't know." Percentages of inmates indicating the problem had only occurred since their incarceration are presented in Table 10.

A brief perusal of the table indicates that bad grades, expulsion and dropping out of school were perceived problems, particularly among male inmates for the latter two. Both sexes indicated children were experiencing problems with guardians and friends. Interestingly, female inmates were more likely to report alcohol problems among children, whereas male inmates were more likely to report drug problems among their children. Finally, high percentages of both males and females reported their children had experienced depression.

All of the effects of incarceration on families were not necessarily harmful, however. For example, many inmates reported using drugs in the home. Drug use around children is reported in Table 11.

As Table 11 indicates, women were significantly more likely to report using drugs at home while a child was present. Almost half of the women but only one-third of the men reported using while the child was in the home with them. More than half of both sexes reported keeping paraphernalia in the home, but only seven women and two men admitted to drug use with their child.

Table 10: Inmates' perceptions of effects of their incarceration on their children

Has become a problem for child since inmate was incarcerated	Females	Males	Total
Bad grades	16.0%	14.2%	15.2%
Expelled from school	3.8%	8.0%	5.7%
Dropped out of school	6.2%	8.0%	7.0%
Trouble with friends	12.2%	9.8%	11.1%
Trouble with parent/guardian	12.3%	12.4%	12.3%
Running away	3.8%	4.4%	4.1%
Child arrested	2.3%	3.5%	2.9%
Child incarcerated	0.8%	2.7%	1.6%
Problems with alcohol	6.1%	2.7%	4.5%
Problems with other drugs	3.8%	6.2%	4.9%
Depression of child	27.5%	16.8%	22.5%
Child suicidal	1.5%	0.9%	1.2%
Child became pregnant or got somebody pregnant	4.6%	1.8%	3.3%

Table 11: Drug use around children

Variables	Females	Males	Total	χ^2	p
Used while child was in home with you?	62 (n = 131)	33 (n = 100)	95 (N = 231)	4.808	.05
Used with your child?	7 (n = 129)	2 (n = 100)	9 (n = 229)	1.721	ns
Kept paraphernalia in home?	88 (n = 141)	65 (n=118)	153 (n = 259)	1.426	ns

When asked about ways in which their families may be faring better as a result of the incarceration, inmates mentioned placing the family in danger, having drugs around the children, causing worry for family members and poor parenting skills:

> They are not in the danger they were in when I was with them selling drugs (male).

> Because of all the drugs and riff-raf associated with drugs are not around (male).

> They don't have to worry about me getting killed, going to jail or getting in trouble. They can relax when they here (*sic*) sirens (male).

Inmates gave similar responses about ways they had endangered their children. In particular, they viewed drug use and gang involvement as potential threats to family well-being:

> Anything could have happened to harm them. Drugs and violence usually go hand in hand (male).

> Yes someone could have tried (*sic*) to rob me and kill me and my family for drugs or money (male).

Discussion

The primary purpose of this research is to explore the unintended effects of incarceration on children and families. By examining the pre-incarceration situations as well as the inmates' perceptions of family circumstances since incarceration, we are able to provide a representation of how incarceration may have affected their children and families. It is important to recognize the gender differences in pre-incarceration family situations in order to explore more fully the effects of incarceration.

Overall, the quantitative data and the inmates' own words support the second research hypothesis (children of female inmates would be more likely than those of male inmates to be placed in a non-parental household), and to a lesser degree they support the first (families of male inmates would experience more economic disruption as a result of incarceration). Females are more likely to be serving their first sentence, with less than one-third of the females reporting prior incarceration as compared to almost half of the males. Females are also almost twice as likely as males to report that they had a child of their own living with them prior to their arrest. Thus, their imprisonment is more likely to disrupt their children's living arrangements. Females are also significantly less likely than males to say those children are now living with the other parent. Taken in conjunction, these two statistics emphasize the fact that almost 50% of children of incarcerated mothers may find themselves not only without their mother but also without their home.

Almost half of the married inmates in our study had either discussed divorce or had filed for divorce. This represents a disintegration of almost half of the legal marriages. If the same trend occurs in common-law relationships, the implications are depressing. Incarceration could lead to the disintegration of almost half of the intact families. This could then result in a larger number of children living in single-parent households after their parents have been released from prison.

Although the numbers are low, there is an interesting pattern among those indicating divorce or potential divorce. Males are much more likely to indicate that the spouse has filed for or discussed divorce. Female inmates, on the other hand, are more likely to have filed for divorce themselves. One explanation may be that female inmates are very likely to be married to other offenders, whereas male inmates are unlikely to be married to an offender. Thus, it may be that individuals, whether incarcerated or not, tend to divorce offenders. Female offenders also report being married to men that were violent or drug-addicted. Therefore, they may be divorcing a violent or drug-addicted spouse. This may then be a positive effect of incarceration.

The loss of contact between parents and children is another adverse effect of incarceration. Male inmates are more likely to have lost contact with their children than female inmates. However, it is unclear if the male inmates had regular contact with their children prior to incarceration since they were less likely to be living with their children. If the loss of contact between male inmates and their children precedes incarceration, the mother's incarceration may be more traumatic for them. It is important to gather more information to ascertain more specifically how incarceration has disrupted parent-child relationships. It is clear, though, that families in Oklahoma appear to be experiencing negative effects of incarceration similar to those found by other researchers (Gabel and Johnston, 1995; Hairston, 1995; Johnston, 1995; Kampfer, 1995).

Another important area of concern is the high percentage of female inmates who report histories of abuse. This has important implications in terms of future problems that they and their families may experience. Inmates may need therapy to resolve prior trauma in order to remain drug-free and to stay out of abusive relationships upon parole. Without intervention, the cycle of abuse and chemical dependency may continue, and the children of these inmates may in turn become drug users and victims of abuse. Furthermore, the trauma of imprisonment may exacerbate the problems of inmates with a history of abuse, which may affect the inmate's ability to function and be productive once released. These findings confirm other research conducted in Oklahoma (Marcus-Mendoza, Sargent and Chong Ho, 1994) and in other states and countries (Chesney-Lind, 1997; Heney and Kristiansen, 1998; Merton, 1938; Messner and Rosenfield, 1993; Sommers, 1995).

There is another related concern for the children of female inmates. Substantial numbers of female inmates report being physically or sexually abused as children. We have also demonstrated that the children of female inmates are often living with the inmate's family of origin. The implication is that children of female inmates may be living with persons who abused the inmate. Thus, the children themselves may be living in potentially abusive situations. Family members with histories of inflicting abuse may become primary caretakers for the inmates' children. This points out the importance of gaining additional information about the abuse histories of the inmates, as well as information about whether the caretakers of inmates' children are, in fact, past abusers.

Inmates report that their incarceration has many other negative consequences for their children. Many inmates believe that their children are getting less supervision than prior to their incarceration, which could lead to a host of problems for children. Depending on the age of the child, safety considerations, alcohol or drug use and legal complications are potential problems. In addition, inmates report pervasive problems with their children's academic performance, conflicts with friends and caretakers, alcohol and drugs, and depression. Many children are experiencing these problems for the first time, possibly as a result of their separation from their parents. These findings suggest that children in Oklahoma experience the same traumas as those documented in previous research on children of incarcerated parents (Bloom and Steinhart 1993; Gabel and Johnston 1995; Hagen 1996; Hairston 1991; Merton 1938; Messner and Rosenfeld 1993; Weisheit and Klofas 1989).

We have less detailed information about the impact of incarceration on income as many inmates failed to answer income-related questions. However, over half of the male inmates indicate that their paid employment helped support their families prior to incarceration compared to slightly less than half of the females. Comparing pre-incarceration sources of support with current sources, we find some interesting patterns. Since more than half of the male inmates state that their own employment was a primary source of family support, a significant number of families are experiencing the loss of this income. Forty-three percent of the female inmates also report their own job as a primary source of family income, with additional reliance on AFDC and child support as sources of support prior to incarceration. So again, there is the potential for a devastating financial crisis for spouses and children.

It is important to note that "family" is not necessarily the same for male and female inmates and, therefore, the financial impact of their incarceration differs. Males are far less likely to report children in the home at the time of their incarceration. However, over half the males either lived with a spouse or common-law partner prior to incarceration, so their incarceration has reduced their spouse's income. Prior to incarceration, only twenty men reported their spouse's employment as a primary source of income. In contrast, thirty-seven male inmates report their spouse's employment as the current primary source of income. The children who were living with the male inmate at the time of his incarceration are highly likely to currently live with the other parent, suggesting that the mother of these children has taken a job to help support the family. And since women earn less on average than men, the family income may be considerably lower. Also, men are more likely than women to have been paying child support before incarceration, so their incarceration may leave their children without their financial support. These findings mirror those of other researchers (Daniel and Barrett 1981; Girshick 1996).

Conclusions

Many of the same devastating effects of incarceration that have been found in other parts of the United States are apparent in Oklahoma. As suggested by previous research, family functioning diminishes as marital relationships dissolve and parent-child relationships frequently disappear or diminish in quality. Incarcerated parents in Oklahoma feel that they have lost their parental status and identity, and that their children are suffering as a consequence.

Incarceration also has economic repercussions for these families in Oklahoma similar to those documented in other studies. Frequently, inmates' families face a reduced income and the loss of their homes as bills, mortgages and child support may remain unpaid. Inmates are distraught because they are no longer able to provide financial support to their spouses and children, further harming their families and their own parental identity.

Our research suggests that children of incarcerated parents in Oklahoma are experiencing trauma. Divorce, reduced standard of living, new living arrangements, personal problems, adjusting to new caretakers and, possibly, abuse, are among the problems that Oklahoma's children are facing while their parents are in prison. According to their parents, children also have difficulties at school such as bad grades, expulsion or even choosing to drop out and may experience problems with alcohol, drugs and depression.

Prior research has also stressed the positive effects of helping inmates maintain family ties (Gabel and Johnston 1995). For instance, research has linked maintaining ties with families to maintaining order in prisons, particularly among prisoners lacking formal college education (Davis 1998). In addition, keeping the family unit intact is also associated with more successful rehabilitation and reintegration into society (King 1993; Light 1993). Therefore, it would seem to be in the best interest of the families and society at large to help maintain family relationships when offenders and their family members desire it. Innovative correctional programming is available to address the needs of incarcerated parents and their children (Blinn 1997; Pollock 1998). Many correctional systems have started implementing such programs as the Parenting from a Distance Program (Boudin 1998) and Girls Scouts Beyond Bars (Moses 1997). Oklahoma should implement similar programs to address the problems documented by this study.

Although this study does not specifically address the impact of incarceration on communities, some of the problems suggested by other researchers seem to exist in Oklahoma. Incarceration creates financial and emotional hardships on the remaining residents of the communities here as in other studies (Moore 1996; Watts and Nightingale 1996) Parents in our study express concern about their children becoming desensitized to prison or thinking it is "cool," which Clear (1996) suggests leads to future criminal behaviour in children. Is this creating a scenario for "backfire" in Oklahoma?

Even though some inmates see positive aspects to their incarceration (less of a burden to their family, a deterrent to their children, not endangering their children), we cannot overlook the harm of incarceration. Such alternative sanctions such as day reporting centres or nighttime incarceration may protect children and address problems faced by offenders and their families without creating devastating new ones. It is imperative that we explore these and other alternative forms of corrections to avoid further harm to families.

This project points to the need for more research in this area. This study is limited to a particular subgroup: drug offenders. We selected this target population for two reasons. First, drug offenders comprise the fastest growing segment of prisoners. Additionally, we initiated this study in response to a solicitation for research on this population. However, it will be important to determine whether the issues identified in this study are of concern to other groups of offenders.

Furthermore, we have only examined the inmates' perceptions of the effects of incarceration. It is equally important to explore the effects from the perspective of the families themselves. Insight into the unintended effects of incarceration might be garnered through tracking the intergenerational patterns of incarceration. Research should explore the proportion of inmates' children who follow their parents into crime. As the numbers of incarcerated increase, the potential number of future criminals would also increase. Estimates could help policy-makers make informed decisions about future policies. Research should also examine more fully the effects of incarceration on marriages and parent-child relationships, the safety of children who are separated from their parents and the financial status of offenders' families.

Moreover, this survey does not address the issue of children born during the period of incarceration. Both male and female inmates told research team members they felt this was an area that was important. Future research needs to explore the effects on these children and the long range plans for them: Will they remain in the care of others or will they return to their mothers or fathers ? How will this affect them? Finally, research should also explore how offenders and their families fare when offenders are released from prison.

Bibliography

Blinn, C. 1997. *Maternal Ties: A Selection of Programs for Female Offenders.* Lanham, MD: American Correctional Association.

Bloom, B. and D. Steinhart. 1993. *Why Punish the Children? A Reappraisal of the Children of Incarcerated Mothers in America.* San Francisco: National Council on Crime and Delinquency.

Boudin, K. 1998. "Lessons from a Mother's Program in Prison: A Psychological Approach Supports Women and their Children." *Women & Therapy* 21(1): 103-125.

Bureau of Justice Statistics. 1994. *Women in Prison.* Washington, D.C.: US Department of Justice.

Chesney-Lind, M. 1997. *The Female Offender: Girls, Women, and Crime.* Thousand Oaks, CA: Sage Publications Inc.

Clear, T. 1996. "Backfire: When Incarceration Increases Crime." *Journal of the Oklahoma Criminal Justice Research Consortium* 3: 7-17.

Daniel, S.W. and C.J. Barrett. 1981. "The Needs of Prisoner's Wives: A Challenge for the Mental Health Professionals." *Community Mental Health Journal* 17(4): 310-322.

Davis, R. 1988. "Education and the Impact of the Family Reunion Program in a Maximum Security Prison." *Journal of Offender Counseling, Services and Rehabilitation* 12(2), 153-159.

Elliott, D. 1993. *National Youth Survey (United States): Wave VI, 1983.* Boulder, CO: Behavioral Research Institute [producer], 1992. Ann Arbor, MI: Inter-university Consortium for Political and Social Research [distributor].

Fishman, L.T. 1995. "The World of Prisoner's Wives." In T.J. Flanagan (Ed.). *Long-term Imprisonment: Policy, Science, and Correctional Practice.* Thousand Oaks, CA: Sage Publications, Inc. Pp. 148-154.

Fulbright, K. 1996. "Foreword." *Journal of the Oklahoma Criminal Justice Research Consortium*, 3: 5.

Gabel, K. and D. Johnston. 1995. *Children of Incarcerated Parents.* New York: Lexington Books.

Girshick, L.B. 1996. *Soledad Women: Wives of Prisoners Speak Out.* Westport, CT: Praeger.

Girshick, L.B. In press. "The Importance of Using a Gendered Analysis to Understand Women in Prison." *Journal of the Oklahoma Criminal Justice Research Consortium.*

Hagan, J. 1996. "The Next Generation: Children of Prisoners." *Journal of the Oklahoma Justice Research Consortium*, 3: 19-28.

Hairston, C.F. 1991. "Family Ties During Imprisonment: Important to Whom and for What?" *Journal of Sociology and Social Welfare*, 18(1): 87-104.

Harris, J.W. 1993. "Comparison of Stressors among Female vs. Male Inmates." *Journal of Offender Counseling, Services and Rehabilitation*, 19(1/2): 43-56.

Heney, J. and C.M. Kristiansen. 1998. "An Analysis of the Impact of Prison Women Survivors of Childhood Sexual Abuse." In J. Harden and M. Hill (Eds.). *Breaking the Rules: Women in Prison and Feminist Therapy.* Brnhamton, NY: The Hawthorn Press, Inc. Pp. 29-44.

Johnston, D. 1995a. "Effects of Parental Incarceration." In K. Gabel and D. Johnston (Eds.). *Children of Incarcerated Parents.* New York: Lexington Books. Pp. 59-88.

Johnston, D. 1995b. "The Care and Placement of Prisoner's Children." In K. Gabel and D. Johnston (Eds.). *Children of Incarcerated Parents.* New York: Lexington Books. Pp. 103-123.

Kampfer, C. 1995. "Post-traumatic Stress Reactions in Children of Imprisoned Mothers." In K. Gabel and D. Johnston (Eds.). *Children of Incarcerated Parents.* New York: Lexington Books. Pp. 89-100.

King, A.E.O. 1993. "Helping Inmates Cope with Family Separation and Roles Strain: A Group Work Approach." *Social Work with Groups* 16(4): 43-55.

Light, R. 1993. "Why Support Prisoner's Family Tie Groups?" *The Howard Journal* 32(4): 322-329.

Lindsey, L.L. 1997. *Gender Roles: A Sociological Perspective* 3rd edition. Upper Saddle River, NJ: Prentice Hall.

Marcus-Mendoza, S.T., Sargent, E. and Y. Chong Ho. 1994. "Changing Perceptions of the Etiology of Crime: The Relationship between Abuse and Female Criminology." *Journal of the Oklahoma Criminal Justice Research Consortium*, 1: 13-23.

Merton, R. 1938. "Social Structure and Anomie." *American Sociological Review* 3: 672-82.

Messner, S. and R. Rosenfeld. 1993. *Crime and the American Dream*. Belmont, CA: Wadsworth.

Moore, J. 1996. "Bearing the Burden: How Incarceration Policies Weaken Inner-city Communities." *Journal of the Oklahoma Criminal Justice Research Consortium*, 3: 43-54.

Moses, M.C. 1997. "The 'Girl Scout Behind Bars' Program: Keeping Incarcerated Mothers and their Daughters Together." In C. Blinn (Ed.). *Maternal Ties: A Selection of Programs for Female Offenders*. Lanham, MD: American Correctional Association. Pp. 35-49.

National Institute on Drug Abuse. 1993. *National AIDS Demonstration Research Project Public Use Data*. Rockville, MD: National Institutes of Health.

Oklahoma Department of Corrections. 1996. *Oklahoma Department of Corrections 1996 Annual Report*.

Pollock, J. 1998. *Counseling Women in Prison*. Thousand Oaks, CA: Sage Publications, Inc.

Sobel, S.B. 1982. "Difficulties Experienced by Women in Prison." *Psychology of Women Quarterly* 7(2): 107-117.

Sommers, E.K. 1995. *Voices from Within: Women who have Broken the Law*. Toronto: University of Toronto Press.

US Department of Justice. 1996. *Bureau of Justice Statistical Bulletin: Prison and Jail Inmates, 1995*. Washington, D.C.: Office of Justice Programs.

Umberson, D. 1995. Men's Relationship Project. Unpublished work in progress.

Watts, H. and D.S. Nightingale. 1996. "Adding It Up: The Economic Impact of Incarceration on Individuals, Families, and Communities. *Journal of the Oklahoma Criminal Justice Research Consortium*, 3: 55-62.

Weisheit, R.A. and J.M. Klofas. 1989. "The Impact of Jail: Collateral Costs and Affective Response." *Journal of Offender Counseling, Services and Rehabilitation* 14(1): 51-65.

First Nations People and Law Enforcement: Community Perspectives on Police Response

Robynne Neugebauer
York University

T his paper examines First Nation perspectives on policing. Accordingly, the discriminatory treatment of First Nations people by the police has been highlighted. This study was designed to build on the need for improved police treatment of First Nations communities, which cannot be achieved without an understanding of various levels of community involvement. More specifically, this study follows up on issues raised by current scholarship: themes noted in state sponsored task forces on Aboriginal people and people of colour within the criminal justice system; Solicitor General of Canada (1985, 1989); Manitoba Metis Federation Justice Committee (1989); Aboriginal Justice Inquiry (1989); Hale (1974); Royal Commission of the Donald Marshall Jr. Prosecution (1989); the Morand Report (Ontario, Lieutenant Governor's Office 1976); Pitman Report (1977); Ontario, Ministry of the Solicitor General (1980); Lewis (1989); S. Lewis (1992); African Canadian Community Working Group (1992); the Commission on Systemic Racism in the Ontario Criminal Justice System (1994); as well as a number of concerns raised by a variety of communities.

Conceptual Overview

For First Nation communities, a study of police-community relations encourages an appreciation of the conditions and consequences of being set apart and relegated to the margins by authorities. Specifically, this study demonstrates that police-community relations are largely defined by wider cultural values. Aspects of the wider culture, such as racism, misogyny, the marginalization of youth and classism, and the respective system of values that inform the police, such as the occupational culture, legal and administrative rules and the communities—history, colonialism, exclusionary practices, religions/traditions and ethno-specific approaches to authority—are all implicated. Thus, this inquiry has transformative possibilities when it forms part of a larger set of counter-hegemonic strategies such as feminist and anti-racist perspectives, thereby enabling a rethinking of police roles and racialized and gendered subjects in discourse.

A critical framework explains the impact of social structures in the development of social relations. This critique invites a discussion of racism, misogyny, classism and the marginalization of youth. Ultimately, the social construction of reality is analyzed in terms of wider issues, that is, the reproduction of dominant values. Given that elements in both the dominant culture and policing cultures marginalize First Nations people and equate colour with crime, communities undoubtedly expect trouble from the police. Clearly, police-community relations are relations of domination. As Gramsci (1971:52-55) notes, given the different world views or cultures (consciousness, action, history and folklore), there is resistance to the dominant hegemony to control the subordinate group, the working class as well any minority or subgroup being dominated by hegemonic powers. In response to perceived challenges, insidious tactics are used to absorb resistance, and distort and commodify challenges (Das Gupta 1994). Police-community relations programs and agencies and consultative committees are examples of state co-optation and absorption of community resistance.

To First Nation communities, policing is a fundamental expression of power, protected by the cultures inherent in the dominant order, law, occupational norms and bureaucratic administrations. That is, policing is a cultural practice. Additionally, all of the comments from respondents indicate that police-community relations are cultural products.

First Nations People and the Criminal Justice System

The law discriminates against First Nations people by denying them justice in all aspects of the criminal justice system. First Nations people are over-represented in the criminal justice system due to overpolicing of their communities and judicial decision-making. Moreover, the constant surveillance or over-policing of First Nations people is the result of cultural stereotypes (Jackson 1989; Hylton 1979, 1980; Harding 1991). First Nations people are arrested for offences that would otherwise be ignored if committed by non-Aboriginals. These exaggerated public order infractions include petty thefts, trespass, loitering, public drunkedness, driving offences, prostitution or the consumption of drugs. The visibility of First Nations people—their dress, location and physical characteristics—makes them conspicuous. The visibility of poverty and the ideological orientations of police officers render First Nations people even more vulnerable.

The over-representation of First Nations people in the criminal and juvenile justice systems has been well documented (Moyer et al. 1985; Harding 1991; La Prairie 1987, 1998). Some evidence suggests even higher rates of imprisonment for First Nation women and youths in particular (La Prairie 1987). These legal systems alienate and thereby prevent any meaningful participation by the First Nations. In general, the legal culture is restrictive; the mystified language, convoluted arguments and turgid reasoning preclude any informed and open dialogue. The bias in the courtroom is manifested in a number of ways. Judges seldom clarify to First Nations people the nature of the charge let alone their rights. A plea of guilty is frequently advised by duty counsel who wish to expedite the case. As a result of inadequate legal representation, First Nations people are advised to plead guilty, a term which is conceptualized quite radically from the Western interpretation of it. Aware of the impoverished living conditions of their defendants, judges still rely on fines as dispositions. The inability to pay fines or even post bail money ensures penal detention. Although judges are fully cognizant of the poverty, unemployment and homelessness of many of their defendants, judges continue to consider their respective employment records (Havemann et al. 1985: 7). It is here that factors of class and race are used to criminalize in many subtle ways. Many of these economically disadvantaged offenders default in paying fines, causing an even greater representation of First Nations people in prison. Clearly, the denial of bail significantly influences both the likelihood of conviction and the severity of the sentence imposed (Griffiths and Verdun-Jones 1989). First Nations people make up approximately 1.5-2% of Canada's population, yet in federal penitentiaries they account for 8-10% of the population, and an even greater proportion of the provincial and territorial correctional institutions (La Prairie 1998). According to the *Correctional Law Review* (1988: 3) First Nations people comprise 10% of the male federal prison population and 13% of the female federal prison population. Provincially, the figures are staggering particularly in the prairie provinces (Task Force on Aboriginal Peoples 1988:23). In Saskatewan, for example, First Nations people comprise 60% of the provincial prison population (Jackson 1989: 216) while only 10% of the population in Saskatewan is Aboriginal (CSC, Centre for Justice Statistics, Federal Bureau of Indian and Northern Affairs-*Globe* p. A4, July 1995).

Legal practices accept race as a natural fact and fail to consider race as socially and historically constructed. Legally, the experience of racism is ignored or simply denied. Colonialism, the history of domination, looms large in contemporary practices of institutionalized racism. Law has always been a technique of persecuting "stigmatized minorities" (Kallen 1982: 12). That is, racism, as Fitzpatrick (1990) argues, is an integral feature of law. The law, however, articulates the dominant culture. This is the case despite the rhetoric of cultural pluralism that continues to be promoted in statues and case law. Essentially, Canadian law seeks to incorporate minorities into the dominant culture by claiming to celebrate the equal contributions of ethnocultural, racial and religious groupings in the Canadian mosiac. Interestingly, the First Nation respondents in the study which I will refer to momentarily consider themselves to exist outside of Canada's multicultural mosaic.

The criminal justice system is the most coercive state apparatus. Within this site, the state exercises a legal and legitimate monopoly over force and violence. At every stage of the justice system—from arrest, pre-trial hearing, conviction, sentencing to classification and parole hearings—First Nations people and other racial minorities receive harsher penalties (Staples 1975; Koch and Clarke 1976; Lieber 1994). The criminal justice system amplifies threats and popularizes criminal mythologies. What is especially significant about the role of the police in this process is that the police are on the front line; they are the vanguards of the system—they begin the process of criminalization, they are the first to encounter alleged offenders, they make the critical decision to criminalize individuals. Their discretionary decision-making power influences the course of events. Yet, what is even more peculiar about their role is that in many instances they act as judge, jury and executioner. A recent example of police discretion and abuse and government inaction is the attack on First Nations people that erupted over a land claims dispute at Ipperwash Provincial Park. Ipperwash Provincial Park, northwest of Sarnia, Ontario is the site of a sacred Native burial ground. After being fed up with over twenty years of promises and inaction on the part of the government, a protest began with the occupation of a former military training base in June 1995 and spread to the park in September. Ontario Provincial Police officers opened fire on protesters leaving Anthony (Dudley) George dead, three other protesters injured from gunshot wounds and one injured from a beating by police. To add insult to injury, George's brother Perry and sister Carolyn were thrown in jail after driving their dying brother to the hospital; they were released twelve hours later and could not be at their brother's side when he died.

The police violence exhibited at Ipperwash has remained a strong symbolic reminder of the ongoing police violence, discriminatory treatment and the abhorrent coercive state apparatus used against Aboriginal people in Canadian and American cities on a daily basis. It is this issue to which this paper will now turn.

Methodology

The methodology adopted for this research was critical ethnography (Thomas 1993, 1995; Smith 1987; Maguire 1987). Critical ethnography refers to the reflective process of choosing between conceptual alternatives and wittingly making value judgments of meaning and method. Critical ethnography does not silence opposition but rather hears voices that move toward social action.

Within feminist and anti-racist perspectives, critical ethnographies advance a unique standpoint that has been neglected in traditional scholarship. As Dorothy Smith (1987) notes, mainstream methods exclude the voices of women and men of colour, of Native peoples and of homosexual women and men. The data used for this research were based on interviews and focus groups with thirty-five members and representatives of community-based organizations in the Native community of Metropolitan Toronto. Interviews and focus groups lasted approximately two-and-one-half hours. Many participants expressed fear of the police; therefore few interviews were actually taped. Further data were obtained through participant observation of community members at community functions and meetings. Central to critical ethnographies is the notion of "triangulation" (Denzin 1989). Triangulation is the application and combination of different research methodologies in the study of the same phenomenon. In this research, multiple methods were employed to overcome the biases of a single method. To safeguard ethics, subjects were provided with informed consent and were encouraged to read the manuscript. To ensure confidentiality and trust, pseudonyms were used and confidentiality was promised.

Findings: Voices of First Nation Communities

This section details how the police are problematized as a result of their relations with First Nations people. Respondents express serious concerns about the stereotypic attitudes of the police, their lack of confidence with the police, and the degrees of dehumanization, helplessness and dependence that enhance a sense of inferiority. Community members reported that they are mistreated by the police as a result of the pervasive disrespect. First Nations people experience a great degree of police derision expressed in rude, cruel and provocative verbal exchanges, aggressive and belligerent acts and an overall hostile demeanour. In these encounters, racial epithets are common:

> The words of police officers. They commonly refer to us as 'savage,' 'squaw' or 'beast.' The white man has many terms to describe my people. Really, we get used to their nastiness. This abuse is actually quite common. (Frank, 43: August 5, 1996)

According to key informants and respondents the above excerpts describe common attitudes and typical occurrences in exchanges between Native peoples and the police. Comments by police express sentiments that reflect a culture that perpetuates and naturalizes superiority. Respondents admitted that they refused to report crimes primarily because they had little faith in police investigations or feared reprisals.

Consequences of Disrespect: Police Encounters with Aboriginal Civilians

Disrespect is consequential, especially when manifested by an institution that enjoys a legal and legitimate monopoly over physical force. The use of force during discriminatory practices of arrest, search and seizure were noted. Given their general failure to understand the experiences of First Nation peoples, police officers subscribe to the values of their own occupational culture, which disregards any claims of innocence made by individuals who have been charged and arrested. Respondents allege that the police treat members of their communities as if they are guilty until proven innocent. Specifically, 80% of participants disclosed that they were stopped by the police, often for no apparent reason. Even when they requested an explanation, officers were unwilling to provide one, or begrudgingly justified their behaviour in terms of superficial criteria of suspiciousness or perceived drunkedness or loitering.

Youths were particularly targeted by police. Stopping a motorist or pedestrian often on a flimsy pretext is one of the most frequent ways stops and searches are executed against youths. In addition to stops and searches of individuals, the police seek to contain or control certain communities through surveillance and intelligence gathering.

All youths maintained that police perceive their associational activity as gang related:

> They seem to think that we are gang members who get together to drink, maybe sniff some glue....But, ya know , we just say that we are not into that stuff. I wish they'd just leave us alone. (Graham, 17: January 13, 1994)

Once stopped, these "suspects" are questioned in a rude, hostile and provocative manner. Frequent stop and searches cause considerable anger and frustration. This frustration is in turn interpreted by the police as a sign of guilt or suspicion. These random stops tend to initiate lengthy processes of confrontation. Arbitrary arrests characterize many of these encounters. Youths were seldom told why they were stopped or searched. When they resisted these arbitrary arrests, they were subjected to unfair interferences, including charges of assaulting a police officer. For youths, excessive police force, therefore, is presented as an inevitable aspect of arrest. As Graham asserts:

> Native kids are in a really bad spot when coppers are checking us out...You know that they threaten and stuff. It can be freaky but, you know we can always see them coming after us. You just can't move 'till they're finished with us. And if you put up a fuss they'll bang you or even make it look like you broke the law or something.(Graham, 17: Jan. 13, 1996)

Although all youths perceive a willingness on the part of the police to use force; all youths knew at least one person who was the victim of police violence. The following testimony about police violence was provided:

> I've been beaten up and hassled by the cops so many times I just lost count. They follow me till I'm close to home and then they start grabbing, punching, choking...I don't know why I wish they'd stop.... But I know a lot of Native guys that they like to pick on like they're Rambo or something. (Mickey, 18: July 13, 1994)

Interestingly, youths perceived themselves as victims of violence who generally refuse to register a complaint with the police. They were reluctant to complain for many legitimate reasons, including fear of reprisals, insensitivity of the criminal justice system and inadequate or limited options, to name only a few. Despite the availability of well-established police-complaint procedures, all youths perceived themselves as marginal and thus voiceless in formal institutions of authority. It is apparent that they lacked the requisite intellectual and political modes of resistance; they did not have the effective resources to counter the accounts proffered by the police. Youths were especially reluctant to respond to police. In general, First Nations people acquiesce to problematic police behaviour (Neugebauer forthcoming).

Irrespective of both the nature of the encounter and the situational role assumed by the civilian as witness, complainant, victim, bystander or suspect, the police tend to be cynical of the accounts provided by interactants who happen to be Native.

In brief, this section reviewed the general perceptions of respondents regarding issues of respect and trust. All respondents reported a lack of reciprocity on the part of the police. For the respondents, police officers typically reacted with contempt, aggression and incredulity. The legitimate claims of the community were frequently dismissed as inconsequential by the police. According to the respondents, colour is a commodity to be exploited by the police for crime purposes. Again, officers tend to generalize situations in terms of fixed stereotypes available in the occupational culture and in the wider culture (Neugebauer forthcoming).

Police Discretion: Situational Discrepancies for the Over-enforcement and Under-enforcement of laws

The non-enforcement and under-enforcement of laws whenever First Nations people are the victims of crime were themes consistently raised in interviews with respondents. There is a widespread perception that the police fail to respond effectively to calls for service in First Nations buildings and neighbourhoods. Again, all respondents generously commented on the low standards of police professionalism when policing involves less privileged communities. According to the perceptions of an overwhelming number of respondents, that is 97% of participants (thirty-four out of thirty-five), criminal incidents wherein First Nations people are the victims are under-reported to the police or alternatively assigned low priority by the police. Moreover, these communities further fear recrimination from the police should they complain about the unsatisfactory levels of service. Respondents noted that community activists have long argued that the police pay lip-service to reforms as they continue to harass Aboriginal communities. All respondents believed that calls for police service, especially complainants or victims from neighbourhoods with a higher representation of Aboriginals, are not taken as seriously as those from white victims or complainants. Participants expressed frustration and anger when learning about the slow response time of the police, the excessive delays and lengthy waiting periods.

These findings demonstrate the elasticity of law. The police transform situational identities: victims are treated as suspects and suspects as convicted criminals. Moreover, as the previous section highlighted, whenever First Nations people are victims there is an under-enforcement of the law. But, as the following section argues, whenever First Nations people are potential suspects there is an over-enforcement of the law. Along with these discretionary practices, respondents identified abuse of powers as salient.

A consistent thread running through the comments of respondents pertains to the routine abuse of police discretion in encounters with First Nations people. Police abuse the vulnerability of crime victims by harassing them and inventing charges against them. Community representatives complained about multiple charging. Given the susceptibility and imposed marginality of these disadvantaged communities, respondents noted that charges were stacked to force confessions. Respondents maintained that some accused individuals are coerced into entering plea bargain situations. Six respondents spoke candidly of hearing about the police planting of evidence. A common crime for which people of colour were too easily arrested concerned the charge of assaulting police officer. It was noted by ten respondents that the police provoke individuals into a confrontation. As Warren astutely admonished: "They wouldn't dare do this to the white man, what they do to us—they're always in our face. My people are always charged with public mischief. This is their gratitude for stealing our lands" (Warren, 53: Oct. 26, 1992).

The treatment of First Nations people in Canada and the US is rooted historically in Anglo-centric assumptions of superiority. Institutional practices equate colour, for example, with criminality. For Du Bois (1985:81), standards of justice vary on the basis of colour:

> Too many people are funnelled through the criminal justice system. They are charged with petty crimes. This is a complete waste of taxpayers' money. It's no accident that

you have so many Natives in prison. They're doing time for things that others would be on probation. Putting some Natives in jail justifies putting many more in jail. (Lily, 40: May 4, 1992)

Police officers enjoy a legal and legitimate monopoly over force. From their early days of training at their respective police colleges and from images represented in the popular culture, police officers have learned to rely on the use of deadly force. Researchers (Stansfield 1993; Hodgson 1993) have argued compellingly that within the occupational culture physical force is celebrated.

Given the fatal consequences of some police decisions, respondents suggested that police powers ought to be based on trust. Trust cannot be blindly ceded to the police given the sheer volume of police shootings. For the communities, this dangerous trend towards an increase in police violence demands a firm measure of public accountability. Similarly, First Nations people equally complained of police neglect in the investigation of serious cases. In this study, twenty-four of the thirty-five respondents indicated that reports of violence in the Aboriginal community were never explored by police. They noted that violent incidents against First Nations individuals, sometimes involving death, are inadequately investigated. Individuals described the case of a man who was killed. It took three days before the police decided to investigate the matter. The lack of trust in the police is discussed by the following respondents:

Far too many people in the community are picked up for minor things like public drunkenness. Yet, the penalty is so harsh. These people end up in jail for minor offences. They [Natives] do not trust the police or the entire system. Natives do not want to deal with the police. They would rather go quietly to jail than deal with the police even when they are innocent. (Michelle, 50: Aug. 24, 1993)

The only time that Natives are boisterous is when they are under the influence of alcohol. They only react to police when they are drunk. Otherwise they are passive. They are passive even while being attacked by the police and arrested for crimes they never committed. (Lance, 41: March 21, 1991).

For these respondents, this disregard for the legal rights of First Nations people is attributable to the police insensitivity to their cultures. They noted that police ignorance to cultural differences has become an excuse for further abuse:

> They become suspicious of Crees who won't make eye contact with them. They take this as a sign of guilt. (Mark, 37: April 4, 1996)

> Native youth are hassled for jaywalking. Natives get hassled and abused just because they're Native. (Warren, 53: Oct. 26, 1992)

Multiple Oppression: Policing First Nations Women

The manner in which the police deal, respond to and interact with First Nations women is an area of great concern. The police frequently deal with First Nations women in cases concerning spousal violence. These women are victims of multiple oppression due to their combined discrimination based on race and gender. It is argued herein that First Nations women, as victims of disadvantage, experience greater neglect due to their status as female and as members of a racial minority group.

The juxtaposition of a patriarchal culture, capitalism and racism grossly enhance the vulnerability of First Nations and racial minority women. For Lorde (1984: 10),the location of women of colour at the margins ensures their silence and subordination. Women of colour are severely disadvantaged within the wider political economy and therefore over-represented among those who are poor, under-employed and unemployed. Within a social order founded on and fuelled by inequality, there are very few supportive environments for helping women of colour who have been violated. The social system, especially the ethos of liberalism and its emphasis on individualism, perpetuate their isolation. Given that the Canadian and American cultures are blatantly ethnocentric, women are expected to satisfy the different cultures of which they are part (ibid.).

First Nations women and women of colour are forced to face numerous disadvantages as minorities. It is argued that it is precisely because of inextricable links between race, gender and class that violence against women is further perpetuated by institutions mandated to respond to violence. The cultural representations of subjects in terms of race, gender and class not only code (Bannerji 1993) processes of being and becoming but also order power. The layering of colour, class and gender cannot be ignored. The dominant order colonizes women of colour.

In situations where white officers were summoned to these homes, explicit forms of racism surfaced. Many victims and shelter workers complained that officers employed sexist and racist terminology against victims. In interviews with both shelter workers and victims, there was much discussion about the police use of terms like "bitch" and "whore," which were commonplace. These sexist terms were repeatedly combined with such racist epithets such as "squaw," "savage" and "redface."

Another study (Neugebauer 1992) reported that one shelter worker attributed this practice not to the social psychology of the officers but to the institutional character of policing:

> They (the police) use racial slurs not realizing that they are racial slurs...Slurs within the police force have become normalized. (Bonnie, 33: May 6, 1992)

Community Action and Institutional Police Change

In the following sections, respondents moved beyond an identification of the problems inherent in police-community relations towards a program of action. These responses implicate various immediate and long-term, isolated and multi-tiered remedies emphasizing the significance of culture at the interpersonal, institutional and systemic levels.

Over the years, citizens' groups in various minority communities have demanded more education and training for police officers in order to reduce community-police tensions. Although the educational levels of police officers have risen in recent years among new recruits, there is no evidence to demonstrate that college-educated police officers perform better or are more respectful of citizen's rights than less-educated officers. Likewise, the training of police personnel has also improved significantly in recent years. Police colleges have added a number of important courses to their curricula: race relations, domestic violence, handling youth and integrated training. A professionally trained police force would serve to de-escalate violence given the development of non-violent skills, especially in the areas of conflict management, communications and community sensitivity training. Regrettably, advances could be easily subverted by seasoned officers who remain loyal to the traditional occupational culture.

All respondents expressed the view that improved anti-racist training would ameliorate police working relations in the community. They also believe that such training must begin very early at the police college. Some indicated that prospective recruits must be selected on the basis of their demonstrated resistance to the systemic racism prevalent in society.

While the recruitment and promotion of more First Nations officers was recommended by some, others stated that greater representation will not make a difference because, once recruited, First Nations officers will feel compelled to fit in—to look, sound, think and act like the rest of the organization. Twenty respondents feared that these officers become cheap tokens in the process. Their self-concept is shaped by the occupational culture and the administrative rules. In order to be accepted by their peers and to move through the ranks, their skills must conform to the demands of the job as defined by extant values. The bureaucratic, paramilitaristic and conservative nature of the police department inhibits flexibility, community dialogue and innovative change.

Community representatives firmly believe that the police are not accountable for their actions. In fact, police officers act with impunity, condemning anyone who seeks reform let alone challenges them. Accountability will serve to reduce the officers' social distance to their superiors and to the public, the communities which they are expected to serve and protect.

Accountability safeguards against individual and institutional wrongdoings. Professionalism requires a code of conduct to which everyone in police services is accountable. Despite well-established traditions that compel officers to be responsible to the law, officers tend to act too independently as a power unto themselves. Much of what officers do is not only invisible to the public but remains protected by a wall of secrecy within the police culture. Accountability is difficult to secure if processing the investigation, adjudication and review of police misconduct is solely left to police officers or their supporters. Policing is far too important to leave exclusively in the hands of a close-knit organization. Accountability invites the development of remedies that confront systemic or structural problems. Respondents maintained that a failure to effectively remove the symptoms and the causes of abuse erodes a sense of public trust, and they unanimously called for an examination of promotions and the involvement of community representatives.

Police-Community Relations

In this study, police officers are unanimously perceived as prejudiced towards First Nations peoples to the extent that community members reveal little faith in meeting and dialoguing with the police; they maintain that relations are strained. However, communicating with the police is ineffective in allaying community fears and mistrust of the police. According to the perceptions of the respondents, the police do not appear to be serious about developing genuine relations with diverse communities.

> When there are meetings with the police Natives tend not to show up. It is difficult to foster an understanding between police and the community because police see themselves as authority figures—not operating at the same level as community members. There is no real equality in the exchange. (Matt, 33: Oct. 27, 1992)

Respondents did not believe that police initiatives were designed to succeed given the police reluctance to be accountable to the public. They also maintained that communication with the police was neither open nor reciprocal. Such efforts to improve police-community relations were very superficial, an exercise in impression management based on self-serving police priorities. Interestingly, respondents maintained that the police were only interested in enlarging community control by gathering information on community members. In other words, police involvement in community relations was a form of policing the community through a seemingly benign agency. The repeated denial of racism drives a wedge between the community and the police.

One method of countering racism involves anti-racist strategies. However, a commitment to anti-racism requires the ongoing development of strategies that move beyond the police organization. Institutional change will alter the cultural traditions of police work; yet, congruent with internal changes are external practices. Changes from within the institution, ranging from internal regulations, training, acceptance of responsibility, accountability and professionalism, will presumably result in changes in the behaviour of officers, priorities, deployment of personnel, law enforcement and discretion.

Community Action

The theme of resistance has been consistently articulated in the data. Respondents have argued that current police-community relations is based on a continued colonialism thinly disguised as multicultural integration. Problematic police-community relations emerge whenever police policies and practices silence the voices of those rendered vulnerable and designated as marginal. Change is long overdue in restoring a more balanced approach to police treatment of First Nations communities.

Institutional police changes, however, are also inseparable from fundamental structural changes. The police apparatus is derivative of wider relations of domination. Hegemonic discourses and images are not only well anchored historically but cast widely across institutional sites. Impaired police relations with First Nations do not exist in isolation from widespread defective relations imposed on disadvantaged communities. In this regard, law is perceived as promising. Given that policing is a legal invention, legal reforms are necessary to improve the quality of policing. Respondents provided detailed programs of action oriented towards the reduction, if not the eradication, of police intolerance. For respondents, police abuse and the culture of racism must be attacked by a more active lobbying of government for more progressive legislation. Changes in the Police Services Act were frequently cited in terms of accountability, improved training and anti-racist action. These participants believed that advocacy groups should pressure government for change. But at the same time they expressed a sense of trepidation given the lack of political will and the general apathy displayed by many Canadians.

They fully realized that governments are usually slow in introducing progressive legislation.

Hegemonic forces produce "docile" citizens (Foucault, 1977). Relations of domination are not always visible and do not necessarily involve coercion. But rather, these relations of domination involve consent. In this regard relations of domination become more negotiable than rejected outright. For many respondents, consent becomes a cultural marker. The more one agrees with the police, the more successful one's integration. Consent emerges as a signifying practice denoting affirmation by, and membership and status in, Canadian society. Interestingly, this consent to relations of domination has become part of common sense. The concern in this regard is that some members in the community have internalized the values of the dominant classes.

Coalition-Building within and beyond First Nations Communities

It is necessary for anti-racism to broaden its agenda as a mode of opposition. It is incumbent upon all sectors of society to understand the significance of cultural factors, to confront insidious forms of white supremacy in all institutions and to become conscious of the impact of institutionalized racism, sexism, heterosexism, age discrimination and the like. An important recommendation made by participants was that networking within First Nations communities and with other communities and interest groups is necessary for change to occur. White supremacy and concomitant benefits of privilege are so well entrenched that coalition building among oppressed groups is imperative. In other words, to connect all forms of oppression in order to provide a more powerful unified movement toward full equality for all oppressed groups is needed. Communities are encouraged to negotiate and hybridize their social agenda. The building of coalitions with other disadvantaged groups is imperative.

White communities occupy an important place in anti-racist struggles. For far too long, white people simply deferred to First Nations people to initiate real anti-racist action. This reluctance or at best superficial support fundamentally denies both individual and collective responsibility for racism. Similarly, Kahn-Tineta Horn, a prominent activist and leader in the Native community, maintains:

The white power structure doesn't respond to minorities—Natives and others. We have no clout. But it will attend to whites. It is up to you to get off your seat and help in the struggle against racism. (November 20, 1996, personal communication)

White anti-racist organizations must also make themselves important constituencies that will not be ignored by politicians.

Conclusions

Finally, police-community relations is an exercise in control. Community problem solving has become appropriated by the police. This persuasive practice has become and apparatus of social control and a mechanism of moral regulation established within the "carceral network" (Foucault 1977: 187). This paper demonstrates that respondents, individually and collectively, perceive the police as authorities who not only protect the status quo but ideologically represent a dominant value system that devalues the so-called foreigners, outsiders or those others. This paper examined how communities exist as embodied social subjects. They are socially positioned and culturally identified and identifiable. Police relations with First Nations communities are contextualized within the culture of difference, with varying sets of images used to interpret interactions.

The data disclosed that the policing of First Nations peoples is qualitatively different from that of white communities, especially since formal social control is a reflection of historical and colonial attitudes towards First Nations. Participants believe that police forces rely on stereotypic classifications and mental images that corroborate their negative beliefs. These views reflect wider socio-cultural conditioning, institutionally sanctioned police practices and informal occupationally derived subcultural attitudes. In this investigation the abuse of police powers was noted. The range of police problems includes excessive use of deadly force, excessive use of physical force and discriminatory patterns of arrest. Also noted were patterns of harassment, overly harsh enforcement of petty offences and verbal abuse including racist and sexist slurs. Other notable patterns of harassment were discriminatory non-enforcement of the law such as the failure to respond to calls in areas recognized as heavily populated by First Nations people and apathetic investigations of violence against women. Finally, lack of accountability, such as the failure to discipline or prosecute abusive officers and the failure to deter abuse by denying promotions and/or particular assignments because of prior abusive behaviour, was an area of concern.

Many recommendations for eradicating discriminatory behaviour were made. One of the main areas for change was police accountability. Participants unanimously maintained that there was a complete absence of police accountability, and they therefore demanded a more effective system of civilian review that more closely monitors and disciplines police misbehaviour.

Theoretically, this paper addressed the conditions and consequences of police-community relations. Both subjective and objective qualities regularly exist and impinge upon all relations. Within these relations, respondents felt that they pacified the police by being objectified. Once they were reduced on the basis of their colour or culture, they were reconstituted as if they were objects. Objectification permits authorities to under-enforce the law when First Nations people and people of colour are victims of crimes and to over-enforce the law when they are suspects.

Respondents indicated that the police reflect the white society and a white government that are not serious about eradicating racism, and neither of which is too disturbed by police racism. The general lack of response from the wider community is seen by respondents as a reinforcement of police violence. In Canada, however, there is a tendency to opt for the costly proliferation of state-sponsored commissions of inquiries, token gestures by ill-informed politicians and reports. Despite all these reports for which millions of dollars were spent, the same recommendations surface, such as the need for Native awareness and race awareness training, public education, more effective outreach, improved public relations and an equitable system of hiring and promotion. A considerably more valid approach to anti-racist struggles, let alone race relations training, that is rarely adopted involves the simple process of hearing the messages of those affected and to move beyond accounts from privileged sites. Throughout Canada's history authorities have marginalized communities and silenced the voices of First Nations people.

Community coalition building and mobilization toward anti-racist change were serious recommendations. Advocacy groups should continue to pressure the government for change. The role of whites in the struggle for social justice and change for First Nations people was noted. This research highlights the plight of those experiencing multiple oppressions, the layering of racism with misogyny and the marginalization of youth. In his treatment of racism and anti-racism, Dei (1995) espouses the importance of "integrative anti-racism"— the relational aspects of social difference. In the discourse of anti-racism, the working knowledge of the intersections of race, class, gender and sexual oppressions enhances the struggle for social justice and change (Dei 1995). Resistance and struggle are central features in police-community relations challenging official versions. Accordingly, this cultural criticism is essential in locating the marginalized other (hooks 1981). This study is part of a long tradition in critical sociology that argues for integrated communitarian solutions. A more emancipatory and transformative potential for police-community relations, grounded in struggle, is required.

Bibliography

Aboriginal Justice Inquiry. 1989. *Aboriginal Justice Inquiry Proceedings.* Winnipeg: Four Seasons Reporting Services Inc.

African Canadian Community Working Group.1992. *Towards a New Beginning: The Report and Action Plan of the Four Level of Government/African Canadian Community Working Group.*Toronto.

Bannerji, H. (Ed.). 1993. *Returning the Gaze: Essays on Racism, Feminism and Politics* Toronto: Sister Vision.

Cain, M. 1990. "Towards Transgression: New Directions in Feminist Criminology" *International Journal of Sociology of Law,* 18(1):1-18.

Carmichael, S. and C. Hamilton. 1967. *Black Power: The Politics of Liberation in America.* NY: Random House.

Carter, G. E. 1979. *Report to the Civic Authorities of Metropolitan Toronto and its Citizens.* Toronto: Ministry of the Solicitor General.

Chen, H. 1994. "Asian Women Face Problems as Minorities." *Lantern* (July 01)

Commission on Systemic Racism in the Ontario Criminal Justice System. 1994. *Racism Behind Bars, Interim Report.* Toronto: Queen's Printer.

Correctional Law Review. 1988. *Correctional Issues Affecting Native Peoples.* Ottawa: Solicitor General of Canada. Working Paper #7.

Das Gupta, T. 1994. "Multiculturalism Policy: A Terrain of Struggle for Immigrant Women." *Canadian Women's Studies,* 14(2): 72-75

Dei, G. 1995. "Integrative Anti-Racism: Intersections of Race, Class and Gender."*Race, Gender and Class,* V.2(3), spring: 11-30.

Denzin N. 1989. *The Research Act: A Theoretical Introduction to Sociological Methods,* 3rd edn. Englewood Cliffs, N.J.: Prentice-Hall.

Du Bois, W.E.B. 1985. Against Racism: Unpublished Essays, Papers and Addresses, 1887-1961. New York: Russell and Russell.

Fitzpatrick, P. 1990. "Racism and the Innocence of Law." In D. Goldberg (Ed.) *Anatomy of Racism.* Minneapolis: University of Minnesota.

Foucault, M. 1977. *Discipline and Punish.* New York: Pantheon.

Griffiths, C. and Verdun-Jones, S. 1989. *Canadian Criminal Justice.* Toronto: Butterworths.

Gramsci, A. 1971. *Prison Notebooks: Selections* (translated by Q. Hoare and G. Smith). New York: International Publishers.

Hale, E. B. l974. *The Police are the Public and the Public are the Police.* Task Force Report on Policing in Ontario. Toronto: Ministry of the Solicitor General.

Harding, J. 1991. "Policing and Aboriginal Justice." *Canadian Journal of Criminology* 33(3-4): 363-383.

Havemann, P., K. Couse, L. Foster, R. Matonovich. 1985. *Law and Order for Canada's Indigenous People.* Regina: School for Human Justice, University of Regina.

Henry, F., C. Tator, W. Mattis, and T. Rees. 1995. *The Colour of Democracy: Racism in Canadian Society.*Toronto: Harcourt Brace and Co.

Hodgson, J. 1993. *Police-Community Relations: An Analysis of the Organizational and Structural Barriers Inhibiting Effective Police-Community Relations.* Unpublished doctoral dissertation, York University, sociology.

hooks, b. 1981. *Ain't I a Woman.* Boston: South End Press.

Hylton, J. et. al. 1979. *Public Attitudes About Crime and Police in Regina.* Regina: Prairie Justice Research, University of Regina.

Hylton, J. et al. 1980. *Public Attitudes About Crime and the Police In Moose Jaw.* Regina SK: Praire Justice Research, University of Regina.

Hylton, J. 1981. "Locking Up Indians in Saskatchewan: Some Recent Findings." *Canadian Ethnic Studies,* 13:144-151.

Institute of Race Relations. 1987. *Policing Against Black People.* London: Institute of Race Relations.

Jackson, M. 1989. "Locking Up Natives in Canada." *University of British Columbia Law Review,* 23 (2): 215-300.

James, C. 1995a. *Seeing Ourselves: Exploring Race, Ethnicity and Culture.* Toronto: Thompson Educational Publishers.

Kallen, E. 1982. *Ethnicity and Human Rights in Canada.* Toronto: Gage.

Koch, G. and S. Clarke 1976. "The Influence of Income and Other Factors on Whether Criminal Defendents Go to Prison." *Law and Society Review,* 2(1) Fall: 57-93.

La Prairie, C. 1987. "Native Women and Crime: A Theoretical Model." *Canadian Journal of Native Studies,* 1:121-137.

La Prairie, C. 1998. "The Role of Sentencing in the Over-Representation of Aboriginal People in Correctional Institutions." In T. Hartnagel (Ed.), *Canadian Crime Control Policy: Selected Readings.* Toronto: Harcourt Brace and Company.

Lewis, C. 1989. *Report of the Race Relations and Policing Task Force.* Ministry of the Solicitor General of Ontario.

Lewis, S. 1992. *Report on Race Relations in Ontario.* Office of the Premier of Ontario (June). Toronto: Queen's Park.

Lieber, M. 1994. "A Comparison of Juvenile Court Outcomes for Native Americans, African Americans and Whites." *Justice Quarterly,* 11(2) June.

Lorde, A. 1984. *Sister Outsider.* Freedom, Ca.: The Crossing Press Freedom Series.

Maguire, P. 1987. *Doing Participatory Research: A Feminist Approach.* Amherst, Massachusetts: The Center for International Education, University of Mass.

Maloney, A. 1975. *Report to the Metropolitan Toronto Board of Commissioners of Police.* Toronto: The Metropolitan Toronto Review of Citizen-Police Complaint Procedures.

Manitoba Metis Federation Justice Committee. 1989. *Research and Analysis of the Impact of the Justice System on the Metis: Report to the Aboriginal Justice Inquiry.* Winnipeg: Manitoba Metis Federation Inc.

Moyer, S. B. Billingsley, F. Kopelman, C. LaPrairie. 1985. *Native and Non-Native Admissions to Federal, Provincial and Territorial Correctional Institutions.* Ottawa: Ministry of the Attorney General.

Neugebauer, R. 1992. "Misogyny, Law and the Police: Policing Violence Against Women." In L. Visano and K. McCormick (Eds.), *Understanding Policing.* Toronto: Canadian Scholars' Press.

Neugebauer, R.(forthcoming). *Police-Community Relations.* Toronto: University of Toronto Press.

Ontario, Lieutenant Governor's Office. 1976. *The Royal Commission into Metropolitan Toronto Police Practices.* The Honourable Mr. Justice Donald R. Morand, Commissioner. Toronto: Lieutenant Governor's Office.

Ontario, Ministry of the Solicitor General. 1980. *Policing in Ontario for the Eighties: Perceptions and Reflections.* Report of the Task Force on the Racial and Ethnic Implications of Police Hiring, Training, Promotion and

Career Development Reva Gerstein (Chair). Toronto: Ontario Ministry of the Solicitor General.

The Pitman Report 1977. *Now is Not Too Late,* Volumes I and II. Task Force on Human Relations. Toronto: Council of Metropolitan Toronto (W. Pitman, chair).

Royal Commission on the Donald Marshall Jr. Prosecution. 1989. Halifax: Government of the Province of Nova Scotia.

Smith, D. 1987. *The Everyday World as Problematic: A Feminist Sociology* Toronto: University of Toronto Press.

Solicitor General of Canada. 1985. *Native and Non-Native Admission to Federal, Provincial, and Territorial Correctional Institutions.* Ottawa, Solicitor General of Canada.

Solicitor General of Canada. 1989. *Task Force on Aboriginal Peoples in Federal Corrections: Final Report.* Ottawa, Solicitor General of Canada.

Stansfield, R. 1993. *The Evolution of Police Forms and Structures:A Transpersonal Perspective.* Doctoral dissertation, graduate programme in sociology, York University, North York.

Staples, R. 1975. "White Racism, Black Crime, and American Justice: An Application of the Colonial Model to Explain Crime and Race." *Phylon,* 36 (1)March : 14-23.

Task Force on Aboriginal Peoples in Federal Corrections. 1988. *Final Report.* Ottawa: Solicitor General of Canada.

Thomas, J. 1993. *Doing Critical Ethnography.* Newbury Park: Sage.

Thomas, J. 1995. "Variants of Participatory Research" (thomas@well.sf.ca.us).

Valverde, M. 1990. "The Rhetoric of Reform: Tropes and the Moral Subject" *International Journal of the Sociology of Law,* v.18.